Psychological care for
ill and injured people

Psychological care for ill and injured people

A clinical guide

Keith Nichols

Open University Press
Maidenhead · Philadelphia

Open University Press
McGraw-Hill Education
McGraw-Hill House
Shoppenhangers Road
Maidenhead
Berkshire
England
SL6 2QL

email: enquiries@openup.co.uk
world wide web: www.openup.co.uk

and

325 Chestnut Street
Philadelphia, PA 19106, USA

First published 2003

A catalogue record of this book is available from the British Library

ISBN 0 335 20997 1 (pb)   0 335 20998 X (hb)

Library of Congress Cataloging-in-Publication Data
CIP data applied for

Typeset by RefineCatch Limited, Bungay, Suffolk
Printed in Great Britain by Biddles Limited, *www.biddles.co.uk*

To my wife Lorna, my perfect companion and helpmate. She has given truly valued assistance in the preparation of the manuscript of this book. Also as an encouragement to my daughter Elene who I hope will take the cause of improving psychological care for ill and injured people much further.

Contents

Acknowledgements

My thanks for helpful discussions go to: Polly Woodhams, Clinical Nurse Manager, Exeter Renal Unit; Clare Penny and Alison Copp, occupational therapists; Jonathan Blood-Smythe, physiotherapist; Corrie Spencer, speech and language therapist; Clare Hardman, cardiac rehabilitation nurse specialist; Gillian Slade, dietician.

PART 1
Psychological Care: Concept, Provision and Clinical Basis

1 Psychological care: the neglected element of medicine and nursing

A greeting

Rather curiously perhaps, given that this is a serious minded book, I want to use my first few sentences as a greeting. In so doing, I can make clear whom I have in mind while writing on the theme of providing psychological care to people who are ill or injured. Basically, the greeting is to any member of the caring professions who has significant contact with people who are ill or injured. The list of professions is, therefore, quite long. It includes hospital nurses, community and practice nurses, physiotherapists, occupational therapists, dieticians, social workers, health visitors, speech and language therapists, audiologists and technical staff providing diagnostic procedures such as echo-cardiogram or treatment procedures such as radiotherapy – in fact, *any health care practitioner who has significant or extended contact with medical patients and their partners*.

Naturally, since this book is concerned with situations in medical settings, the medical profession is also very much in my mind. This is because where doctors or surgeons have no understanding of psychological care there is quite likely to be little by way of encouragement for psychological care, so that a situation of psychological neglect may prevail. A further profession that does not fit the pattern, but nevertheless has a strong impact, is that of hospital or community health service managers. Again, where managers are ill-informed on the key issues to do with psychological care in illness and injury they may exert a direct influence that has the effect of suppressing the provision of psychological care.

Why does it matter and why should all these professions have an involvement in psychological care for the ill and injured? There are several good reasons, as I will demonstrate in stages throughout the book. Here, though, let us simply note that *the absence of psychological care in hospitals or health centres will sometimes undermine medical and nursing efforts to provide effective treatment.* It can also cause much distress for patients and their partners. Psychological care is thus something that should concern all professions engaged in providing a health care service.

I do realize that at first sight this long list of those who should be involved might cause raised eyebrows. Is it really the case that I am about to suggest that hard pressed staff repeatedly break off their work to sit in a corner with distressed patients conducting informal counselling sessions? No, that is not the case. As will be made clear in the following pages, the psychological care of patients and their partners should be pitched on one of three levels. *At its most basic level it is as much an attitude as a procedure.* This attitude promotes the habit of good, effective communication and a raised awareness in noting patients' psychological state – that is, how they are reacting to their situation and how they are handling the information that has been

Figure 1.1 Some of the community of heath care practitioners who should be involved in the provision of psychological care.

given to them. The only time demand might then be passing the word that a particular patient is in need of further help to other staff better placed to provide it. So, at its most basic level, your involvement with psychological care in general medicine, nursing or therapy roles means that 'you have to have attitude' – but it has to be the right attitude. That is what this book is about.

The key concept: psychological care in general hospitals and health centres

As the book unfolds the full meaning of the phrase 'psychological care' will be developed. I cannot offer you a crisp definition of one sentence length because the construct is complex – although in no way difficult to understand. Essentially, *psychological care refers to an approach to looking after the ill and injured that can be integrated with nursing or the various therapies to provide an organized and practical psychological content to overall care.* It represents a big step towards meeting the requirements of truly holistic care for the ill and injured. Although the scheme of psychological care to be presented is designed particularly for adoption by nurses and therapists in general hospitals and health centres, other professions are also encouraged to become involved, as you will have realized from my opening paragraph.

To avoid confusion, it should be noted that there are similar terms in current use: psychosocial care, for example. This is essentially similar in general meaning to psychological care.

Rather than leaving the description of psychological care as a no doubt irritatingly vague statement, I set out the basic components of the approach in diagram form in Figure 1.2 in order to give you an immediate preliminary picture. The message within the diagram is simple. Psychological care for people who are ill or injured requires an organized approach with an associated set of disciplines. It involves various skills and objectives, with the involvement of certain staff in specific tasks. The key aim is to monitor the psychological state of our patients in a systematic way and then either to provide or to arrange for preventive interventions designed to deal with psychological issues arising from their illness and injury. If this preventive effort is not successful then the work refocuses on therapeutic and supportive interventions in an attempt to help the person cope with the psychological reactions that have arisen. Following Figure 1.2, the next section gives you a brief overview of psychological care on the three levels of intensity identified. Note that the description of level 1 is organized in relation to various categories of health care profession.

PSYCHOLOGICAL CARE

Level 1: awareness

> Awareness of psychological issues
> Patient-centred listening
> Patient-centred communication
> Awareness of patient's psychological state: relevant action

Level 2: intervention

> Monitoring the patient's psychological state: records kept
> Informational and educational care
> Emotional care
> Counselling care
> Support/advocacy/referral

Level 3: therapy

> Psychological therapy

- -

Self-care

> Self-care by staff providing psychological care (participation in support, supervision and self-monitoring schemes)

Figure 1.2 The components of psychological care.

Level 1: awareness

Concerning managers in general hospitals and community health services

As mentioned above, personal involvement with psychological care can be pitched on one of three levels, depending on one's role within health care. For those with no direct patient contact, but who nevertheless exert an influence on the range of care procedures made available in an institution – managers, for example – the minimum asked for would be an informed and *facilitating* stance to psychological care. Sadly, if I may divert for a moment of general comment, in my 25 years of personal experience in British hospitals, I have not often met hospital or community health service managers with much real understanding of the key issues concerning psychological care in medicine. It is not often that one meets managers who hold the essential concept of psychological care as being an 'investment' that underpins physical medicine. Nor, in my experience, is psychological care usually seen by managers as a potential means of saving expenditure in specified areas of medicine (e.g. cardiac medicine). Often it is confused with psychiatry and construed to be of minimal relevance to a general hospital or health centre. As a result, the organized provision of psychological care in our hospitals and health centres is often neglected, or it is conducted at a patchy, low-key level, with little involvement by the managers. Fortunately, there are some notable exceptions, but I do worry they might be a minority. In the British, state-funded National Health Service, managers are, to be fair, constrained by the dictates of the government of the day and, effectively, told what is to be considered important and fashionable. Even so, a manager with an understanding of and sympathy for the aims of psychological care can make an enormous difference. *Thus, at the distant level of involvement that befits managers, the key requirement is informed, supportive awareness and an effort to facilitate psychological care within their organization.*

Concerning health care practitioners with patient contact
With reference to level 1 in psychological care, the hope is that a loose but broad group of health practitioners will be involved. As you look at Figure 1.2 you will notice that what is sought is a continuing effort to make contact with patients in a manner that allows some awareness of their general status in terms of their information and general coping. For example, the medical physicist who conducts an echocardiogram or the practice nurse who is taking a blood sample at the start of a warfarin regime is, in reality, free to work in an interpersonal style that is quite 'minimalist'. They may be bright and cheery but somehow manage to avoid all meaningful conversation concerning their patient's current experiences. But this is not good care and it does not have to be like this.

The alternative would be that, just before, just after or while carrying out the procedure, they might engage with their patient briefly to explore the level and accuracy of information held and the understanding of what is happening. Following this they might pose one or two comments that would allow a patient to voice any emotional distress. *This is the task of making oneself aware of the patient's psychological state.* It involves some moments of face-to-face contact and some 'listening skills' on the part of the staff. If poor levels of information are detected then there needs to be a brief effort at further explanation, pitched at a level that is suitable for the particular person in the clinic. In the example, the practice nurse might make a note to set aside five minutes when taking the next blood sample in a few days' time to consolidate the conversation that she started. The cardiology technician could offer a similar brief review of information on the spot. However, probably having no further contact with the patient, she would, if concerned about the patient's state, leave a note for the cardiac liaison nurse, the GP or the referring cardiologist.

At first encounter this might sound like more hassle for you when you almost certainly have hassle enough as it is. In reality though, it is more an issue of attitude, values and style. At this basic level psychological care rarely takes much out of the day. For one thing the number of cases needing much intervention are unlikely to be that high unless something is badly wrong in your locality. *In short, for a health care practitioner to walk away from a patient with no knowledge of how they are coping or whether they are confused or in distress is the opposite of holistic care. In my view it is very unprofessional.* Added to this, attending to patients' needs in the simple manner required for psychological care on level 1 usually leads to a greater sense of professional completeness and therefore job satisfaction.

Concerning hospital doctors, GPs and psychological care

I once asked a consultant oncologist roughly how much time he managed to spend with the average patient whom he had diagnosed as having cancer and was treating on an outpatient basis, with perhaps occasional admissions to hospital. He replied, 'About an hour a year.' At the other end of the scale I have also watched young senior house officers (SHOs) scurrying about, often at a half run. Clearly, they can have periods when they are under exceptional pressure too. It has to be recognized, therefore, that some consultants are very hard pressed, with very demanding case loads. Similarly, doctors in more junior grades can have patches of rush and extreme busyness.

An important question thus has to be faced. Should hospital doctors who are often under extreme time pressure be exempt from a call to improve psychological care? The answer is *of course not.* As Dixon and Sweeney (2000) reveal, the current leaning towards a more holistic

---

Box 1.1   The psychologically minded dietician

Gillian, a dietician in a general hospital, attended a ward to meet her third patient contact of the day. This was Ruth, a middle-aged woman who had recently been diagnosed as having insulin-dependent diabetes. Ruth was unexpectedly angry and difficult in her manner to begin with and then became a little tearful. Gillian, noting the obvious risk that, if the situation was not dealt with in a supportive and exploratory manner, compliance problems could well result, decided not to deal with dietary issues in a standard way. Instead, she gave a little time to letting Ruth talk about why she was angry and distressed.

It transpired that the young registrar who had informed her of her diabetes had been brief and 'matter of fact' in his manner, leaving her both offended and somewhat frightened. The diabetes was a surprise to her and she feared it, since a friend with a history of diabetes had suffered badly with microvascular disorder, leading to very poor sight and kidney failure. Ruth also, it emerged, had a mild fear of needles and injections and so did not want to administer two insulin injections everyday. She believed that the doctors could give her tablets instead. Nor was she keen to start changes in the way she was used to eating and so she was very negative about instruction in new diet plans.

Being quite psychologically minded and having had some training in psychological care, Gillian put her initial effort into building rapport and offering a reassuring and supportive presence. On this first contact she settled for answering any questions that Ruth had and assessing what Ruth actually knew and how she felt about managing her situation. Another meeting was organized, which was designed as an information and support session. Gillian also told Ruth that she could arrange for help from a clinical health psychologist for her fear of needles and her general distress. On the second meeting Ruth proved to be rather more welcoming, if still indignant about her encounter with the registrar. She did settle to the information session, did accept the need for insulin and diet management and did accept referral to the psychologist for assistance with her difficulties.

---

approach in nursing is, quite rightly, mirrored by the beginnings of a parallel movement in medicine. There is a growing awareness of the importance of a doctor's style of relating and communicating with patients as an influence on the outcome of medical treatments.

Similarly, a patient's psychological status (which includes information held and expectations derived from this information) is known to influence the physical progress that a patient makes in recovery from illness. If doctors of any grade ignore this then, to be blunt, it becomes a case of them opting to follow an approach that undermines their own efforts and reduces the chances for a full and efficient recovery by their patients – in other words it is a form of negligence. *The involvement of hospital doctors in the overall provision of psychological care is, therefore, essential.*

A similar argument holds good for general practitioners. GPs have a greater spread of responsibilities than hospital doctors and a wider set of roles. Some would argue that there is a more obvious holistic component and more generalized caregiving emphasis contained within the role of the general practitioner than in that of the technically focused hospital doctor: hence the alternative title 'family doctor'. It is essential, then, as indicated in Dixon and Sweeney (2000), that these elements of the role of the GP are developed and available to all patients. This is a good start from the perspective of providing psychological care on level 1, since, as Dixon and Sweeney illustrate, an effective consultation process with an emphasis on good listening skills and an ability to help the patient to express important issues is fundamental. They do not develop things far enough, in my view, but at least their recommendations take a GP to within a step of consciously providing psychological care. With good communication and listening the doctor will be in a position to monitor psychological state, arrange for informational and emotional care and refer for psychological therapy should this be necessary – that is, involvement on level 1 in psychological care.

Some GPs will occasionally have the time to function on level 2 by providing some of these interventions themselves on an individual case basis, which is even better. Time constraints may prevent this from being a frequent event, however. Crucially, though, involvement on level 1 should be routine, since the GP is often the eyes and ears of a practice in relation to an individual patient's needs. If he or she does not have an orientation towards monitoring psychological state (and the skill to do it) then the practice functions ineffectively and neglect of psychological issues will undermine the medical effort at times, as is described in case studies later. Hence, *the involvement of general practitioners in the overall provision of psychological care is essential.*

Box 1.2   How poor psychological care by doctors influences treatment outcomes

Ray, a 43-year-old builder with lower back problems, attended hospital for an epidural injection procedure. Unfortunately, this procedure did not go well and he was left with continual, distressing sciatic pain and a very weak leg as a result. He became exhausted physically and emotionally by both the pain and the physical effort of coping with reduced mobility. He was also very angry because he found that he could get very little information about the event. His experience was that the doctors involved, although concerned, seemed reluctant to talk with him. Above all else, he resented the failure of any of his doctors to sit down and explain to him what might have happened, why it went wrong and what the long-term outcome was likely to be. Ray was prescribed various pain killers and other chronic pain treatments but none of the treatments produced a significant reduction in the pain. He became more demoralized and depressed. He withdrew socially and exercised little. He was in steady decline and, as the months went by, was on a deteriorating trend in terms of pain and mobility.

Ray then moved from the area and his care was transferred to another hospital. The range of his treatment then, belatedly, expanded to include more emphasis on psychological care. A consultant anaesthetist at the local pain clinic teamed up with a clinical psychologist and met Ray in a sequence of sessions. Together they emphasized good communication, full information, full discussion and an opportunity for emotional expression. An atmosphere of close engagement with support and encouragement was created. It was not a rapid process but Ray's anger did ease and his depression became patchy rather than continuous. He slowly re-engaged with his friends and hobbies and took part again in gentle exercise. His leg was not miraculously cured, nor was the pain eliminated, but it became less troublesome to him as an experience. Over the next year he slowly acquired a greater degree of mobility, to the extent that he was able to participate once more in his sport of bowling.

The telling point in this case was that *no new treatments were introduced to bring about this change*. The only alteration was in the move to include an effort at psychological care and deal with the voids in supportive, patient-centred communication, information and emotional care. His physical treatments had been undermined by his doctors' failure to provide psychological care, but when it was provided and his psychological status changed the physical treatments seemed to acquire more power.

My main assertion is now emerging. It is the claim that the psychological status of people who have experienced serious illness or injury can influence the outcome of medical treatment and recovery. Thus, doctors should feel an obligation to include psychological care in their approach to all cases in terms of patient-centred communication, together with an ongoing effort to note a patient's general psychological status. However, the extent to which doctors personally offer interventions in psychological care beyond this level will depend on circumstances. Sometimes it will not be possible, I recognize that. However, what is absolutely vital is that the hard pressed doctor who has little time to take things further with a patient personally ensures cover by referral to someone else on the team who can deal with it – be it nurse, therapist or clinical psychologist. In other words, the presence of a doctor who has a positive attitude to psychological care and who 'sponsors' it by means of making sure that it is dealt with and not overlooked is vital.

Level 2: Interventions

A deeper involvement in psychological care is needed for those working on level 2. Typically, these tasks fall to staff who maintain some sort of extended contact with patients. For example, this might be during a period of admission to a hospital for surgery or following a heart attack. Alternatively, where repeated outpatient visits are required with, say, people with diabetes or those attending for regular haemodialysis sessions, psychological care interventions of the level 2 type are essential. It is equally important that this sort of provision of psychological care exists in the treatment routines offered by therapists. Patients recovering from accidents, surgery or illness will usually attend for a sequence of therapy sessions with the same member of staff – an ideal situation. Obvious opportunities are found in the roles of *physiotherapists, occupational therapists and speech and language therapists*, for example. Primary care also provides an important option for psychological care work on this more involved level. When a health centre is solely or jointly managing the care of a person suffering from serious illness or injury, the staff will be in regular contact with the person involved. *Practice or community nurses* and also *health visitors* will encounter important opportunities to improve the care of their patients by interventions of the level 2 type.

Although the interventions needed to provide psychological care

are dealt with at some length later in the book, let us take a very brief look at the sort of activity involved on level 2. With repeated contacts, the task of being aware of the psychological needs (including information and education) of the patient hardens up into an active role of monitoring psychological state using brief, simple records. The nurse or therapist (who is probably the only health care practitioner with regular contact) becomes the 'psychological eyes and ears' for the case. Thus, as part of routine work with a patient, at each contact there will always be a little conversation initiated by the member of staff that is designed to check the information, understanding and expectations of the patient and, if relevant, their partner. Similarly, there will be a question or two that should reveal how the patient is coping generally. This in turn will usually give an insight into their emotional state. The

---

Box 1.3 Psychological care by the dialysis nurse

Linda was assigned as named nurse to Sheila, a 58-year-old woman who had collapsed in renal failure and been taken on to a unit-based haemodialysis programme. She was dialysed three times a week. Not surprisingly, Sheila was in great distress and confusion. She was initially very anxious, in part because her understanding of the situation and the techniques of dialysis was poor. Later, she became more depressed than anxious as the implications of survival by dialysis became clearer. She worried about the strain she was imposing on her husband and began to see herself as a burden and nuisance to him and her family. As her named nurse, Linda covered the majority of her dialysis sessions. As part of her routines she would spend a little time talking with Sheila during sessions, checking her information and exploring how she was emotionally. To assist with adaptation to life on dialysis and to help emotional processing, Linda regularly gave her patient an opportunity to express her feelings and talk through her shock and subsequent reactions. They also edged into problem-solving discussion when troublesome issues arose.

Sheila later commented that she found her nurse to be a true emotional companion, and this was a great comfort. She also found her nurse to be a helpful teacher who worked with her to improve understanding and keep her up to date on the clinical plan. Sheila valued this psychological care and regarded it as an important contribution to her first two months of treatment. It helped her through the early emotional reactions and enabled her to achieve a stable pattern of coping.

whole emphasis is on brief but 'patient-centred' communication with the aim of providing a more complete picture of the patient's status through these routine contacts – even though the main work of the day might be physiotherapy or speech therapy.

When significant needs are revealed a little time can be set aside for information work or emotional care along the lines described in later chapters. Where the member of staff has some training and capability this work can extend into basic counselling if required. On level 2 it is the nurse or therapist who, in the first instance, is active in providing information and offering an opportunity for emotional expression and processing. It is also for the nurse or therapist to engage further help with the patient if it seems necessary – that is, if the patient or partner requires psychological therapy provided by a specializing psychological therapist, such as a clinical psychologist.

A note on 'preventive psychological care versus psychological therapy'

Before I introduce the third level of psychological care it is timely to point out an important distinction, namely that psychological care work with the ill and injured can either be preventive in nature or oriented towards dealing with cases where prevention has failed. *The general scheme for psychological care that I offer in this book is heavily biased to the preventive approach*: hence the involvement of nurses, therapists and other health care practitioners who are not psychological therapists. Being realistic, though, there will, despite this preventive effort, be many occasions when people dealing with illness and injury do cross the clinical threshold and will need assistance from a psychological therapist – they will have become '**psychological casualties**'.

The borderlines between preventive psychological care and psychological therapy are not at all distinct. I regard it as something of a waste of time trying to find tight definitions that denote sharp boundaries, other perhaps than noting the related distinction between staff trained to offer psychological therapy and those not so trained, which is a fairly objective distinction. I will, though, give brief expansions of the terms 'preventive psychological care' and 'psychological therapy' as a guide.

Preventive psychological care. When people become seriously ill or injured it is *normal* that they will react psychologically, usually experiencing various reactions as described in some detail in Chapter 2. *It is important to understand that, in many ways, a lack of reaction is the more abnormal state.*

This progress through psychological reactions takes the person involved into important cognitive and emotional processing as the impact of their situation is grasped and the effort towards adaptation and coping is begun. Naturally, there is considerable individual variation in the type and strength of these reactions, so we should beware of relying on stereotypes only as a guide. It should also be said that not all reactions are negative; sometimes there are positive psychological gains. However, one thing is certain: a significant proportion of the patients and their partners that you will encounter in a career as a health care practitioner will manifest negative psychological reactions such as anger, anxiety, grief and depressed episodes. These should not, in the first instance, be construed as something wrong. *Often they are normal reactions, signs of emotional processing.* However, if the reactions become prolonged and intensify then they can become disabling in various ways and possibly impair physical recovery. At this point the phrases 'psychological disturbance' and 'psychological casualty' begin to be more relevant to a case. It clearly makes great sense to try to reduce the likelihood of this type of deterioration into psychological disturbance by means of preventive psychological care – that is, intervening in a way that supports and helps people through their initial reactions and then on to adaptation and adjustment. This includes providing a situation where efforts are made to minimize the stress and threatening impact of illness or injury by effective communication, information provision and education.

In earlier approaches to both medicine and nursing little heed was given to this psychological side of illness. Medical treatment was generally seen as a physical event, while psychological reactions were usually held to be (as much by patients as doctors) some sort of weakness or failure that was best kept hidden. A stroke or heart attack was just another of life's trials that one bravely dealt with. If there was emotion this was better kept out of sight.

Fortunately, this bias is giving way to a much more informed and balanced view. If, for example, you spend an hour or two just browsing through Baum *et al.* (1997), you will find over 200 short, briefing chapters that demonstrate beyond question the predictable, parallel psychological processes that accompany illness and injury. The importance of emotional state, levels of information, effective communication and supportive counselling or psychological therapy is a recurring theme. Thus, a key argument in the rationale for preventive psychological care emerges. *If we know that, during illness or injury, psychological processes are often set in train that both affect physical outcome and lead to people being much more stressed and uncomfortable than is their norm, then, as part of our caring procedures, it makes sense to work with these psychological processes from the outset. The aim in such work is, where possible, to prevent patients and partners from becoming psychological casualties and to prevent progress in physical recovery being hindered by adverse psychological status.*

However, while this effort will pay off in many cases, some patients or their partners will become psychological casualties despite the preventive interventions. At this point it is relevant for us to take a brief look at the place of psychological therapy as part of the scheme of psychological care.

Level 3: psychological therapy

As a simple scheme for organizing thoughts on this topic I tend to think of psychological care as being offered at a basic level by staff with relatively basic training and supervision in psychological interventions. These interventions include monitoring psychological state, information, education and emotional care, as described above. Those staff who have gained experience and taken further approved training are able to extend their contribution to include a valuable form of basic counselling, which can be a very powerful form of support and greatly help people with problem-solving. Beyond that, the role of staff who feel that their client needs assistance at a greater depth has to be one of *acting as a referring agent*, since 'greater depth' implies psychological therapy and that is the specialist function of the clinical or health psychologist. Thus, if you feel that the routines of psychological care (as outlined in detail in later chapters) are not sufficient because your patient is clearly in considerable difficulties, then a referral to a clinical health psychologist is an important link in the chain of care. I should mention that referrals do not have to be to clinical health psychologists exclusively, since there may well be other members of staff who have recognized qualifications in psychological therapy. Some psychiatrists and professional counsellors may be able to function in this role. To illustrate the basis for this sort of transfer I will sketch out the background of several referrals that have been made to a health psychology department in recent years.

Eileen, a nurse specialist in dermatology, usually found 10 minutes or so once every other week to talk with Tamsin, a 31-year-old woman receiving PUVA treatment for severe psoriasis. Eileen realized that her patient was becoming increasingly stressed with a difficult situation at work. It was clearly affecting her greatly and possibly responsible for the flare-ups of her psoriasis. This was the third flare-up in 18 months. From the content of her conversations Eileen formed the impression that Tamsin's difficulties had to do with her inability to deal with male authority figures. She therefore sought Tamsin's consent and then contacted the department of clinical and health psychology with a referral request. The five sessions of therapy offered by the clinical psychologist explored her approach to managing the work situation and why she might have difficulties with the particular figures involved. Tamsin found this useful and was able to alter things to reduce the levels of work stress. She certainly was not psoriasis-free as a result but there were no more flare-ups for quite a while.

Cheryl had experienced a difficult childhood, in the sense that she felt unwanted within her family. Her parents had been adequate rather than loving and she never felt that she had their true interest or concern. Two marriages in succession had failed because she found that the pattern of lack of love and true interest repeated itself. At the age of 47 she required surgical treatment in the form of a fusion of two lumbar vertebrae to deal with increasing back pain. This surgery was not entirely successful and left her with further pain and a weak leg. Following sessions with a physiotherapist and with the surgeon, she felt great anger because she experienced both of them as being indifferent and lacking true concern with her problems. She felt angry and abandoned and became so distressed that she consulted her GP. The GP referred her to a clinical health psychologist. This psychologist opted first to work at rebuilding her basic trust and rapport with professional figures. They then looked at the situation she found herself in and worked on understanding how Cheryl had transferred expectations and feelings of anger from her earlier childhood into the situation of her surgery and relationships with the health care professionals involved. Cheryl realized that, in part, her anger was more to do with her expectation that the staff would not be truly interested in her and the angry, defensive style that she rapidly adopted with the surgeon and physiotherapist made things worse. Further work led to the discovery that she tended to adopt this difficult style with many people in her life and had done so for years. The behaviour was based on defensive expectation of being let down in relationships. Her habitual perceptions of people in her life and herself were explored in some depth. Cheryl emerged from this therapy feeling much less distressed. She felt that she had a greater understanding of situations that troubled her and a better capacity for managing them. This in turn helped her to relax with her pain problems and eventually accept a place on a back pain management programme, from which she gained considerably.

Jane had suffered a surgical accident and consequent cardiac arrest. She spent four days on a ventilator in an intensive care unit as a result. At follow-up clinic six weeks after discharge she was found to be suffering stressful and frightening flashbacks related to her stay time on the ventilator. She was showing all the symptoms of post traumatic stress disorder. The consultant anaesthetist and sister in charge of the unit gave her some time to talk through her experiences and reassure her, but decided on an immediate referral to a clinical health psychologist for therapy. Three months later, after six sessions of therapy, she was much less troubled by flashback and generally stronger emotionally.

Having worked with David for a year, Becky, a diabetes nurse specialist, began to feel that he was coping with his diabetes and with life in general increasingly less well. He continued to work as an architect but was emotionally up and down with the shock of the diagnosis, and found himself lacking in concentration. Then his wife was diagnosed as having ovarian cancer. Becky thought that David was near to breakdown and also judged that his health was being badly affected by events. She referred him to a clinical health psychologist, who set up an extended support regime and helped him with issues to do with anger and fright for the future.

After a coronary artery bypass operation followed by numerous admissions with chest pain and two further angiograms, Robert, a Methodist minister, was again present for review with his consultant cardiologist. The cardiologist was convinced that there was now no vessel pathology and that the pains, lassitude and low-key sense of illness that Robert reported were psychological in origin – hence he referred Robert for assessment by a clinical health psychologist. In the first interview it emerged that Robert, who was disposed to the classic Type A coronary-prone behaviour pattern, had blamed himself for his heart attack and felt that he was letting his congregation and God down by his enforced retirement. He felt enduring guilt and a strong sense of failure. These feelings had undermined his sense of well-being and rehabilitation. After some time of personal reflection and exploration of personal issues in therapy sessions, Robert began to relax rather more with his situation and was able to see a path for returning to a less driven part-time role in the church. He managed to move on from his preoccupation with guilt and failure and, over the next year or so, suffered less chest pain and became more confident. There were no further admissions to hospital.

Psychological therapy is, of course, a blanket term for a diverse collection of approaches and theoretical influences. I will not attempt to describe these here. But it may be helpful to outline some of the basic features that most approaches to psychological therapy in a medical setting have in common.

Referral will be because a health care practitioner will at some point have sensed 'caseness'. This is a phrase that you may find used sometimes to imply that a person has passed a threshold of psychological discomfort, disturbance or impairment, as a result of their illness or injury, that justifies psychological therapy to halt deterioration and deal with a crisis. Sometimes the problems may involve longstanding interpersonal or behavioural difficulties, and therefore be less of an emergency but still need psychological therapy to facilitate all-important change.

In terms of obvious psychological status, patients or partners meriting referral for therapy may be in distress and disabled by strong emotions, such as overwhelming worry, anxiety, general anxious tension, panics, phobic reactions, hypochondria, depression, anger or grieving. A second large group of patients or partners may be in a generalized stressed state, feeling that they cannot deal with what is demanded of them and fearing some sort of breakdown. In contrast, other patients struggle (or, perhaps, fail to struggle) with issues that may be more to do with a pattern of behaviour that is damaging their health and well-being – eating disorders, excessive dependency, damaging lifestyles (e.g. excessive workload and work hours), non-compliance with treatment and so on. Much less often, fortunately, a few clients may be found to be suffering mild organic effects, such as minor brain damage resulting from surgery (e.g. coronary artery bypass surgery) or anoxic incidents. These patients also need referral.

On receiving a referral a psychological therapist will have two initial tasks. The first is to begin the work of creating a genuine rapport that will lead on to the development of a therapeutic alliance. In basic language this means that the therapist sets up a situation in which the client feels truly safe, accepted and free of any need for defence or evasion. Then begins the work of assessment, which is, in reality, a joint task. With the therapist's help the client explains the situation and then explores the perceptions and feelings related to it in increasing depth. Some therapists will then move on to rather directed therapy systems, such as cognitive behaviour therapy or cognitive analytic therapy. As used here, 'directed' means that the content of the therapy follows a loose schedule of objectives linked to a particular theoretical system – for example, tracking down the identity and origin of automatic negative thoughts that, in the system called cognitive behavioural therapy, are believed to trigger anxious or depressive feelings. Other therapists work in a less scheduled, more exploratory way. Sometimes they put much more emphasis on the relationship between therapist and client, using this as a springboard for assisting personal development away from damaging past interpersonal relationships, which, in turn, lead to failing present patterns in relationships (as in some of the clinical examples above). Davidson and Neale (2001) give a brief, manageable breakdown of the theoretical and practical elements of contemporary approaches to psychological therapy, together with references, should you wish to read further.

The key problem: lack of psychological care in general hospitals and health centres

At times you might find that this book expresses views in a rather forceful, perhaps passionate, manner, especially with reference to the lack of organized psychological care in hospitals and health centres. In fact, in places, I even refer to this as negligence. In view of this, it is probably best to reveal to you the origins of my vehemence early on in the book rather than later. To do so takes us straight to a case example and, later, a little personal history. The case of Peter J serves well as an illustration of the issues I have in mind.

Case study: Peter J

Peter J, a 46-year-old man, was eventually referred to me for assistance by his general practitioner. Two months previously, while visiting his daughter in the north of England, he had been admitted to an emergency medical unit with chest pains that were thought to be an ongoing heart attack. This took place after a family row that had been quite upsetting for him. He was transferred to a cardiac unit for diagnostic tests and treatment. After five days of observation he was discharged as stable and well. He returned home, and was transferred to outpatient and GP care while on the waiting list for an exploratory angiogram. The basis of the referral to me (as a clinical psychologist attached to the coronary rehabilitation programme) was that he was extremely anxious and had been in and out of the doctor's surgery numerous times complaining of chest pains and associated panic attacks. On two separate occasions he had called for an ambulance to take him to casualty, believing that he was having another heart attack. He had then spent a day or two on a cardiac unit under observation and was discharged on both occasions with no significant finding.

In a sense there is nothing remarkable about this history. Many people do have heart problems and many of these people do become quite anxious about their situation, but it is worth recording some of the statements that Peter made to me in our first session together. For example:

'Lack of information is my real complaint. What has made me really angry is that nobody told me anything in the hospital up north and I've not been told anything much since I left either. I don't know what I am supposed to do about exercise or eating – I've been eating little more than toast for two months, it's very frightening. I don't know what state my heart is in. They said I'd get all the information at the coronary rehabilitation class, then they said I could not go to that until after the angiogram, which is another four months to wait. The nurse on night duty at the cardiac ward said that I must have fallen through the hoop somehow and missed out on information. I'm in limbo, I've lost all my confidence and I have panics now – I've never felt so bad.'

One element of psychological care comprises regular and organized checks to establish the accuracy and depth of information that patients hold. Another element is the task of assessing the patient's psychological condition in simple everyday terms. If action needs to be taken in relation to these then it follows in natural progression. The problem for Peter was not that he was being dealt with by negligent and unhelpful people, quite the opposite in fact. They were a caring team. The problem was that the cardiac units and the health centre involved had no practice of *organized* psychological care. Thus it became possible for him to be discharged in an ill-informed state and to develop increasing levels of confusion, anger and anxiety without this being identified. The situation persisted until he had, effectively, become a psychological casualty. As a result of his state of insecurity and emotional upheaval, together with worries about his future, Peter developed panic attacks with hyperventilation that were sometimes accompanied by chest pains. These chest pains were possibly caused by episodes of dynamic angina. This term refers to a contractile spasm of one of the coronary arteries rather than an actual blockage. It causes angina-like pains and it is thought that it can be provoked by stress and emotional states. Not unreasonably, Peter interpreted these epi-sodes of chest pain as another heart attack and so panicked and sought immediate medical help. It happened on several occasions, leading to call-outs for the general practitioner and two admissions to hospital. These emergency interventions were necessary but a waste of resources, since his heart was in fairly good order and no physiological signs of a further heart attack were ever detected.

Much of Peter's problem seemed to be insecurity caused by a lack of understanding of his situation combined with a sense of being abandoned when not fully recovered. Quite possibly nurses or doctors had given him some explanation, guidance and information during his stay in hospital, but this clearly had not been delivered in a way that enabled Peter to retain and make use of the material. Given, as described above, that the basic routine of psychological care is to check what people know about their situation, then to amplify or correct this information as necessary, it was a clear example of absent or failed psychological care procedures. He was discharged with little useful information and left in a bewildered, frightened state.

With Peter's care being transferred to his primary care team, a further opportunity was on hand for monitoring and checking his understanding and handling of his situation. Nothing much was done, presumably because the general practitioner and practice nurse felt they had too little available time for such interventions and believed that the cardiac unit would have done what was necessary. Paradoxically, assuming that lack of time had prevented interventions to provide support and education for Peter, this effort at saving time directly caused a situation to build up, where the same staff then had to find the time for frequent consultations and call-outs to Peter. His psychologically induced problems – that is, panic attacks, hyperventilation and possibly dynamic angina – all of which indicated another heart attack in Peter's eyes, then necessitated further admissions and diagnostic efforts by the cardiac team. *The lack of psychological care caused more time consumption in the end.*

The moral in this case (and hundreds of others that I have encountered) is that with the monitoring and support that comes with good, organized psychological care Peter's general situation would have been picked up and he would probably not have ended up in this state. He would certainly not have consumed anywhere near as much of the doctors' and nurses' time. Nor would he have had to endure so much personal stress and distress. This provides our first example of a key point that I highlight below. *If some small amount of time is not given to psychological care work with the ill and injured, then, in a proportion of cases, this will lead to a larger amount of extra medical and nursing time needing to be found.*

By way of clinical evidence to support my view of this case I should record that, after a couple of sessions with me in which I offered little more than the typical content of nurse-provided, preventive psychological care (including basic informational and emotional care), Peter settled and the panics and chest pains receded. He had no further admissions and his contact with his GP became routine only. Any cardiac nurse, practice nurse, physiotherapist or occupational therapist could have achieved the same. If there had been a scheme of preventive monitoring and psychological care in the hospital units and the health centre that dealt with him it is unlikely that he would have become a psychological casualty.

Other evidence?

Am I making a fuss about one patient and over-generalizing? Clearly, when observing clinical practice in one's own locality it is important to guard against the risk that local approaches are seen as applying to the rest of the country in an unfair generalization. Therefore, as we reflect on Peter's situation, it is worth mentioning at this point that I have kept a particular form of record with regard to over 200 cardiac patients I have met in recent years who have received cardiac surgery. The record has been of their response to the following two questions:

1 When you were in hospital did anyone on the staff discuss with you how you were reacting personally to your illness or surgery and what you were thinking and feeling about your future? (Emotional care work.)

2 Before you were discharged did anyone review with you your understanding of your situation and the information you had received? (Informational and educational care work.)

Now what is of interest to us in this group is that my own hospital does not have a specializing cardiac surgery unit, so all these patients were treated at quite a wide range of units elsewhere in Britain – all for coronary bypass or valve repair/replacement surgery. While I do not claim that the information is anything more than informal survey material, the average answers are not very encouraging. Very few people, less than 10 per cent, have any memory of any such interventions. In fact, none of these people has related their experiences in a way that suggests that they benefited from organized psychological care; quite the opposite in fact. Most had similar, although less strident, complaints to those of Peter J, noting that they had not had sufficient information and guidance and felt rather abandoned and unsupported until (often months later) they were offered a place on coronary rehabilitation courses, which are specifically set up to give exercise training, information, guidance and support. *The regrettable indication here is that organized psychological care was weak or absent at the various hospitals involved.*

One slightly more encouraging finding was that over 20 per cent spontaneously said something like 'but my own doctor has been very helpful to me', indicating that things might be a little better at the health centres receiving patients back into their care after hospital treatment. My conclusion is, then, that there are indications of inadequate psychological care at a significant number of cardiac units throughout the country – it is not, therefore, just a problem in my own locality. Incidentally, I also have similar information from a group of patients who have received general or orthopaedic surgery from hospitals around this country. These are people who have run into problems with post surgical pain and been referred to me through the local pain clinic.

Finally, I might also mention that four years ago I was able to be a first-hand observer in the cardiac care situation when I had to have open heart surgery to repair a failed mitral valve. My finding was that all the staff gave excellent medical and nursing care that was well supported by good physiotherapy. It was noticeable though that, while all the staff involved were supportive and helpful on an individual basis, I encountered no established, organized practices in psychological care. It was also obvious that the staff were generally untrained in the business of monitoring psychological state (including levels of information) and not required to provide appropriate psychological interventions. There was no instance in any of the diagnostic or treatment units that I visited that might be identified as a conscious intervention linked to a scheme of preventive psychological care. This was a disappointment because, like most cardiac patients, I would have found it helpful.

Others think this way too

We are reviewing the issues around my claim that, although routine, preventive psychological care of ill and injured people, particularly by nurses and therapists, can make a significant contribution to patients' general progress, this type of care seems to be the exception rather than the rule in our general hospitals and health centres. There are some types of unit where developments are more likely to have taken place with staff who are more psychologically minded. I recognize and applaud this. Often it is in specialist units that have specialist staff. Breast cancer screening nurse counsellors and diabetes nurse specialists are such examples. Even so, it is often the case that these specialist staff work in isolation in units that do not have an overall, organized scheme of psychological care and where the rest of the staff are neither required nor trained to provide psychological care.

It might be argued that such practices are yet to be developed because the notion of psychological care is relatively new. In reality this is not the case. The general awareness of the importance of patients' psychological state is not at all new. Added to this, the importance of doctor–patient and nurse–patient communication with effective information provision has been recognized for quite some while. For example, Janis and Levanthal (1965), writing under the title

'Psychological aspects of physical illness and hospital care', describe typical reactions to illness and the potential role of a counsellor to assist with these reactions. They also recommended 'setting up and maintaining a therapeutic milieu in the general hospital'. During the 1970s and 1980s there were a steady stream of publications in both psychological and nursing journals and, occasionally, in medical journals that brought the issue to our attention. There are many examples, including the issue of *Nursing* (number 27, July 1981) that was composed of 12 articles all designed to illustrate the importance of good nurse–patient communication and information provision in a hospital setting. This theme was consolidated by Ley (1989) who has proved a vigorous campaigner for improved communication and information provision by all health care practitioners. Lynch (1977) wrote an impassioned book using research and clinical observation to support the psychosomatic theory that loneliness was associated with increased illness and death rates. On this basis he argued that human physical contact, emotional support and continual effort at communication in settings such as cardiac units were vital for patient recovery. Later publications, such as Lacey and Burns (1989) and Davis and Fallowfield (1991), reflect the development of knowledge concerning the psychological impact of illness and injury and the importance of attention to psychological status and psychological reactions among patients and their partners. Baum *et al.* (1997) is one of the latest examples, and gathers together a huge amount of material in this field from many authors. Curiously, though, even their authors fail, in general, to grasp the importance of improving basic psychological care through organized schemes that guarantee basic psychological monitoring and preventive interventions for all patients. This is exactly the scheme proposed in this book.

A formative experience

I, among many others, have been a campaigner for improvements in the provision of psychological care in general hospitals and health centres since 1978. In that year I first started some clinical sessions in a renal unit and then slowly developed links with various other sectors in general hospital activity, including the care of patients with cardiac problems, cancer, chronic pain, neurological disorders, orthopaedic difficulties, diabetes and so on. It was a valuable if rather sobering experience that led me to conclude that *the average patient in the average*

general hospital or health centre receives little or no psychological care, and
this is often to the disadvantage of everyone involved.

This period of general clinical duties and observation was then
followed by some research into what might best be described as the life
and times of patients in renal failure (Nichols and Springford 1984).
This research did not produce a very encouraging picture. Both renal
patients and their partners were often very stressed by the circumstances and responsibilities of home or unit haemodialysis and clearly
suffered psychologically. It was also clear that the provision of information to patients and partners was unreliable and that the staff did
not have a habit of communicating in depth with their patients about
their experiences, expectations and feelings. They were kindly and
well motivated staff with good technical skill. Somehow, though, they
sustained a situation in which patients and partners, although sur-
rounded by caring staff, felt that the staff were out of touch with their
feelings and needs and often did not manage to keep them informed in
an effective way.

This led on to some proposals for the improvement of psychological care in general hospitals. Essentially, these involved a simple
model from which Figure 1.2 was derived. The early proposals
advanced the idea that nurses and allied professions become the front-
line agents of psychological care in hospitals under the training, support and supervision of clinical psychologists, as described in Nichols
(1993). This book develops these proposals further.

Psychological care as an 'investment'

On one level psychological care in medicine is an expression of the
human capacity to support and care for those in distress or distressing
situations. It is, effectively, an extension of the physical caring provided through nursing and the therapies. But there are dangers with
this fine notion of psychological care as simply a higher form of
human expression. There is a sense in which it is too closely linked to a
'tissue box' image – that is, limited to dealing with emotional casualties in weepy sessions in the counselling room, with constant recourse
to the tissue box. Inevitably, a smaller proportion of psychological care
activity does involve this type of emotionally laden interaction, but I
would prefer that you think of it in quite different terms from this
right from the start.

The important (vital) alternative perception is that *psychological care is seen as an investment of effort that underpins medical, nursing and therapist interventions*. Investment might seem a curious word when applied to the context of a person arriving in hospital with a myocardial infarction or attending a renal unit for their first session of haemodialysis. Indeed, the definition of investment describes the term as referring to an initial laying out of money in order to make a return and end up with more money than you started with. Here, partly in metaphor, I assert that if organized psychological care is provided the patient will often end up in a better state physically or further down the road of rehabilitation than if there is no psychological care provided – it is a good investment of effort. This is such a fundamental point that I will repeat it from time to time through the book, rather like a mantra. Thus:

> **In serious illness and injury good psychological care complements and underpins physical treatment regimes. Psychological care contributes to recovery. When there is no psychological care physical treatment plans may sometimes be undermined, and thus the power of medical, nursing and therapist interventions will be reduced.**

Writing a decade ago in Nichols (1993), I set out the basis for this notion of psychological care as an 'investment' by advancing some rather bold claims. It is relevant to review these in support of this point. Thus, when people become seriously ill or injured but no psychological care is included in their regime of care or therapy, there is a definite risk that:

- the patient (and partner) will suffer more stress and distress.

- the patient may have less understanding and therefore less motivation, leading to poorer levels of compliance with treatment.

- the patient may exercise less self care or fail to rehabilitate, and thus there will be greater utilization of doctor or nurse resources.

- medical, nursing and therapist achievements with an individual patient may be undermined or reversed when there is no psychological care.

At first sight you could be forgiven for rejecting these claims as dramatic and overstated, particularly when combined with my other major claim that the provision of psychological care in general hospitals and health centres is usually inadequate or non-existent. It suggests quite a severe problem. However, when you stroll through the wards of the average general hospital or visiting the average health centre there is not usually an immediate impression of many people in distress or, for that matter, distraught staff battling with endless problems of non-compliance and readmission. In these terms you might well say 'He's got to be wrong.' I have to accept that there is local variation but, overall, both my past and my ongoing experience consistently takes me to the position that the effects I describe are actually quite widely occurring. The little case vignettes given above indicate the type of clinical evidence that repeatedly presents itself when one talks in depth to patients or their partners. In the next chapter the weight of clinical evidence is quadrupled and supplemented by evidence from research sources.

Research supporting the concept of psychological care as an 'investment' that underpins medical treatments

The claim that psychological care should be regarded as an investment of effort that underpins medical treatments is so important that some supporting research should be presented, especially in the current climate of 'value for money' within our health service. I will present evidence only from the field of cardiology at this point but material from other specialities will be found in Chapter 2. The material cited is all from respected, peer reviewed journals and is therefore of reliable quality.

Maeland and Havik (1987) reported a prospective study that sought to establish the psychological features that predicted failure to return to work after a heart attack. A total of 249 patients were involved. They found that the following features were strongly linked with *failure* to rehabilitate and get back to work:

- marked feelings of hopelessness;
- anxiety and depression at nine days and six months;

- poor knowledge of coronary-prone lifestyle;
- expectation of reduced physical abilities;
- expectation of reduced autonomy;
- expectation of reduced work capacity;
- expectation of reduced emotional stability.

Put simply, patients who sustain a heart attack, are treated and then returned home with negative expectations, lack of information and emotional distress are much less likely to return to their job than those who have the reciprocal, positive features. This demonstrates that the psychological status of patients can undermine their overall progress to normality. Without psychological care as an attempt to identify and deal with these negative features, one of the primary aims of the medical and nursing effort with post infarction patients (to return them to as near a normal life as is possible) may be undermined, possibly to a significant degree.

A more recent analysis that lends general support to the work of Maeland and Havik is that of Hemingway and Marmot (1999). They reviewed a large collection of research papers of a prospective design and derived a consistent pattern of findings within these studies. The psychological features that were associated with a *second* heart attack were clearly identified. The main culprits were:

- depression and anxiety following the first heart attack;
- low levels of social support (including emotional support);
- work characteristics (e.g. job strain, in jobs featuring low levels of control and conflicting demands).

Again, the import is that failure to monitor and attend to emotional state in post infarction patients increases the likelihood of a second heart attack. As you can see, this allows a rather startling deduction that is so important that it is worth emphasizing. *If relatively cheap and easily provided psychological care to detect and deal with adverse psychological reactions is not offered by the health care practitioners involved with cardiac care, then this situation itself becomes an indirect risk factor for further heart attacks. The investment of psychological care must be made to minimize the risk of second heart attacks.*

Incidentally, issues concerning a return to work where the situation is one with job strain characteristics might possibly be included within the routines of coronary rehabilitation education, but this may be beyond the range of everyday psychological care on the ward. Referral to a psychologist might be the best route.

Though I am running the risk of becoming repetitious with supporting evidence (which, anyway, is a comfort when seeking to establish a point), other recent research has demonstrated that depression adversely affects a person's survival following a heart attack. Frasure-Smith *et al.* (1993) show that patients who meet the criteria for major depressive disorder following a myocardial infarction were five to six times more likely to die during the following six months. They report a 16 per cent mortality rate for depressed patients, in comparison with 3 per cent for patients who were not depressed. Later, Frasure-Smith *et al.* (1995) assessed the impact of lower levels of depression – that is, patients who recorded scores on the Beck Depth of Depression Inventory that fell into the mild (as opposed to major) depression category. At 18 months after the myocardial infarction depression was still associated with an increased risk of death. As Tabrisi *et al.* (1996) comment, 'Despite the high prevalence of depression and associated risk of death in CAD [coronary artery disease] patients, depression is infrequently diagnosed or treated in this population.' That would not occur if the investment of effort in providing psychological care were part of the overall provision of care in cardiac units and the health centres caring for patients after discharge.

The stress of illness and the immune system

As a further addition to my collection of arguments justifying developments to provide psychological care in hospitals and health centres, I want to mention the expanding area of knowledge linking the performance of the immune system to the experiences that people have and the general psychological state that they are in. Evans *et al.* (1997) note that current research lends some credence to the claim that differing psychological states have an effect of either up-regulating the immune system's activity or down-regulating it. In other words, the experience that people have had during, say, the preceding six months may affect *immunocompetence*. Kennedy *et al.* (1988) review various experiments in which cell counts, proliferation rates and the attacking power of various elements of the immune system (natural killer cells and T helper lymphocytes, for example) were explored in relation to psychological state. There were strong indications that exam stress in medical students, stressful life change, loneliness and enduring stressful situations such as divorce or being the caregiver for a partner with Alzheimer's disease caused a reduction in the power of the immune system. Martin (1997) offers a very readable review of the current state of knowledge in this area. He concludes that long-term demanding and stressing situations can make us more vulnerable in health terms.

This is an issue that we, as health care practitioners, should reflect upon. Chapter 2 includes plenty of research and case studies to confirm the obvious. Illness, injury, hospitalization and treatment can sometimes be enormously stressful and affect people's lives in a long-term, negative way. The implication for us is that if we do not work to identify those patients in stressed states or affected by other adverse psychological reactions, then we face the risk of standing by, complacently, while the health of these people is further threatened. We must, therefore, remain mindful of the basic *psychosomatic premise* that is mapped out in Figure 1.3.

The theory is clear. Eventually our body systems develop a hormonal and physiological emphasis in response to what is going on in our lives. If it is long-term stress, struggle and emotional upheaval, as can happen with serious illness or injury, this can affect health through increases in such hormones as cortisol. This hormonal change

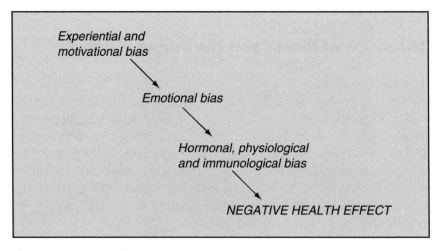

Figure 1.3 The psychosomatic premise.

can, in turn, *downgrade* levels of immunocompetence, so making us more vulnerable to infection and cancer onset. Alternatively, it can increase levels of fatty acids in our blood and add to the risks of coronary heart disease. Here, then, is yet another reason to attend to psychological care in the ill and injured. It is about protecting physical health.

Comments concerning the 'user perspective'

As we will see in Chapter 4, there is evidence to show that most people prefer doctors and health care practitioners to spend a little time with them to give good information concerning diagnoses and treatments. These days, many medical and nursing conferences include talks by patients. A common theme in these is of a general need for good communication, combined with a general effort by health care practitioners to give empathic, emotionally sensitive care. Most seriously ill or injured patients and their partners have a natural need for basic psychological care. I find this demonstrated over and over again in situations such as coronary rehabilitation, the pain clinic or the diabetes clinic.

I would like you to assess your own needs too. What response would you have given concerning your own family in the situation described below?

A somewhat hard minded, financially orientated hospital manager recently asked of me, 'What evidence is there in terms of cost effectiveness or increased turnover of patients if you introduce this sort of thing [psychological care]?' Well, as has been shown already and as will be shown throughout the book, there is evidence to support such developments, but from the users' point of view the case is already established. Thus, I replied to the manager, 'Imagine that your wife needs some distressing surgery to deal with cancer. There are two units available to choose from. One is technically good but being traditional has no special scheme for keeping patients properly informed and caring for them emotionally. The other has staff who, as well as medical and nursing competence, have also been trained in the basics of psychological care and operate a scheme of psychological care – monitoring how their patients are and giving good informational and emotional care with supportive counselling if required. Which unit would you choose and why?' He replied 'Point taken.' I hope that you will see it that way too.

JUST IN CASE - - - I will pause in my flow for a moment to try to head off the risk of offending some readers. Some psychologically minded nurses, physios, dieticians, speech and language therapists etc. will almost certainly be saying something like, 'What a cheek, who does this guy think he is? We already do give psychological care as part of our work and we do think that it is important.' It is, most certainly, a reasonable protest.

I am well aware that there *are* many individual health care practitioners who provide elements of psychological care – often as a personal initiative. There are others who provide aspects of psychological care as part of their job requirement. I have met and been impressed by a breast cancer screening programme's nurse counsellors, for example, and home dialysis nurse counsellors. But this is not exactly what is in my mind when I campaign for psychological care to be introduced into hospitals and health centres. What I have in mind is reflected in the following question:

> If you and I were to go to your hospital, select a ward at random, go in with the clinical nurse manager and select, say, the third bed on the right and then ask 'What is being done about the psychological care of this patient, and who is handling it?' would we get a satisfactory reply? (A modified version of this question could clearly be put to a practice nurse or GP at a health centre.)

In other words, does the average patient at the average general hospital or health centre have the resource of an organized scheme of psychological care? That is the key question.

I hope that you can see the distinction. It is not so much a case of my complaining that individual staff do not offer psychological care. Many will do so, which is pleasing. However, it then falls to the luck of the draw for the patients as to whether or not they are cared to by such members of staff. This will not do. We cannot allow an important resource to be so 'hit or miss' in distribution. Hence my complaint is about the relative rarity of units, wards or health centres that have an organized provision of psychological care. That is, they are organized at a level that provides an effective guarantee that all patients will at least be monitored for psychological state.

As a follow-up point look at the questions below and decide if your particular unit, ward or centre provides psychological care according to the criteria given.

Discussion time

Is there psychological care in my unit?

- Have the nurses and therapists had relevant training?

- Is there an *explicit scheme* for psychological care interventions?

- Is there a systematic allocation of 'psychological care duties' to staff?

- Are there prepared materials (e.g. brief psychological report sheets)?

- Are brief records kept of significant psychological interventions, including educational work?

- Is there a guarantee of basic psychological monitoring and care for all patients?

- Do medical staff support the effort at psychological care and coordinate their work with the psychological care programme?

- Is there an established link with a clinical psychology or counselling service for referrals? Are referrals made?

2 Understanding the psychology of illness and injury: the clinical perspective

> The crisis of physical illness is an unusually potent stressor that may extend over a long period of time and lead to permanent changes among patients and their family members. The potency of the crisis stems from the typically sudden and unexpected onset and the pervasive threat to the essence of an individual's life and adaptation.
>
> (Moos 1977: 130)

What really goes on in the hearts and minds of people who become seriously ill or injured? What do they feel, what do they think and how do these responses affect the outcome of their situation? There is no short answer to these questions other than to comment that people will *always* have some sort of psychological reaction to serious illness and injury, but we are unlikely to find these reactions to be simple and predictable.

The culture of 'masked reactions'

Perhaps the quotation from Moos given above does seem rather to overstate things, especially with the improved medical capabilities that our society has now achieved. It is certainly the case that, if you are regularly in and out of a modern hospital, you do not find it to be strewn with people in evident crisis or florid psychological reaction – rather the opposite in fact. This is partly, I believe, because of the British culture in general and, more specifically, the evolved culture within our medical environments. In short, this culture encourages an effort towards the denial and repression of feelings or a considerable effort to mask them. I began to recognize this effect in the early stages of my interest in renal failure, when I spent many hours at a renal unit. The open haemodialysis unit with its eight dialysis stations was a place with a kindly and cheery atmosphere. There seemed to be a special effort at cheeriness on the part of the staff that became echoed by many of the dialysis patients. The interactions tended to be functional (about dialysis) or trivial and light hearted. There was little invitation for patients, many of whom were seriously ill and at risk of dying within a few years, to reveal what was actually in their thoughts or feelings. Thus, I felt compelled to write of Myrtle, a 40-year-old mother who, after several years of haemodialysis, had experienced the bitter blow of her kidney transplant failing after seven months. She was back to being treated by haemodialysis, which she hated and feared, and for which vascular access was becoming increasingly difficult. She was exhausted and emotionally broken, giving up in fact:

> Myrtle . . . was noted for her cheeriness towards other people. She clearly made enormous efforts to put aside her personal grief and make the best of things. What intruded upon me most powerfully was experiencing how isolated she was with the weight of her sadness. She was in decline, her spirit broken, conscious of the realisation that she no longer wanted to carry on while attempting to deal with her fears of death together with the intense grief of a mother saying goodbye to her child and husband. The staff at the Kidney Unit at the time were kindly and concerned but, it seemed to me, a hundred miles away in terms of knowing about and understanding her experiences. She was truly alone, surrounded by caring people who were unable to offer the kind of care she needed – that is, companionship and understanding. They wanted to 'cure' her with anti depressants, persuade, cajole, in some ways shake her into struggling on again.
>
> (Nichols 1984: 12)

Perhaps the most obvious feature to be recognized in understanding people's reactions is that of the enormous human diversity in perception, thinking and feeling when illness or injury has to be confronted. There is a huge range of reaction, sometimes negative and sometimes positive. Characteristically, the majority of people 'battle on' bravely. *However, one thing is certain. A proportion of people will have a type of reaction that takes them into stress or distress. Such reactions may then adversely affect their physical and mental well-being and sometimes directly affect the outcome of treatment, therapy and rehabilitation efforts.* How many react in this way? The last section of this chapter reports research that gives an indication of what levels these proportions might run at. There are also occasional references to survey type data in the main body of the text.

As I outlined in Chapter 1, it is often possible to identify and *understand* the negative reactions and attitudes held by patients at an early stage of their care. Thus, with appropriate psychological care, we can attempt to reduce the adverse impact of these negative reactions on their treatment and rehabilitation and, at the same time, reduce the stress and distress that patients and their partners can experience. I hope this ambition will now be familiar to you as my key objective, namely to help to establish within our hospitals and health centres the knowledge that *preventive psychological care is an investment that underpins and secures medical and nursing achievements.*

Seeking evidence

My claim that the absence of psychological care can threaten the well-being of patients and undermine efforts at physical treatment will, by now, sound familiar. Probably, though, you will be looking for rather more by way of supporting evidence and detail before committing yourself to agreement with or rejection of my position. Such support does exist and comes from two sources: clinical evidence (observation) and clinical research. This chapter draws particularly on clinical observation gained from contact with thousands of cases, together with general pointers from clinical research. It is designed to provide you with a guide to some psychological reactions and processes that you may well encounter when working with the ill or injured. This complex clinical picture helps to establish why psychological care is so important within our general hospitals and health centres.

Box 2.1   Clinical versus research evidence

In medicine, nursing and all forms of clinical work, evidence to support one view or another can be found through two areas of activity. First is the evidence collected from the observations and experiences of thousands of clinicians and health care practitioners going about their clinical duties and making systematic observations, usually referred to as *clinical evidence*. The great strength of clinical evidence is that it is often based on a wealth of personal experience and allows flexible and readily adaptable forms of inquiry. It also caters for in-depth case studies that allow access to the uniqueness of individuals and the specific context of their health and illness issues. Clinical evidence is always somewhat personalized, though, in the sense that observations usually come from one clinician or, at best, one clinical team, and so are governed by the perceptual habits and biases of those clinicians. Independent observers may well come to the same conclusions, but that is not necessarily demonstrated or guaranteed in clinical observation.

What tends to happen, therefore, is that when claims are made that are based on clinical observation, *formal research investigations using controlled comparisons* are undertaken to provide independent evidence in support, or otherwise, of the claims. These are the studies that are more likely to be found in the professional journals. This research route to our knowledge of psychological reactions to illness and injury has the strength of established scientific method, often using formal assessment techniques and measurement 'tools' – for example, reliable psychometric scales. However, research-derived knowledge also has limitations, especially when we are faced with individual cases in the clinic. The problem is the tremendous human diversity likely to be encountered. While research-based knowledge helps a great deal in establishing general findings that can be relied upon, confident *individual* case work also calls for a breadth of clinical knowledge through one's own case experience and observations, combined with that of fellow clinicians. This combination is the bedrock of psychological work.

Behind the mask: psychological reactions to illness and injury

As we begin to look at some of the psychological effects of illness and injury I will set the scene by a simple description of a variety of cases that I have been involved with during the past few years. These are typical rather than exceptional and, I hope, impart some idea of the range of reactions that are to be encountered. Of course, many people do not manifest much by way of disturbance or florid reaction to illness. Quite often the reaction is repressed or the person has sufficient coping skills and support to deal with it within their own resources. The following cases are drawn from the group who do end up struggling in some way or another.

Liz was a 49-year-old unmarried primary school teacher. After a visit to India she appeared to develop a viral infection that affected her hearing. After some months of struggling to hear the children in the classroom, she consulted her GP once more and was referred to the audiology department at her local hospital. Her visit to the audiology department was brisk and efficient. The male audiologist said little more than 'I'm afraid you have developed a fairly severe upper frequency deafness. There is nothing we can do about it. You will need a hearing aid. There also are some good lip reading classes.' Armed with a booklet that she had been given explaining hearing loss, Liz wandered home in a daze. Later she felt a growing level of panic as she thought of the implications for her work and the effect the hearing loss might have on the rest of her life. There was no further spontaneous contact from the audiology department. (For further comment see under 'Shock at the event and its implications' below.)

Ken was 41, had two children and worked as a technician in a small electronic manufacturing company. His passion was motorbikes. He was admitted to an intensive therapy unit after a near fatal collision with a stationary car while travelling at speed on the bike. He was sedated and kept ventilated for eight days. During this time (as frequently happens with people in this situation, see Skirrow et al. 2001) Ken experienced vivid traumatizing hallucinations. He believed himself to be forcibly restrained. The nursing and medical staff were experienced as torturers who pushed painful tubes into his body and were trying to take his life from him. Over the months, as he recovered, these experiences were relived as nightmares and flashbacks. Ken struggled to rehabilitate but found himself needing to avoid much social contact, and was generally in a state of tense disarray. He had developed post traumatic stress disorder. (For further comment see under 'Post traumatic stress reaction' below.)

Katherine was 23 years old. She had been diagnosed as diabetic two years before and completed the usual training and education at a diabetes centre. She worked as a beautician, had a partner she hoped to marry and coped well enough in life. However, she was prone to emotional ups and downs, especially since her diagnosis. Unfortunately, Katherine was not reliable with her twice-daily insulin injections. In fact, on being asked at interview when she had last injected insulin she replied, 'Well, I haven't really bothered for the last month.' She was also open about daily 'binges' on chocolate bars. Asked if she understood about the future effect of high blood sugar levels on her retinas and kidneys she said, 'Yes, but it doesn't happen until you're fifty.' (For further comment see under 'Denial' below.)

Martin was 44 years old. He worked in the south of England as a senior sales manager for a large petroleum company. Martin was noted for his very driven approach to work. He worked an extended week, often 12 to 14 hours a day, and rarely took holidays. He was also noted for his jovial, extroverted social presence and his competence in solving problems in the work situation. He sustained a moderate myocardial infarction in 1998. He made a reasonable physical recovery but deteriorated psychologically, losing all his confidence. He became increasingly anxious and was reluctant to leave his house. A year after his heart attack he was still off work, quite agoraphobic and suffering frequent episodes of depression. (For further comment see under 'Collapse of denial and assumptions of health, power and longevity' below.)

James was 60 years old. He owned and ran a small hotel. The business was his life. Regrettably, autumn bookings dropped off and his business became at risk of closure. A significant booking for New Year's Eve was secured but on the night preceding the event there was fairly heavy snow, which blocked the rather long drive to the hotel. James set about digging out the drive after serving breakfast to a handful of guests next morning. His mood was of urgency and some anger because if the evening event had to be cancelled he might fail on loan repayments.

After an hour of digging snow James felt suddenly ill and collapsed in the door of his hotel. He was admitted to the stroke unit. Two weeks later he was discharged. He had a fairly severe dysphasia and the right-sided hemipareisis that often affects stroke victims. James was increasingly troubled by a deep depression and, over the next year or so, his eyes would often stream with tears. (For further comment see under 'Responses to physical symptoms, handicaps and lowered personal control' below.)

Sheila was James's wife and was of roughly the same age. She felt great sorrow and compassion for James, both for his disability and because of the loss of the business and his all important occupation. She put a lot of effort into helping him and nursing him at home. Progressively he became more dependent on her and less inclined to take initiatives himself. If she did not bring his drugs to him he went without. If she wanted to go out to see friends or play bridge he protested in subtle ways. Eventually, Sheila gave up most of her social activity and would only leave the house for brief, essential visits to the shops. She became lonely and stressed, especially with the effort of holding back her anger at times. At one point she made the statement, 'My life is so narrow now I might just as well have had a stroke myself.' (For further comment see under 'Partner crisis, stress and guilt' below.)

Brenda, at 47, was a career nurse. She had suffered from menorrhagia for some time and had eventually elected to have a hysterectomy. The outcome was disappointing, leaving her with disturbing pains and a fever. After some months of attempts to manage this the medical team suggested an investigation through laparoscopy. To the horror of all concerned, this surgery resulted in an accidental puncture of Brenda's bowel. To survive she had to have a reversable colostomy, which she endured for 12 months. This was a terrible time for her and even two years after the colostomy was gone she remained deeply shocked. Physically she was very low on power and felt that she had lost most of her energy. She was unable to work. Psychologically she was preoccupied with the event and made remarks to the effect that her body and life had been destroyed. Her thinking and feelings regarding this surgical accident were very similar to those described by women who have experienced rape. (For further comment see under 'Damage to self-image, loss of self-worth, self-rejection and shame below.)

Bob was a 48-year-old policeman. He had noticed a proneness to chest pains and some breathlessness during the preceding months and so had consulted his GP. His GP referred him to a cardiologist, who, in turn, had booked him in for an angiogram. After monitoring and recovery from the procedure for an hour or so the consultant came out from the 'cath lab' and told Bob that he had fairly advanced coronary artery disease and that three of his coronary vessels needed bypass surgery. Bob was stunned by this news and spent ten minutes wandering around the small ward talking to other patients, saying, 'It is the last thing I expected to be told – that I've got to have heart surgery.' There was a seven-month wait for this surgery and during this time Bob found himself quite changed – sufficiently so that he was referred for counselling. In his first sessions he described how his ambitions for promotion, his plans for savings and retirement, even his plans for a forthcoming holiday, felt of little importance and interest to him. His future seemed insecure and he no longer trusted his heart and health. Somehow, magically, he wanted the security of 'guaranteed' health back. (For further comment see under 'The collapse of denial and assumptions of health, power and longevity' below.)

So far I have not mentioned Sue, who broke her neck and became quadraplegic, Mike, whose legs were severely burnt when he used petrol to light a bonfire, Debbie, whose first child was stillborn, Joy, who developed emphysemia, or Ian, who was paralysed for three months with Guillain-Barré syndrome. Frankly, the list stretches on at great length and we need to move on. However, I will again note that the uniqueness and detail of each of these cases often becomes buried in the cold statistics of general research data. Hence my reliance, at this point, is on clinical observation and evidence.

Recognizing psychological reactions to illness and injury: description with brief case examples

I would like now to provide you with an explanatory briefing on some of the types of psychological reactions that, over the years, you will almost certainly encounter in your work as a health care practitioner – especially if you include psychological care as part of your job description and make the effort to talk with your patients in any depth. Some of these reactions will be in the acute phase and perhaps more likely to be encountered within a hospital setting. Others are more long term and so more likely to be seen at the primary care level or in follow-up at outpatient clinics. Box 2.2 names the main reactions that I will be introducing.

One preliminary word of caution, though: this is a personal set of observations that I am sharing with you. It is based mainly on my own clinical experience. Therefore, the observations will be biased in the sense that they record the features that *I* frequently notice in therapy sessions with people who have been referred to me by doctors and nurses. All of us perceive selectively – influenced by our personal history and training. This means that, in the clinical situation when we are attending to human reactions, the picture that each of us develops of the person and what is going on will have a bias and will probably differ slightly one from another. Each of us may have a tendency to notice certain types of features with regularity, and at the same time have personal blind spots. It is inevitable. In these terms you may feel that you want to add some items from your own experience to the list. Excellent, do so, that is how clinical evidence is built up into a powerful body of collective knowledge. Please also bear in mind that the bulk of these observations are drawn from my own experiences in certain specialities, namely cardiology, renal medicine, diabetes, pain management, dermatology and plastic and reconstructive surgery, with some clients from oncology, trauma, general surgery and intensive care. Hence, if you are a health care practitioner in another type of speciality or in general practice you may well have variants of these observations or additions that can be added in. Note, finally, that this book concerns the psychology of adults. I do not deal with the psychology of children and their parents who are dealing with illness or injury.

Enough of qualifying comments. Box 2.2 lists the psychological reactions that have become familiar to me in my contact with various types of illness and injury. The next sections set out some detail of these reactions.

We will take the general situation of patients who have developed a serious illness or sustained a serious accident. They will usually be in hospital for a while if it has been an illness of sudden onset, or back and forwards for diagnostic assessments and treatments. Eventually, though, they will be discharged back into the care of the primary health care team. Initial psychological reactions (in the first few weeks) are about responding to the event and trying to come to terms with the implications. These first perceptions may well shape reactions in the

---

Box 2.2 Observed psychological reactions to illness and injury

- **Shock at the event and its implications: threat and anxiety.**
- **Post traumatic stress reactions.**
- **Collapse of denial and assumptions of health, power and longevity: the psychodynamic origins of anxious hyper-vigilance and hypochondria.**
- **Distress with hospitalization, treatments and medical crises.**
- **Responses to physical symptoms, handicaps and lowered personal control: anxiety, loss, grief, anger and depression.**
- **Damage to self-image, loss of self-worth and self-rejection: perceptions and feelings of being damaged and diminished as a person.**
- **Sexual changes and losses.**
- **Existential impoverishment.**
- **Denial.**
- **Exaggerated independence versus collapse into dependency.**
- **Partner crisis, stress and guilt: the 'care trap'.**

---

longer term, perhaps six to twelve months later. Again I will acknowledge that a good proportion of people do manage to end up in a stable, coping, relatively positive state (although their task will be easier with good psychological care). A good many do not, though, and if you can engage them in gentle, exploratory conversation, you will find evidence of reactions that you may recognize in one or more of the following.

• Reactions: Shock at the event and its implications – threat and anxiety

Individual histories differ, of course, but when illness has a rapid onset there will have been no time for preparation of any sort. Thus, many people will then experience a shock reaction. By shock I mean the sudden, jarring intrusion of menacing events that break up the sense of personal safety and security. In the instance of a totally unexpected heart attack, for example, there may follow a pervading apprehension linked to the sense of being threatened by something that is not, at the outset, understood and that is out of personal control. Worries may crowd in to the extent that some patients and partners can feel terribly vulnerable and barely able to function normally. Worrying may be the dominant form of thinking, with either patient or partner preoccupied with a range of issues. If you want a glimpse of the issues that invade people's thinking simply imagine for a moment that you have just been diagnosed with breast or testicular cancer and project this into your current life and near future. Worries to do with premature death, surgery and hospitalization, effects on finances, the mortgage, employability, the effect on one's partner and children are likely to gain ground on you in a predatory manner.

If the feelings of shock and the persistent worries last for more than a few days then the people involved may develop the physical signs of acute stress. Stress is an adrenergic type pattern of physical change, dominated by raised heart rate and blood pressure, physical tension, distractibility, disturbed sleep and sometimes night sweats. It is very unpleasant and very undermining, both of mental health and, in the long term, of physical health. Furthermore, it is not something that can be banished by effort of will – it is powerful and intrusive. Naturally, at this stage, the gentle support of a member of staff who can give time, listen and offer a stable, reassuring presence with useful information and help with 'reality checking' (that is, helping people to check that their perceptions are realistic) can be immensely valuable – more on this later. Remember also that, in some illness states, limiting the power and duration of the shock and consequent stressed state can be a positive contribution to conserving physical health.

> Belinda, at 34, was a single parent with two children aged five and eight. She worked as a receptionist in a car hire company, her own mother dealing with the children immediately after school. When a lump in her breast was diagnosed as malignant Belinda became very frightened. She was regularly up at night fretting with worries about money and coping with the children when she had surgery and radiotherapy. After several days of extreme anxiety she was forced to go to her GP for assistance. The GP was a significant help and so too were several sessions with the breast cancer nurse counsellor. Even so, she had a very poor time waiting for surgery, losing weight and much sleep.

As emphasized above, this general section is primarily devoted to clinical observations. It may be helpful, though, from time to time, to have brief mention of research evidence that substantiates the observations. There is no shortage of research literature that reports on the anxiety and shock that can be provoked by the onset of illness. For example, Hughes *et al.* (1986) assessed women with clinical signs of breast cancer for 'stress response'. They used both interview measures and self-report questionnaires. The data returned indicated that 42 per cent of women later found to have cancer scored in the 'high' anxiety category. Jacobsen and Holland (1991) give a very useful review of the stressing effect of a diagnosis of cancer and Fallowfield and Clarke (1991) offer a similar perspective specifically on breast cancer. These two reviews give similar sorts of figures for the incidence of anxiety and stress attendant on diagnosis and the immediate aftermath in cancer. In Baum *et al.* (1997) it is easy to find equivalent pictures for very many of the frequently occurring illnesses and injuries.

• Reactions: Post traumatic stress reaction (PTSD)

I expect that this term is familiar to you. When people are subjected to an unexpected and personally alarming or traumatizing experience a proportion will develop a cluster of reactions that combine together into the PTSD syndrome. People in hospital who have been involved in accidents such as aircraft, car or train crashes, industrial accidents or fires are very likely to suffer PTSD. So too are those who have had difficult experiences, such as personal attack or rape. There is also a group of medical patients who are vulnerable to PTSD in relation to their illness or treatment, in particular post heart attack and ICU (intensive care unit) patients. The key feature of post traumatic stress disorder is the intrusive re-experiencing of the stressing event. This can be very vivid. One patient described it to me as 'Rather like a video playing in my head. It plays the image of the fire, which I can see coming at me, on to whatever I am doing. I can't get away from it.' These experiences are called flashbacks. They are often accompanied by disturbing nightmares, tension and anxious disarray generally. Many sufferers will avoid the circumstances that led up to the event. A surprising number of patients that one meets in a general hospital (especially those who have been involved in accidents) describe experiences that suggest PTSD. Sometimes this is mild and fades rapidly, but occasionally it will persist for many months.

Supporting evidence for these observations concerning PTSD is not hard to find. For example, Owen *et al.* (2001) report studies, including one of their own, which indicate that between 10 and 15 per cent of post myocardial infarction patients experience PTSD symptoms within the first year after the event. Skirrow *et al.* (2001) offer a review concerning PTSD experiences related to admission to an ICU. Generally this was for a duration greater than four days. Various surveys reported indicate that up to 15 per cent of ICU patients in general and 27.5 per cent of patients with acute respiratory distress syndrome may suffer PTSD symptoms after discharge. In particular, there were flashbacks to very frightening hallucinatory experiences while sedated and breathing by means of a ventilator.

Les was 52 and an enthusiastic trainee glider pilot. On making his circuit to land one afternoon he allowed the airspeed of his glider to drop too low and the glider stalled, flicked into a spin and hit the ground. Les did not lose consciousness but his back and legs were badly injured. During his two months in hospital he was continually disturbed by vivid flashbacks and nightmares of the moment when the glider stalled and spun into the ground.

Hussein was undergoing surgery when his heart stopped. He was resuscitated but needed intensive care support. He spent a week in ICU, for much of which time he was on a ventilator. On discharge he suffered badly with recurring hallucinations and flashbacks of experiences he had while sedated in ICU. He was extremely shaken and agitated for many months.

Eve, at 65 years of age, sustained a heart attack during the night. She lived alone. For a while she was in so much pain and felt so breathless that she was completely incapacitated. She was unable to move to telephone for help. She found it frightening in the extreme. After ten minutes or so she managed to make a call. While recovering in the cardiac unit she was continually troubled by flashbacks and memories of these terrifying few minutes.

- **Reactions: The collapse of denial and assumptions of health, power and longevity: the psychodynamic origins of anxious hypervigilance and hypochondria**

Until the middle years in life, at least, the average person is likely to have a picture of their life ahead that does not usually involve the onset of serious illness or infirmity through accident. I am suggesting that a defensive denial is maintained, which holds at bay the recognition of the personal risk of illness and death. For many people this defence leads to the stable assumption that health and power will continue uninterrupted through the passing years. Plans for family matters, investment, business or career development, retirement, later life relocation and travel betray the existence of this denial, which, unless you are unusual or have had experience of illness in your immediate family, you will find in yourself. Thus, the argument goes, for the average person, the broad picture of life assumes health, mobility, physical power and a normal lifespan. However, with sudden and unexpected onset of serious illness for the first time in life, this defensive denial will often collapse, with powerful consequences. The person and perhaps the partner and immediate family are suddenly well able to see the risks and implications of the illness and, where it applies, of the foreshortening of personal lifespan itself. Such perceptions can evoke new feelings of great vulnerability and uncertainty. This psychodynamic (a term used to imply a sequence of psychological changes) is often followed by a marked loss of confidence in the reliability of the body. There is a loss of trust in the failing organ, the heart, say, or the body as a whole. The assumption of health is then replaced by an *anxious hypervigilance*, a turning in of attention to the body and a raised sensitivity to body functions, sensations and pains – in other words, the beginnings of hypochondriacal preoccupation.

This enhanced and anxious awareness of the body will often bring fears that illness is developing or that surgery has developed complications. It can lead patients and partners into becoming what can be called 'difficult' patients, although this is a needlessly disparaging term, I fear. Those of you with experience in cardiology will probably have heard the related term 'cardiac neurosis', a term that has evolved to describe exactly this phenomenon – that is, patients who, following a heart attack, lose all confidence and cannot accept that their heart will become trustworthy and reliable again. They are back and forwards to their doctors and cardiologists with anxious complaints about not feeling well, having chest pains, hyperventilation attacks, unusual sensations and heart rhythms.

Having had some twenty years of regular clinical contact with the victims of heart attacks, I can say with confidence that this is a reaction to illness that I have encountered on very many occasions. The first infarction is usually a complete surprise and shock to people, with no warning at all. In the first few months many heart attack victims go

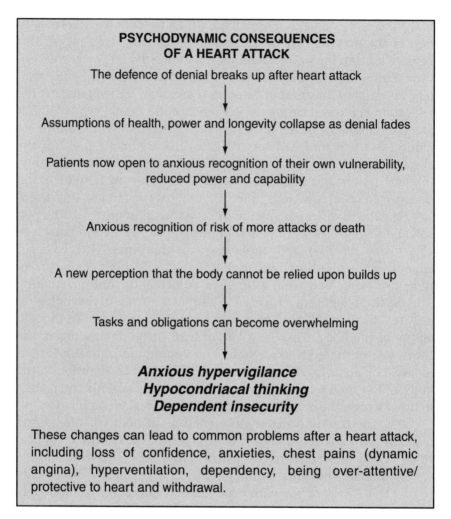

**PSYCHODYNAMIC CONSEQUENCES
OF A HEART ATTACK**

The defence of denial breaks up after heart attack

↓

Assumptions of health, power and longevity collapse as denial fades

↓

Patients now open to anxious recognition of their own vulnerability,
reduced power and capability

↓

Anxious recognition of risk of more attacks or death

↓

A new perception that the body cannot be relied upon builds up

↓

Tasks and obligations can become overwhelming

↓

*Anxious hypervigilance
Hypocondriacal thinking
Dependent insecurity*

These changes can lead to common problems after a heart attack,
including loss of confidence, anxieties, chest pains (dynamic
angina), hyperventilation, dependency, being over-attentive/
protective to heart and withdrawal.

Figure 2.1 Psychodynamic consequences of a heart attack.

through a sequence of experiences that I can best summarize for you in
Figure 2.1. (Note that dynamic angina refers to the effect of a form of
reversible spasm in the coronary arteries, possibly induced by the
physiological changes linked to anxiety.)

Esme, at 55, had been a very busy woman for much of her life. She
came from an industrious family and tended to feel guilty if she was not
busily engaged in tasks or activity. Rest and leisure were not familiar
experiences to her. Esme's career as a nurse had been full and successful,

although she was only working part-time when she had her first heart attack. She found herself surprised and (inappropriately) ashamed of how insecure she felt after this. Seeking help while she was attending coronary rehabilitation classes, she related how her insecurity was causing her to live a very restricted lifestyle. Because she lived alone she felt very unsupported and often had 'nervy' days when she was very aware of her heart and did not want to go out. She knew she should be exercising but did not have the confidence to do it on her own. She feared a further heart attack and would often wake up during the night with sweats, feeling panicky. Sometimes it was all she could do not to call an ambulance.

Bob, at 41, was the regional manager of a tool hire company. He was very competent at his job and popular with his workforce because of his good humour. He travelled a great deal, sometimes more than 2000 miles a month. He was in the middle of a management restructuring project when he had a moderately severe heart attack. Eighteen months later, although his cardiologist regarded him as recovered and fit to work, he was not working. He had suffered a complete collapse in confidence. He rarely left his house on his own. Although he would usually manage to go out if he was accompanied by his wife, he would not go far and certainly would not take on a long journey for a holiday. From a formerly extroverted, confident, professional man he had became an introverted, anxious, near recluse. He accounted for this change by telling how he just did not feel safe on his own and felt mildly panicky if he was more than a few miles away from a good hospital. He continually feared another heart attack.

Naturally, this type of psychodynamic is not just to be found among patients frequenting departments of cardiology. Sudden, unexpected onset of disease, particularly if this involves the risk of further deterioration and, perhaps, reduced abilities, will always make it more likely that people develop a similar psychodynamic pathway leading to loss of trust in their body and the disruptive consequences of anxious hypervigilance and hypochondriacal thinking.

These observations and my claim concerning the mechanism through which insecurity after sudden illness onset can arise invite further empirical scrutiny, of course. While some psychologists might suggest alternative routes to the general effect, there is little doubt concerning actual outcome. This state of anxious hypervigilance and hypochondriacal thinking is widely known in, for example, most cardiac departments, where, as I mentioned above, the phrase cardiac neurosis is sometimes heard. Rough estimates by local cardiologists suggest that between 10 and 20 per cent of post heart attack patients experience the effects I have described at one level or another in the longer term (three months plus). Bennett and Carroll (1997), in their review of the psychological impact of a heart attack, report a general agreement in research that 40–50 per cent of patients experience moderate to severe anxiety while in hospital, which falls to about 30 per cent at three to six months and 20 per cent at one-year follow-up. Similarly, there is general agreement that rates of depression run at about 20–30 per cent early on, rising slightly as the months go by. Bennett and Carroll also indicate that those patients with raised levels of anxiety and depression are less likely to return to work or resume sexual activity, which serves as an indirect indicator of loss of confidence in the heart and hence an anxious notion of its frailty and reliability.

• Reactions: Distress with hospitalization, treatments and crises

The majority of people attend hospital with considerable reluctance and ambivalence. Being away from home and family, dealing with a little known and unfamiliar institutional culture, losing control and privacy, poor communication, not knowing what is happening, noise disturbance and lack of sleep, anticipating painful events and leading one's life in a manner that someone else decides are all issues that can disturb people and lead to discomfort and anxiety. Johnston (1997) describes this well. Similarly, although not as complex an event, even attendance at a local health centre can be something of an ordeal for some, especially if a procedure is involved such as venepuncture or minor skin surgery. Sometimes a gentle, supportive question before the procedure or contact really begins can be quite revealing. Something like 'How are you feeling about this?' might give an insight into a level of tension and discomfort that is greater than appears to be the case from casual inspection.

Having mentioned procedures in a health centre I now want to talk through the issue of general difficulties with diagnostic procedures and treatments. We all vary greatly in our tolerance to pain and discomfort. We also vary greatly in our previous history of sensitizing experiences. These experiences will include previous treatments, perhaps in childhood, or observed illnesses and treatments endured by other members of the family. Family culture and modelling by parents and siblings related to pain, illness and discomfort will have played a big part in shaping our own reactions to medical encounters and treatment procedures. Expectations of pain and discomfort and expectations of not finding these easy to deal with can have a powerful effect on raising anxiety. So too can pain that is unexpected and unexplained; which becomes a poorly understood threat. This point is dealt with in depth using the example of peritoneal catheter insertion procedures in Nichols (1991). Some people admitted for surgery or attending for diagnostic or treatment procedures will be relatively at ease and cope very well. Others may feel very threatened and so be frightened and tense. Some will be anxious at the level of phobic anxiety. For example:

> After her car crash and painful back injury May had waited over three months for an MRI scan of her lower back. She was pleased to receive the appointment and arrived early for her scan. However, as she was prepared and then slowly moved into the scanner she became increasingly anxious and panicky. It felt hot, very confined and noisy, and she started to develop a claustrophobic reaction with hyperventilation. After five minutes she could no longer tolerate the situation and started shouting to be let out. The scan was abandoned.

If events do not unfold in quite the way that our patients had been expecting then a further effect might be the distress and stress of an ensuing medical crisis:

> Don attended for an angiogram. Vascular access was through his brachial artery. He had been quite nervous but managed to cope until the catheter actually entered his heart and set off (as he had been warned it would) a series of strong, irregular ectopic beats. This experience was not what he had expected and was suddenly exceptionally frightening to him because he feared his heart was about to stop. It did not but, nevertheless, he was in quite a shaky state for the rest of the day.

Similar accounts will be found in the literature to do with the treatment of burns, the treatment of cancer by chemotherapy and radiotherapy, experiences in the MRI scanner, endoscopic investigations, the run-up to eye surgery, facet joint injections to control back pain etc. Wilson-Barnett (1989) and Benyamini and Leventhal (1997) give useful reviews of research and practice related to the problem of distressing medical procedures.

- ### Reactions: Responses to physical symptoms, handicaps and lowered personal control: threat, anxiety, loss, grief, anger and depression

A difficulty for me in composing this section is that one might easily take up half a book dealing with items like this one in depth. There are few surprises, but the range of circumstances with their specific effects is dauntingly large. Therefore I must settle for a brief indication only.

It is instructive to take the time to attempt truly to empathize with the experience of some of our patients. We need to focus on *sensing* the feelings of, say, patients suffering the encroachments of motor neurone disease or the restrictions of paraplegia or quadriplegia after an accident; similarly, on sensing the impact of an amputation after bone cancer, the limitations in speech and movement following a stroke, the sense of damage and weakness caused by a heart attack and the continuous, disabling head and neck pain that can result from a severe whiplash injury. It truly is a worthwhile exercise to take the time to project yourself into these types of situation and sense the feelings and thoughts that would affect you. Despite much individual variation it is possible to make some generalizations concerning how we are likely to deal with these sorts of experience in life. When perceptions are dominated by threat many of us will respond with *'threat-laden' thinking*. Consequently, we will feel anxious, sometimes so anxious that it becomes disabling. If perception is more focused on loss then this will usually evoke a type of grieving reaction. We are more likely to experience a great sadness that makes us feel very fragile emotionally, very easily moved to tears. But loss may also provoke anger, resentment and frustration. Early on these more aggressive feelings may be very prevalent, but later they can give way to depression or grief.

Perhaps the most important point to make about reactions of this type is that they are *normal*, we are 'designed' to react this way. In many ways no reaction at all would be the abnormal state, as, too, is a sanitized ward where the hope of the staff is for grateful, smiling patients who, despite worrying illness or disfiguring accident, strive to maintain a cheerful presence. That would be an abnormal expectation. Fortunately, although once common, this pretty much belongs to the past, since our present generations of nurses and doctors are much more aware of the emotional concomitants of illness and injury.

Having made this basic point, I need to make two clarifications. First, these normal reactions of anxiety, anger, grief and depression are considered by most psychologists to be part of the emotional processing of difficult events and experiences. However, sometimes people get stuck with their feeling reactions and their disturbing perceptions of their situation. They do not achieve the adaptation and acceptance that allows progress and rehabilitation. They can thus drift down into an increasingly disabling depth of negative perception and feeling. At this point normality *is* lost to a degree. In such cases assistance and actual psychological therapy will often be needed. Second, whether or not a person develops this type of progressive difficulty, psychological care is usually welcomed by patients and partners and, in my experience, helpful in consolidating recovery.

Malcolm was 37 years old when he was told that he had developed motor neurone disease. Being a very computer literate university lecturer he rapidly gained access to a considerable amount of detail concerning the disease. It was very depressing and frightening reading. He discovered that the average survival time after diagnosis was about 15 months (although he might survive much longer than that) and that he could expect a steady decline in physical capacity and independence throughout the remainder of his lifespan. He had married five years before this diagnosis and had a three-year-old daughter. Both he and his wife were initially struck by a terror of what was to come and by a very emotional anticipation of the end phase of the illness. They knew that during the end phase communication would be difficult and the burden of his intense dependency would be an immense agony to them both. In conversation with me a month after diagnosis Malcolm had many issues to face. At this meeting anger was to the fore. There was much anger at the sudden and alarming shift from health to illness, with the implied loss of control and the end to plans for his career at the university and future generally. He was also very angry at the physical effect of his illness. Malcolm had always been athletic and had worked at keeping a fit, trim body that he was proud of. He was angry at the forthcoming physical decline because he expected to find it humiliating and frustrating. He was also angry at the thought of not being alive to see his daughter grow up – it had been a difficult pregnancy to achieve, requiring the services of the fertility clinic. On talking things through it was clear that Malcolm's anger was related to deeper feelings of fright and anticipatory loss. He bitterly resented the physical changes to come because they frightened him. He grieved already at the thought of not seeing his daughter and wife in the years ahead.

Useful texts for information and research findings on psychological reactions to physical symptoms and handicaps are Lacey and Burns (1989), Davis and Fallowfield (1991), Broome and Llewelyn (1995) and Baum *et al.* (1997). If the issue of the psychological effects of motor neurone disease is something that you wish to take further, then Earll and Johnston (1997) or Goldstein and Leigh (1999) are useful sources.

One further issue merits separate mention in this section, namely lowered personal control. Effectively, this is a form of handicap that can weigh heavily on those who have to endure, as in the case of neurological disorder. However, to widen the scope of our clinical examples, the problem is well illustrated by the situation facing people who have needed stoma surgery to treat abdominal cancer. In an insightful, qualitative study, McVey *et al.* (2001) conducted interviews with patients just before, shortly after and three months after their stoma surgery. A key finding was the strongly resented and disturbing experience of lessening personal control of body function, and the reduced control of one's own cleanliness and one's own sense of being hygienic and socially acceptable. Fortunately, as the months passed some sense of recovery of independence and personal control was achieved.

Can it be predicted how people are going to react psychologically to physical symptoms, handicaps and lowered personal control? Not in any exact sense, no. The reactions described may be immediate or delayed. There may be other psychodynamics, such as denial, which displace reactions for a period of time. Individual context is so important in determining a person's reaction to illness and injury too. The meaning that a person gives to the event is a key determinant of developing reactions. This shapes perceptions concerning the domestic and work-related implications and the impact on self-esteem – which is,

---

Box 2.3   Passing comment: psychological care matters

As an aside that anticipates later chapters it is relevant to note the currently dominant view in psychological therapy and counselling. In general it is held that a number of interventions, including support, the opportunity to express and explore one's emotions and their causes, the opportunity to explore the biases in one's perceptions and guidance in problem-solving are all helpful in medical and medical crisis situations (see Davis and Fallowfield 1991: Chapters 1 and 2). When people are helped to work through their reactions to reduced capacity and disfigurement in this way, potential problems can often be headed off and general psychological progress can, it is hoped, parallel physical recovery. Davis and Fallowfield (1991) gather a collection of articles that review the importance of psychological therapy and counselling in relation to various illnesses and injuries. This is why it is so important that health care practitioners have an orientation towards psychological care. While providing basic psychological care, they can identify those patients in need of special assistance, begin the process of helping and, if necessary, call in a clinical psychologist or counsellor to take things further.

---

itself, linked to how the illness or injury affects a person's personal presentation and power to continue as before.

Nigel had been a paratrooper and had signed up for a full career in the army. At 35 he was diagnosed as having insulin-dependent diabetes. As a result he was discharged as medically unfit. He became bitter and angry over his diabetes, resenting the failure of his body. Even ten years later the anger still burned within him.

Elaine broke her neck diving into a swimming pool in the dark. She recovered in hospital to find that she was paralysed and would be wheelchair-bound. Fortunately, some function very slowly returned to her arms, but she was very disabled and dependent. On the surface she was bravely coping but privately it felt like her life, at 22, had already come to an end. She did her best to be outgoing and take part in as much activity as she could but she would have nothing to do with other disabled people. Two years later she became quite irritable and then badly depressed.

- **Reactions: Damage to self-image, loss of self-worth, self-rejection and shame: perceptions and feelings of being damaged and diminished as a person**

Obviously this type of reaction is closely linked to the last item. Often the two merge into one, but I will separate self-image as a topic because, on occasions, it can be the first indication that you will spot with one of your patients that he or she is struggling with emotional issues. Sometimes, within the safety of a therapy session, people have spoken to me with phrases like 'I'm on the scrap heap now, I'm damaged goods, I'm a burden, I'm weird, I'm a freak, I don't belong any more, the children will be better off without me because I can't be a proper mother anymore.'

These terribly sad statements reveal the great psychological damage that illness and injury can inflict on some people in terms of a sudden, negative change in perception of self-worth. The key point is that positive self-worth is the essential foundation of psychological well-being. This damage in self-image provides a further 'engine' for the anger, agitation and depression that you will encounter in some of your patients. The following fragment from an encounter between a physiotherapist and a patient catches the theme:

Physio: 'Hi, Ken, have you had a good week? Have you been keeping up your exercise walks?'

Ken: 'Oh good morning, Carol. Well, not too bad I suppose. I went out on a couple of days for a bit. But not so much this week as last.'

Physio: 'Doesn't sound quite as much as we had hoped. Has anything particular stopped you?'

Ken: 'No, not really. I suppose I have not felt much like a live wire for the last few days.'

Physio: 'What do you mean, that you have been off physically or are you feeling a bit low?'

Ken: 'It's that really. I have been a bit low. The truth is it feels like I'm out of things from now on – not much of a future. I can't do the things I am used to doing. I tried to lay a few slabs in the garden on Monday and had to pack it in after half an hour. I mean, look at me, it's pathetic. I'm only 43 and I'm like an old man. I know you give good advice about exercise but the truth is I don't like going out for the walks in case I meet people that

I know, especially one of my workmates or customers. I don't want them to see me like this. In fact if I see one of them in the distance I try to avoid them. I would go to the pub but it's the same, I'm bound to meet them there. It sort of feels like they might be pitying me. And they should – it's scrap heap time for Ken.'

As you might have guessed, Ken was one of our clients at coronary rehabilitation. He made similar intimations to various of the staff, usually in an emotional manner. He had been a very hard working builder, rather obsessional in character and therefore sought after for his high standards and reliability in finishing a job well. He worked very long hours, often seven days a week, with little rest or holiday time. His was a familiar reaction to all of the staff on the coronary rehabilitation programme. He felt reduced in power and diminished as a person. He was literally ashamed of his incapacity because it clashed with his self-image. This image put great store on his energy and 'can do' persona. He delighted in his ability at mastering problems and getting difficult building jobs finished. It made him popular with his customers, who clearly admired his abilities. *But*, underneath the surface of this strong, outgoing man existed a real vulnerability. His life to date had shaped into him an unrecognized assumption about himself that is best caught in the phrase:

'I am worth what I do.'

In other words, Ken's sense of personal worth was based on his ability to be 'doing' – that is, industrious, productive and successful as a builder. His sense of personal worth, in fact much of his self-image, did not come from his presence and character as a person, but from his 'doing'.

It is not hard to identify the cause of the collapse in his morale after his heart attack. His health was weakened to the extent that, for a year or two at least, he would suffer a considerable loss of energy and become tired quickly. It would be unwise for him to go back to the pace and strain of the long hours and full work diary of the past. Ideally he would take on lighter work at a slower pace. Ideally he would take six months off work to give himself time for proper progress through coronary rehabilitation, and then resume work on a part-time basis. Combined with the worries concerning income and the loss of regular customers, Ken naturally felt despondent. But the real, underlying issue was one of him feeling diminished and, with that, a sense of shame and self-rejection. Now we can summarize his perception as:

> **'I am worth what I do, but now I can do nothing.**
> **Therefore, I am now worth nothing.'**

I am not suggesting that Ken is literally saying this to himself, but it is another psychodynamic event resulting from his recognition of his diminished physical power. This is responsible for his remark 'I'm on the scrap heap now.' Early on he was quite weak physically and could do little. Hence, his dependency for the maintenance of his positive self-esteem on his work led to a collapse of self-esteem as his work came to a temporary halt. This in turn led to anger and self-rejection and that led on to depression that compounded the loss of energy.

So, we must register and keep in mind the fact that medical treatments can have a severe impact on self-image and personal presentation. The impact is to be found in any age group, but often it is more immediately noticeable with teenagers and young adults. Dialysis by continuous ambulatory peritoneal dialysis (CAPD), for example, is a technique in which two litres of dialysate fluid are run into the abdomen through a permanent catheter implanted in the abdomen. This fluid is then exchanged every four hours. The technique is mildly disfiguring in that it causes noticeable distension of the abdomen and requires a retreat into a sterile environment every four hours or so for a dialysate bag change. Younger patients sometimes struggle with this aspect of their treatment, which, together with fairly severe restrictions on fluid intake, can make them feel odd and different. A clinical example of this is given in the section 'Psychological reactions to illness and "the seasons of life"' below.

In similar fashion, diabetes treatment by insulin injection is another trouble spot with younger patients. Image, in the sense of not being different and hence achieving acceptance with friends, feels extremely important for some young people. Not surprisingly, it is a fairly frequent experience in diabetes clinics for staff to struggle with young diabetics who knowingly miss insulin injections and so run at alarmingly high blood sugar levels. Although they often know that these high blood sugar levels carry the strong threat of microvascular failure in later life (bringing visual problems, renal failure, heart problems etc.), compliance is abandoned. This is because the knowledge has less power in controlling the behaviour of some young diabetics than the need they have for a self-image that does not risk rejection by their peers. Hence compliance with insulin injections and diet can collapse to a disastrously low level.

> Lisa was 17. She had been diagnosed as having insulin-dependent diabetes at 15 years of age and was required to inject herself with insulin twice a day. She was not reliable with this, though, and often missed injections. She explained her situation as follows. 'These injections make me feel freaky. No one else in my group has to do them. I don't care if my friends say they don't mind. I just don't like feeling freaky.'

Damage to self-image and loss of feelings of self-worth are obviously a risk in more disfiguring accidents such as facial burns, amputations or accidents leading to paralysis. It is also the case that some types of surgery that are necessary for survival may have a damaging impact on self-image and, more specifically, sexual self-image. Thus the creation of a colostomy, the loss of breasts through mastectomy or the loss of a testicle through testicular cancer are obviously difficult and complicated psychological events for most people. For some people, though, body image and physical dignity matter very much. For such people this type of disfiguring surgery can be *especially* difficult. As you can imagine, this can apply particularly to people if they are still sexually active. This aspect of reactions to medical interventions must always be explored if care is to be considered to be complete. Rumsey (1997) provides a helpful introduction to issues to do with disfigurement, the effects of which can be profound.

> Moira was 38 and had a colostomy following severe bowel disorder. Replying to the stoma nurse's inquiry about how she was getting on, she replied, 'It has changed my life completely. I feel revolting. I can't look at myself undressed in the mirror – the thing is disgusting. We have not had sex since the surgery. My husband is very kind and says it doesn't matter to him but I feel so gross. I won't let him near me.'

A note on guilt and self-blame

Linked to this general theme of loss of self-worth, reactions of guilt justify separate mention. Where your patient is a key figure in a family situation or where the patient's partner has to respond to the illness with a very substantial input of personal, care-giving support, then some element of guilt and self-blame is not unusual. Often this becomes evident in the form of an apology for trouble caused or burdens created. People who have been self-sufficient and independent in style may be more vulnerable to this type of reaction.

> Melanie was knocked off her cycle and sustained mild brain damage. For several months she was quite badly affected by visual disturbance, vertigo and nausea, which combined with very severe headaches. She was forced to spend much time in bed and therefore was unable to cope with her two daughters, aged five and eight, or do much to help her husband cope with domestic duties as well as a full-time job. She became increasingly despairing and guilty. Although the accident was not her fault, she blamed herself for the strain that her accident imposed on the family. This all added to the depression that often follows head injury.

> Following recurrent episodes of chest pain, Mark was discovered to have considerable narrowing in several coronary arteries. Surgery to bypass two of these was not viable and therefore conservative management was the plan. This arrangement, although unavoidable, left the family with a sense of threat hanging over it. Mark felt particularly guilty towards his wife because the situation was very similar to that during her childhood, when her father became ill with heart disease. He had died prematurely, shortly before their own marriage.

• Reactions: Sexual changes and losses

Sexual drive and function can ebb away in both men and women who have become ill or received injury from an accident. For example, Lewin (1995) provides some useful figures that serve as an indication of the surprisingly high levels at which sexual dysfunction can run in people who have sustained a heart attack:

1   Various surveys reveal that a significant proportion of male heart attack patients have sexual difficulties or report reduced sexual activity and satisfaction after recovering from a heart attack. Some studies indicate that this proportion may be as high as 58 per cent. In part this reduction in sexual activity can

be directly linked to impotency that is induced by anti-hypertensive medication. But it is also the case that many men are nervous of sex after a heart attack because it is seen as a provocation to a damaged heart and therefore a risky endeavour. Naturally, this is common in men who have developed a hypervigilant anxiety reaction.

2 Similar surveys reveal that approximately 65 per cent of women have sexual fears or reduced sexual activity and satisfaction after a heart attack.

3 Approximately 57 per cent of cardiac surgery cases suffer sexual dysfunction.

4 Incidentally, there is also a figure that raises issues that are discussed in Chapter 4. Some 65 per cent of cardiologists did not voluntarily discuss sexual issues with their cardiac patients.

Naturally, the problem is far wider than just cardiac medicine. Literature dealing with neurological illness and neurological injury is another source of similar statistics (e.g. Kennedy 1991).

Depending on the time in life and the importance of sexual function for the individual, sexual impairment can be a hated and resented loss, provoking a destructive loss of self-esteem. This is not inevitable, of course. Viz:

> Glenis had required a full hysterectomy and also needed to have one ovary removed. On discussing her recovery at her 12-month follow-up, the issue of sexual relations was raised. She said that during the year since the surgery she had not resumed sexual relationships. Asked if that disturbed her and whether she would like assistance with the issue she replied, 'No, not really. Sex has always been a bit of a chore for me, I've never really enjoyed it. I'm quite glad to be free of it to tell you the truth.'

In my own experience, Glenis's type of reaction is not encountered very frequently. It is much more common to hear the type of reaction that is a mixture of regret, guilt and failure.

Counsellor: 'What about sex. How has it affected you?'
Patient: 'I know he is missing it. He is very good and never complains but I just can't do it at the moment. My back hurts so

much that I just end up pushing him away from me and bursting into tears. I do want sex back into our life but I can't see how we're going to get back to it. It upsets me a lot. It feels like something in our relationship has died. He used to be my lover but now he is more like a sort of caregiver. I cry about it sometimes.'

British people are not usually inclined to raise the issue of sexual dysfunction spontaneously in the encounters that are likely in a health centre or hospital setting. Again, therefore, it falls to us as health care practitioners to make sure that some exploratory initiatives have been taken to give 'permission' for sexual issues to be included on the agenda. Psychological care will include an effort to provide a safe atmosphere in which people can say what their experience has turned out to be and how they are feeling about any impact illness might have had on sexual relations and functions. It may be trivial to them or it may be the focus of a collapse in self-worth and an area of hidden despair that is undermining general morale.

Wells *et al.* (2000) is a very useful source of information and helpful guidance with this issue. In particular, there are chapters by: Doreen Clifford, dealing with the issue of psychosexual awareness in health care practitioners; Jane Selby, dealing with training in psychosexual awareness for health care practitioners; and Marjorie Rutter, expanding the theory of psychosexual development and the effect of illness on psychosexual function.

• Reactions: Existential impoverishment

Progressing on in this clinical briefing, there is a feature that may not manifest itself in symptoms or behaviour change particularly, but that can underlie a generalized change in the atmosphere of a patient's life – it is to do with the experience of existence itself.

During the 1960s and 1970s there was a flare of excitement and interest in the field of existential psychology. This was, in part, popularized by the writings of Rollo May (e.g. 1960, 1977). May recounts that he had been ill in a tuberculosis sanatorium for 15 months. The experience had troubled him greatly, especially the low-key pervasive anxiety that he experienced. During that time he read both Freud and Kierkegaard extensively. May observed that Freud, the psychoanalyst, 'knew about anxiety', whereas Kierkegaard, the philosopher, 'knew anxiety'. As May (1960) records, anxiety, for Kierkegaard, was the struggle of the living being against non-being. Hence, a branch of psychotherapy termed existential therapy grew into fashion, which Yalom (1980) describes as an approach that deals with four ultimate concerns of existence: *death, freedom, isolation* and *meaninglessness*.

I am not about to suggest that, with the onset of illness, the average person is likely to become heavily embroiled in philosophical struggles concerning the meaningfulness of their life. Living patterns today tend to be slanted towards very busy and full lives. When not working, most of us have a full leisure and entertainment programme. Hence, time to engage in thought about the experience of existence or meaning in our lives tends to be scarce – living pressures eclipse the more contemplative and exploratory thinking habits of the past. Yet existential issues can be involved in people's reactions to illness and injury, but usually more at a very basic level of personal feeling rather than a cerebral exercise that concludes with a set of well put together constructs. Our *sense* of existence, its meaning, the experience of life and the dependability of personal existence can be thrown into change and disarray. Hence, the demeanour of the patients that you work with may change in subtle ways.

One such change I have termed *existential impoverishment*, implying that something rather fundamental to normal existence and experience is diminished or lost for a while. As with the collapse of denial, this change has to do with the normal, intact and usually positive perspective each of us holds on our own life and future: the perspective we have on the holiday already booked for next summer, the possibility of promotion through a job application, the task of looking for a new house, the children making progress or the countdown to retirement and great plans. Obviously, for the average person the list is extensive, for, in truth, although when turning out for work on a grey winter's Monday it may not feel much like it, life is rich and fairly colourful for many of us in Western societies. I choose the word colourful deliberately, because the best way I can communicate the psychological change indicated by the phrase existential impoverishment is with the use of the analogy of colour. When our perspective on the future is untroubled, future plans have an appeal, they draw us on with anticipation. A patient who has just received the news that she has a tumour and it is malignant, or another who has just learned that he has advancing macular degeneration that will lead to a steady decline in sight, may well lose this sense of the appeal of the future. What was a 'colourful' expectation becomes simply a 'black and white' feature in a possible future – it has less value and interest than before the jolt of being given a threatening diagnosis. For a time, at least, life can be experienced in a detached, somewhat depersonalized way. The personal meaningfulness of existence is diminished and the anxiety of non-existence intrudes. This applies especially when it is not clear what the future will be in terms of health or, indeed, *if* there is a long-term future.

> The patient, a fit 57 years old, became increasingly breathless while out for daily jogging sessions. After a week of steady deterioration marked by tachycardia and a general sense of not being well, he saw his GP. She made a quick examination and said that she believed him to be in fairly advanced heart failure. He saw a cardiologist that same day who took a history and electrocardiogram and arranged for an immediate echo-cardiogram. Reviewing the results he told him that, probably because of a constitutional abnormality, his mitral valve had partially collapsed and was leaking very badly. The only real route to deal with the problem was open heart surgery, and that needed to be done soon. Because of his involvement with the health care professions the patient knew that this surgery carried a small risk of being fatal, a significant risk of causing brain damage and the possibility of continuing cardiac problems. Inevitably, though, he opted to go ahead. During the three weeks waiting for the surgery the quality of life changed. Because there was no certainty of a long-term future it was difficult for him to find any involvement with thoughts of the future. The only meaningful question seemed to be 'Can you think of any reason why you might not be alive this time tomorrow?' The three weeks were passed relatively calmly but 'mechanically'. Nothing proved engaging or absorbing. Interest had virtually disappeared. Life felt empty – in a state of limbo awaiting resolution. He experienced existential impoverishment.

In similar fashion, where treatment techniques for survival are onerous, this sense of future orientation and the positive anticipation of the flow of life fades. Surviving renal failure by haemodialysis can be an example. A number of patients have confided to me that, although grateful for their treatment, they do find that the grinding routine of surviving by dialysis makes for a world that is experienced as 'colourless' – it becomes a daily exercise of getting by, the very experience of life and existence is impoverished.

• Reactions: Denial

Psychological defences can be very robust and powerful. I have discussed the profound impact that the collapse of the defence of denial can have. Now, we need briefly to reflect on the opposite – that is, when denial is strong and persistent to the extent that it affects physical well-being.

Our ability to block alarming or difficult perceptions from full awareness or to distort the interpretation of events to fit into preferred hopes can be impressive. One only has to listen to the rationalizations of heavy smokers to sample the full power of denial. Early on in this chapter I sketched out the case of Katherine, a young woman with insulin-dependent diabetes. At the time of meeting me she had not properly administered her twice-daily insulin injection for a month or more. In fact, as with all clients of a diabetes programme, she had attended clinic and met a diabetes nurse specialist on several occasions. During these sessions she had been well tutored in the potential harm of poor insulin administration and consequent high blood sugar levels. On follow-up the consultant diabetologist or his registrar would similarly enforce the message, especially when she was found to be running high blood sugar levels. It had been emphasized that she could ruin her sight, be at risk of heart disease, kidney failure and failing nerve function in her legs. Added to all this, Katherine had been encouraged to read the simple but effective literature that is given to newly diagnosed patients and deals very clearly with the hazards of poor insulin management. She 'knew' all this but *something told does not mean something retained and acted upon.* All this educational effort proved to be of no avail. Katherine hated diabetes and she hated insulin injections. She managed, through a mix of denial and distortion, to arrive at a perception that was more comfortable for her: 'Yes, but it doesn't happen until you are 50.'

Denial can be a particular problem in areas of medicine where changes in behaviour or reliable compliance with diet and long-term medication are needed. It can, it should be said, have a protective function that helps to reduce troublesome worries and anxiety for a while, but it may, in the end, prove fatal.

James was near phobic of medical procedures. He had managed years of quite difficult angina by staying within his own exercise tolerance and using medication. Continually denying recognition of the risk, he had delayed having an angiogram and taking up the option of coronary artery bypass surgery, saying, 'Well, I'm managing well enough, let's wait and see what happens.' Unfortunately, he suffered a fatal heart attack shortly after he had relented and agreed with his cardiologist to undergo an exploratory angiogram.

The local view was that this death could have been avoided had perception of risk not been distorted by denial.

• Reactions: Exaggerated independence versus collapse into dependency

'Patienthood' does not sit well with many people and, consequently, behaviour in the circumstances of illness and injury may change in unexpected ways. It is a familiar experience for me, for example, to meet ex-military patients, often in the context of a pain management clinic that offers assistance to people with the problems of chronic pain and disability following injury or disease processes such as arthritis. We meet the occasional patients in this clinic who are retired marines, paratroopers and army personnel. It has been noticeable that these men (and sometimes women) often put up an enormous fight to hide their disabilities and continue, as far as is possible, with a normal life. It is a form of denial. Often they take on an exaggerated drive for independence because they feel humiliated by the limitations of their pain and bitterly resent being injured and dependent on medical services and pain killers. The net result is that, usually, they make their pain worse and become more incapacitated in the short term. This reaction to injury could be said to be a form of denial that is manifest by a clinging to past codes of behaviour and values.

Mike was 43 years old. He had been a small arms instructor in the army but an awkward fall during an exercise had caused back damage and eventual discharge from the army because of the injury. He was extremely annoyed about his back problems and forced himself through a daily routine of exercise that he had devised himself. This included taking the dog for a long walk over rough ground and some rather fearsome swimming challenges, such as completing 50 lengths at a session. Often he would have to spend the afternoon in bed as a result because his back hurt so much. He dismissed his wife's plea for more moderation and that he should accept more assistance with things such as the dog. His rationalization, which he said was based on his army training, was 'There is no point in exercising unless you get a bit of a sweat up.' It later came to light that Mike was ashamed of his disability and reported that if, when out, he saw an old colleague from the army approaching he would cross the street and go into a shop, because 'I don't want them to see me like this.'

The equal and opposite reaction to this is a shift into unexpected dependency. In many ways this is a regression to an earlier form of more childlike behaviour that manipulates the partner or caregiver into taking much more control and responsibility for the everyday needs of the patients than is truly necessary – rather as if they were a parent. There is not just one cause for this type of reaction, it can be triggered or 'shaped' by a range of circumstances. It is, though, reasonable to say that where feelings of helplessness and defeat prevail and where there has been a strong experience of shock and fright it can be more likely.

Edith, at 68 years old, lived alone quite independently but was supported by her daughter and friends if support was needed. It was a shock to them all when a diagnosis of breast cancer was given, followed by rather quick progress to mastectomy and then radiotherapy. After the mastectomy Edith lived with her daughter for several weeks. During this time she became very regressed and essentially gave up looking after herself. She had to be told to get up and get dressed, had to be persuaded to eat and had to be almost ordered to take medication and exercise. Without the constant intervention of her daughter, Edith would simply lay in bed all day neither eating nor drinking. After some weeks her daughter lost patience. There was a row and Edith slowly began to recover some of her old independence.

• Reactions: Partner crisis, stress and guilt: the 'care trap'

To be the partner or close relative of a person who is seriously ill or injured can be a fairly distressing and often stressing experience. For example, in an interesting study of the partners of male heart attack patients, Bennett and Connell (1998) comment that, 'As in previous research, levels of distress were as high or higher amongst partners than patients.' Thus, you will find that some elements of the reactions that I have described above concerning the patient can also apply to partners and relatives – especially those to do with threat and loss.

Those partnering and supporting the ill and injured are in a caregiver role. Depending on the actual demands of their particular situation, the emotional and physical state of the patient and also their interpretation of the role that they have taken on, partners will sometimes be found to be stressed in a way that threatens their own health. Naturally, the level of commitment and involvement in the caregiving role will differ greatly from case to case. Helping someone through two months in plaster after breaking an ankle will usually impose much less demand than supporting a person declining with cystic fibrosis or recovering from a recent severe stroke.

It would be overly dramatic and inaccurate to say that partners are a forgotten group. At the same time I do believe that it is important for us to be constantly on the look out for signs indicating that a partner is under heavy emotional load or struggling because a good proportion will not tell you so spontaneously. Over the years I have had many encounters with partners who are doing their best to cope with the demands of dialysis or looking after a husband recovering from a heart attack. These encounters have taught me that in sectors of our culture there is often a reluctance to declare oneself in difficulties with the caregiving role. Sometimes this is related to a hesitation to declare that they are having problems but it can quite often be a kind of protectiveness towards the staff. As a somewhat distraught woman said to me only a few weeks ago, 'The staff are all so busy with so many patients to see. It seems selfish to make a nuisance of myself by complaining about my stress.'

Lynn's husband, Robert, had had a moderate stroke two months before Eileen, a community nurse, made a home visit. Talking to Lynn separately, Eileen noted that Lynn was noticeably pale and tense. Lynn confided that she had found the few weeks since he was discharged from the stroke unit very difficult. She felt that she did not know enough to be able to handle the situation. They were not really sure what sort of pains and physical effects were normal and did not have a clear idea of what sort of physical activity he should be avoiding. Lynn worried desperately that there might be another stroke. She found herself restless and tense, both day and night, listening out for him. She was 'on edge', losing sleep and weight. It was clear to Eileen that Lynn was drifting into a state of stress that might affect her health quite soon. She decided to put in another visit for some psychological care work with Lynn without delay.

In my years of work in a renal unit it was noticeable that one in ten (or more) referrals to me from the nursing staff were of partners rather than patients. Admittedly, this was at a time when there was a policy of emphasizing home haemodialysis (as opposed to unit-based dialysis). This placed the partners under very heavy load, with responsibilities for conducting dialysis sessions that some found very onerous. The partners had to set the dialysis machine up, learn and practise venepuncture for blood access and generally run the five-hour dialysis session with a good sterile technique and competent management. It was impressive to see how 'average' people mastered the situation and learned quite advanced medical techniques. But for some it was at a heavy cost and it did produce stress casualties, I fear.

It is instructive to look back at a survey of the difficulties experienced by partners that a colleague and I undertook during the era of this particular approach to renal medicine (Nichols and Springford 1984). This took the form of structured interviews based around the specifically designed 'dialysis problem checklist'. The proportion of partners looking after a patient on a home dialysis basis who firmly agreed with and gave personal details confirming their feelings in relation to a set of statements is shown in Table 2.1.

The days of home haemodialysis are virtually gone now with the advent of CAPD. This is based on bag changes, a technique not requiring access to the vascular system and therefore not as exacting. Even so, there are still casualties among renal patients' *partners* from time to time. This is equally the case in coronary and stroke rehabilitation work, and almost any field of medicine where a long-term, caregiving role is required, especially where there is little likelihood of physical and mental improvement in the patient. A helpful descriptive article by Bigler (1989) further illustrates the issues. This article identifies the burdens placed on the caregiver dealing with a husband with significant brain damage. General reviews and further discussion of this theme can be found in Nichols (1987) and Llewelyn and Payne (1995).

Linked to this situation, I want to focus on one aspect of partner reaction that you may come across from time to time in virtually any speciality involving long-term illness or care for the injured. It is to do with a compensatory reaction that leads on to excessive, dependency-inducing behaviours by partners. Some of the identified problems in

Table 2.1 The experiences of partners dealing with home haemodialysis

	Percentage agreeing
Dialysis issues	
Worried that I won't be able to deal with an emergency	45
Feeling anxious about being in charge of the machine	30
Frightened I'll cause harm or even death during dialysis	30
Feeling anxious about putting needles in	25
Helping with dialysis is a strain: my own health is deteriorating	25
The staff don't realize how difficult life is	25
Feeling anxious while dialysis is in progress	25
General psychosocial difficulties	
Feeling depressed at how he or she has changed	60
Feeling exhausted	55
Finding his or her depression hard to bear	30
Upset by the way our sexual life has suffered or stopped	30
I badly need a holiday	30
Feeling trapped because he or she depends on me so much now	25
Resenting the way he or she won't do things for himself or herself	25
Worried about his or her attitude to other people now	25
Worried about the effects the situation is having on the children	25
Finding his or her tempers hard to bear	25
I need to get away for a day or two but never can	25

the dialysis problem checklist provide indications of the problem while the next case introduces the pattern to be on the look out for.

> Lily's husband Len was recovering from a significant stroke. The stroke had been an immense shock to them both, but by about the third month they had adapted into a pattern of coping and, on the surface at least, were managing. However, during a home visit by a community nurse, issues came out that suggested that Lily was not managing very well at all and was becoming noticeably distressed. The problem was that Len was fairly disabled by the stroke. He had become very dependent and demanding and did not like being left on his own. He would take no initiatives for himself, such as organizing and taking his regular medications. Lily had adopted a pattern of accepting his dependency and doing most things for him while remaining nearby, in the house, so that he had company. Consequently, she had given up her part-time

job and virtually never left the house except for essential shopping. Even this she did at breakneck speed in an effort to reduce the amount of time she was away from the house. Her activities with the church choir and her art and craft group had been abandoned. Social contacts were getting much less frequent.

The community nurse explored the situation with Lily and was a little taken aback when Lily became very emotional and said that she did not know how much longer she could carry on looking after Len in this intensive way. She then said, 'I think that I'm near a breakdown. I can't go on much longer like this. I know that it sounds awful but he has changed. He has become so selfish that I hate him at times. It is so restricting, I might just as well have had a stroke myself because I don't get any life. I just cry myself to sleep at nights. It could go on like this for years. Well, I can't take it I'm afraid.'

Lily's was a fairly extreme case but it is a familiar story for me, nevertheless. In seeking to understand what has happened I have taken to using the term 'care trap', since people like Lily have ended up in a sort of trap. In part, the trap is of the partner's own making and, in part, it is the responsibility of the health care practitioners involved with the case. Their mistake was not providing effective, preventive education and monitoring of psychological state – psychological care in other words.

Understanding the psychodynamics of the care trap is easy enough. I will explain this using the example of a typical marital partnership situation in which one of the two has become ill or injured. The basic theory focuses on those partners who react in quite a strong way emotionally with, perhaps, an initial horror and fright at the effect of the illness on their husband or wife. Such a reaction usually triggers other feelings, including compassion and, on occasions, feelings of guilt that the partner is suffering and restricted. One assumes here a fairly normal, close relationship, but elements of these feelings can still be stirred up and strong where the quality of the relationship is poor. The key point in the theory is that such feelings are contained by a *compensatory recourse to excessive caring*.

These types of feelings are readily triggered in an illness situation and can be seen to affect many of us, although usually at modest levels of intensity. I suspect that most of us are able to remember incidents when we have rushed to do something for someone who is ill when, in reality, they are quite capable of managing alone. Our behaviour in that situation is about dealing with our feelings of compassion and disquiet at the difference between our health and the other person's infirmity. For some partners this combination of feelings becomes very dominant, and therefore the compensatory behaviour of excessive caring can also become dominant and, eventually, harmful and stressing – as was the situation for Lily. Partners like Lily can become locked into a pattern of thinking and behaving that greatly narrows their life and imposes losses of a social, occupational and recreational type. It is meant in a kindly way, initially, but what is being created is often very difficult to reverse. Patterns of excessive caring behaviour induce a growing dependency and a set of expectations of caring 'service'. Attempts to change will often induce resistance and protest – possibly in subtle ways that the ill person is not even conscious of. This protest, in turn, evokes guilt, with a consequent reassertion of the pattern. After some while the partner effectively becomes trapped in the situation. Some settle to the new pattern of life and accept the new arrangement. Others find that it is lonely and stressing. Anger and resentment can start to build, but are held back because of the opposing compassion and guilt. Held-in anger is a difficult emotional state to endure and so the scene is set for a steady decline in the situation that leads to a crisis. The sequence is mapped out in Figure 2.2.

Naturally, psychodynamics like this do not create sharp categories. Instead, there are degrees to which people become caught up in something like the care trap, and only a minority of cases will be extreme. Added to this, in some cases, adaptation can eventually set in and the partner can achieve a more balanced approach with growing experience, especially if the physical and mental well-being of the patient improves, as often happens with stroke cases.

It is worth mentioning a small but helpful study by Beer (1995) involving the partners of stroke victims. Beer was investigating the applicability of the care trap model and conducted extensive interviews with 12 women whose husbands had suffered strokes. She noted that the proportion of women carers who could be classified as poorly adjusted and not coping was 'worryingly high at 50 per cent'. Her general findings led her to conclude that the quality of relationship between a married couple was an important variable in determining whether the destructive elements of the reactions that I have described set in or not. It was not, however, the quality of the relationship prior to the stroke but the quality of the relationship between the two people after the stroke that mattered. She gave special emphasis to the

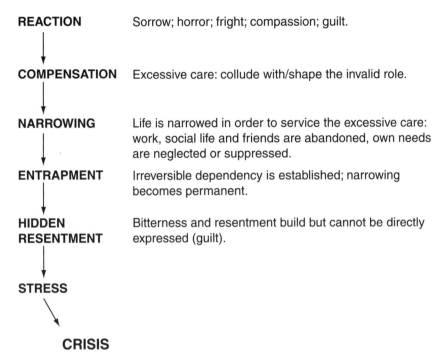

REACTION — Sorrow; horror; fright; compassion; guilt.

COMPENSATION — Excessive care: collude with/shape the invalid role.

NARROWING — Life is narrowed in order to service the excessive care: work, social life and friends are abandoned, own needs are neglected or suppressed.

ENTRAPMENT — Irreversible dependency is established; narrowing becomes permanent.

HIDDEN RESENTMENT — Bitterness and resentment build but cannot be directly expressed (guilt).

STRESS

CRISIS

Figure 2.2   Caregivers and illness: the 'Care Trap' (from Nichols 1989).

impact of communication problems and personality change after the stroke as a basis for the deterioration into care trap patterns of reaction – especially concerning the conflict between resentment of entrapment and guilt. Not surprisingly, she also found that professional input in terms of education and support, together with support from family and friends, was an important variable influencing the outcome of coping and well-being in partners. Beer set out a model closely related to my own but involving two possible pathways to outcome. This model is given in Figure 2.3.

Similarly, on this theme of exploring partner reactions, Bennett and Connell (1998) offer a more substantial study of 40 couples of whom the male partner had experienced a heart attack. *It is of note that the mean Hospital Anxiety and Depression score for the partners was significantly higher than for the patients (on the anxiety component).* They write: 'The primary causes of partner anxiety were the physical health consequences of the MI [myocardial infarction] and, in particular, the perceived limitations imposed on their partner by the MI. The most

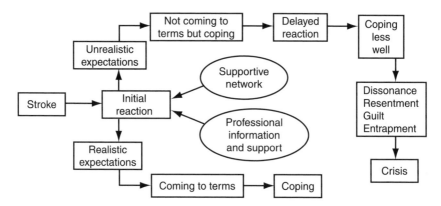

Figure 2.3 Pathways leading to partner adjustment or the 'Care Trap' (from Beer 1995).

important moderators of anxiety were the coping strategies they employed to deal with it. In contrast, the strongest predictors of partner depresssion were the emotional state of their spouse, the quality of the marital relationship and the wider social support available to them.'

How much does all this matter? On an average day in the clinic we have to work with what is in front of us and, unless your clients are incredibly different from mine, you will inevitably encounter *partners* who are struggling one way or another. Occasionally you will meet some who are 'going under'. Obviously, then, from the perspective of complete and professional care, it does matter. We have, as health care practitioners, a responsibility for prevention as well as treatment. Moreover, reminding you of the concept of psychological care as an investment, Bennett and Connell (1998) report studies that imply that when things are not well with the partner it can have a negative effect on the well-being and physical recovery of the patient. This leads us to a familiar position, namely ***we can help to secure our successes in dealing with the patient by keeping an eye on the psychological status of the partner***.

Psychological reactions to illness and 'the seasons of life'

My intention in this chapter has been to compile a set of briefing notes for you as a guide to the 'psychological territory' that you might find yourself in should you become regularly involved in psychological care work as part of your professional duties. This guide has been a composite of my own clinical observations and fairly general knowledge from the research and writing in this field. I have also set out one or two bits of theory concerning the psychodynamics of certain reactions. As a final issue I want to link the type of psychological response that we have been considering to rough age categories. This is not to take an ageist stance, I should emphasize, but it simply recognizes an aspect of psychology referred to as lifespan development. That is, as we progress through life the different demands and tasks of each successive phase of life can be seen as setting before us different psychological tasks that we need to deal with and master.

Erikson (1959), an American personality theorist, was an early writer on this theme. He proposed eight successive stages of human development. Since then there has been a long-lasting fashion in American psychology favouring the notion of stages in psychological process – stages in human development, stages in grief, stages in reaction to illness and so on. My own belief is that some caution is needed concerning the applicability of stages in the individual case, and so we have had little on stages in this book so far. On the other hand, a general answer to the question 'how do people react to their illness or injury?' can be guided *to an extent* by noting the 'season' of life that is involved. I will illustrate this principle with brief descriptive comments and then clinical notes on three cases.

Illness in adolescence

A common view of adolescence held by developmental psychologists is that it is a time where development is focused on establishing personal identity and independence. To facilitate these objectives there can sometimes be a 'pushing away' of parental values and judgements and a preoccupation with belonging to the peer group, which has its own way of thinking, dressing and behaving. Here, the theory reflects that the growing sense of self-identity in the adolescent is sharpened by the *rejection* of the tastes and values of parents and adults. Acceptance into and conformity with the peer group matters very much to some young people – sometimes more than anything else. Goldstein and Hoeper (1987) have provided a helpful outline of the situation in relation to young people with diabetes. This is written under the compelling title of 'Management of diabetes during adolescence: mission impossible?' Some diabetes nurse specialists will know what they mean, I suspect.

Following on from one of the brief clinical examples given above in the section dealing with self-image, I want to illustrate this issue with reference to the relatively rare example of renal failure in adolescence. I will then turn to the increasingly frequent problem of diabetes in adolescence for a second example.

At any age the diagnosis of renal failure is a disaster. It involves a life with the daily inconvenience of peritoneal dialysis by bag changes or the thrice-weekly, five-hour long sessions of haemodialysis (unless a renal transplant is successfully obtained). Compliance with quite severe fluid intake restrictions, necessary changes in diet and adherence to medication regimes are important for long-term survival.

For a young person renal failure is also very much a psychological disaster in the making. The moves in adolescence towards developing self-identity and independence mentioned above will, for some, involve the *device* of rejecting parental and adult values while seeking to maintain conformity with peer group norms. *Peer group norms often conflict quite seriously with the requirements of a dialysis regime.* To some young people it can seem like a constant intrusion by health care practitioners – that is, adults in a semi-parenting role (nurses, nephrologists, dieticians, social workers etc.), with rules, schedules, procedures, advice and all the rest of it. Worse, a style of thinking is required that is very much adult and not at all adolescent, namely to conform to rules with maximum compliance in order to stave off possible health consequences in the distant future. Thus, it has to be said, encounters with clients like Jamie are not necessarily the norm, but they are not uncommon.

> At 18 Jamie was well liked at the renal unit but a very difficult peritoneal dialysis patient. His compliance with fluid limits was very poor and his reliability with bag changes worrying. His parents complained of periods of dark moods, temper and withdrawal. Any attempt to check up on his compliance was met with angry outbursts. From the outset his initial reaction was of anger and resentment.
>
> He conceded one contact with me and, although initially rather unyielding, did eventually confide that 'I can't stand it, it makes me feel like a weirdo. I look fat and am supposed not to drink – what are you supposed to do at the pub all night? And you're not exactly sexy with this lot are you?'

This was a young man who was deeply hurt. He felt that his belonging in his group was at risk. His body image was negative to the point of hatred of his body. He harboured painful worries about looking peculiar and not being likely to achieve good relationships with women. He was at war with his body and also the parents and adults in his life, who seemed to be taking away the things that felt most important to him. It was a case of the needs of late adolescence being in terrible conflict with the requirements of renal failure and its treatment.

(Taken from Nichols 2003.)

I would not want to seem to suggest that all young patients in renal failure, or with other serious illnesses for that matter, endure such conflicts and agonies. Many handle their situation with maturity and elegance. Here, though, special attention is being given to those who struggle badly with adverse psychological reactions. Further illustration is given directly by an anonymous article entitled 'An angry young man with diabetes'. It is written in the style of a diary and reveals to us some of the struggles that diabetes can visit upon a young man:

Monday morning the sudden impact of diabetes began for me on the 24th September, 84. Monday morning (tell me why I hate Monday)
Massive depression.
Anger at the world.
The anger seemed to increase day by day with more advice and explanation!
Why?
At the time my understanding of diabetes was NIL
I had to find a reason!
I had to blame someone or something!
But what? or Who?
Myself or the world
Things like this never happen to me, this can't be true.
These people can't be serious.

The state of confusion roamed through my head leads me to believe this must be a nightmare.
This just wasn't me! It must go away
These people can't be serious

- Injections?
- Blood tests?
- Urine tests?
- Diet?

Most of my favourite foods seem to be foods to avoid

Comments like, 'will I catch diabetes if I drink from the same glass?' (It's not AIDS)
All these people want to talk and talk – doctors, dieticians, psychologists?
nurses, mum, relations, friends – but I don't. Why?
Why do I have the feeling that I don't want to talk to anybody – not even my friends – they just don't understand!!
Getting pissed, smoking and chasing women on Friday and Saturday was natural, Australian way to me, surfacing about midday – then try and relate this kind of life to the one that is being catapulted at me.

The solution – cut off from these people even if they are your family (unfortunate).
Lock yourself away and maybe only talk to the very few who seem to understand.

(Anon, *Diabetes Quest* Autumn 1986: 6–8)

Well, as the Australians often say, 'that's the way it is', or perhaps we should more accurately say, 'sometimes is', for young people with diabetes. You catch, in this diary, something of the dreadful conflict that true compliance brings. The best practice for managing diabetes comes quite close to being the opposite of best practice for gaining full acceptance into a group of average young male friends. Self-image, self-worth and psychological well-being all receive quite a blow. Trouble often follows.

Illness and injury in early and middle adulthood

Generalities are far less reliable when our attention turns to adults in the loose age bracket of roughly 25 years through to the mid-forties. Gender, marital status, parenthood, socioeconomic standing, culture, occupation and parental death are just a few of the factors that shape people's lives and outlook. It is a time of increasingly standing alone and making one's way in the world with, perhaps, a growing responsibility for the well-being of others and perhaps the benefit of a partner to share the experience and burdens.

One thing *is* certain, however. A serious failure in health comes as a menacing threat to assumed security in life. It can topple plans and expectations in a very frightening way. Again, taking an example from the field of renal failure, we can see that this illness can so undermine a person's fundamental sense of personal worth and purpose that depression and decline become a virtually unstoppable consequence.

My involvement with Helen was some years ago now but she was a person whose decline and eventual death teaches us a great deal about the psychological damage that renal failure can bring about and, in particular, the damage that can result from early psychological reactions that become entrenched.

Helen was 28 at the time of diagnosis. She had two children, one of three years and the other of 18 months. She was close to and well supported by her husband, who was a welder. The renal failure resulted from a viral infection and left her shocked, fearful and darkly negative. Early on she felt great guilt to her family.

Unfortunately, Helen was one of those cases where agony follows agony. Her peritoneal dialysis became untenable after a couple of years and a transplanted kidney had to be removed after six weeks following rejection. She was left with the alternative of unit haemodialysis three times a week. This put serious strain on the whole family, since her attendance at the unit involved a minimum of an hour and a half travel each way and then five or so hours at the unit. Thus Helen was effectively away for three days a week, which imposed a considerable strain on her husband, who was also battling with the issue of the care of his children, together with his full-time job.

Helen's initial reactions to diagnosis were personally very damaging and she never really moved beyond these. Early on she would tell me that unless she had a successful transplant she felt that she could not be a proper mother or wife. In a tearful session she confided that she felt in the way – an obstacle to her husband and children having a proper life. 'I can't bear to leave them but I feel in my heart that they will have a better chance if they have a normal mother – they will be better off if I die.' The impact of peritonitis and transplant failure fuelled this belief. Despite tremendous efforts and support by the whole team Helen slowly lost weight and fitness and faded to an eventual death some six years after diagnosis.

Helen had an uncompromising picture of the obligations attending the role of mother and wife. The first few weeks after diagnosis saw her developing the perception of herself as diminished to a level that meant she could not meet these obligations. Her sense of self-worth collapsed and never recovered.

Illness and injury in later life

Compared with 20 years ago a much higher proportion of people in this age group will receive treatment and survive major illness. In general terms, the psychological emphasis is often more to do with the reducing years of life, the wide range of physical problems to be dealt with and the sense of eventual death being in sight. Some, though, will have just retired and have been looking forward to starting a new, well earned style of life. Again, there is much diversity and it is not very productive to go beyond these very broad generalizations. I did consult the clinical nurse manager of my local renal unit and asked her for any observations concerning the psychological reactions of older people who are in renal failure. She mentioned immediately the problem of smiling denial – that is, older people who are motivated not to be a nuisance and who try their hardest not to let on that they are struggling emotionally or finding the life on dialysis difficult to cope with. The following case provides an example of a situation apparently not uncommon with older patients (P. Woodhams, personal communication, 2000).

Alan's first encounter with renal failure was finding himself in an air ambulance, having, at the age of 67 years, collapsed after two weeks of misdiagnosed illness. His reaction during the first weeks of treatment was to maintain a fragile denial made evident by a false levity. For a while he held to his stated belief that things would get sorted out and life get back to normal. He was a model of compliant gratitude at the unit, desperate not to cause a fuss, and determined in his claim that he was not too bothered by the events, 'one of life's little trials'. However, a chance remark by a dialysis nurse led to an unexpected torrent of tears and embarrassed distress. When I met him what was most evident was that right from the start he had been gripped by a strong sense of guilt. He was not used to being cared for physically and was horrified at the physical strain on his wife, in particular the lengthy drive to the haemodialysis sessions. They had various retirement plans, including travel and a house move, and he felt very much to blame that these were to be abandoned. He was also horrified at his own hidden emotional state, which was 'not allowed', since he was an ex-marine. It was clear that his initial shock had been followed by a masked depression that had finally broken through. For weeks he had held it back with a false jollity.

A reminder concerning general statistics on psychological reactions to illness and injury

Most of this chapter has been concerned with clinical observations on the nature of individual psychological reactions to illness and injury. At points I have included relevant details taken from research or review reports. These indicate the approximate proportion of people who develop psychological distress or disturbance. It will be useful to 'wind down' from this overview with a few more reminders of the situation that we face in general hospitals or health centres concerning the psychological status of our clients.

Coronary heart disease

Lane *et al.* (2002) in a prospective study of 288 patients suffering a myocardial infarction, assessed levels of depression and anxiety using the Beck Depression Inventory and the Trait–State Anxiety Inventory. They recorded responses during the first two weeks (during hospitalization), then at four and at 12 months. Elevated (clinically significant) levels of depression and anxiety were found, as shown in Table 2.2.

Lane and her colleagues conclude that 'Symptoms of depression and anxiety are prevalent, persistent problems during the first year

Table 2.2 Levels of depression and anxiety in patients suffering a myocardial infarction

	Depression (%)	Anxiety (%)
During hospitalization	30.9	26.1
At four months	37.7	41.8
At 12 months	37.2	40.0

following MI. This study highlights the importance of routine psychological assessment for MI patients both in hospital and after discharge.'

Cancer

- *Breast cancer.* Fallowfield (1997) notes that approximately 35 per cent of women receiving either a mastectomy or lumpectomy become moderately to severely anxious and/or depressed. A large proportion experience continuing worries concerning the risk of the cancer developing further.

- *Digestive tract cancer.* Allen (1997) reports studies in her review that indicate that some 22 per cent of patients receiving colostomies will still be experiencing moderate to severe psychological disturbance 12 months after the surgery.

- *Head and neck cancer.* Again, Allen (1997) reports that 50 per cent of patients have adjustment disorders, with anxiety, depression or mixed mood states.

Renal failure

Long (1995) gives a general review of studies that indicates initial levels of at least moderate anxiety ranging between 30 and 50 per cent in the early months of dialysis, with rather higher levels of depression (although note that the physiological changes involved in renal failure do incline a person to depression). Kaplan De-Nour (1994) found considerable variability among studies of psychological disturbance in patients surviving by dialysis, mainly because of the variation in assessment methods and scales. However, one objective indicator is suicide by withdrawal from dialysis. Studies here indicate levels of suicide about 15 times higher than in the general population, at about the 7–9 per cent mark of recorded deaths. Incidentally, 'psychological disturbance' implied a range of anxiety-based and depressive reactions sufficient to impair life and cause considerable anguish.

Gynaecological surgery

Gath *et al.* (1982) used the Present State Inventory (a very extensive, interview-based, semi-structured assessment schedule) to assess 147 women four months before their hysterectomy and again at six and

18 months after. The indications were that 58 per cent revealed 'psychological disturbance' before surgery, 38 per cent at six months and 29 per cent at 18 months.

Intensive care patients

As noted above, recent studies reveal that a stay in ICU while on a ventilator and kept sedated often creates long-term psychological 'casualties'. These studies are reviewed by Skirrow *et al.* (2001). Indications are that an average of 15 per cent (one study recorded 27.5 per cent) of ICU patients are disturbed by post traumatic stress disorder, anxiety and depression for a year or more after discharge.

Hospital patients in general

We might round off this reminder by noting that none of this is exactly breaking news. Nearly 30 years ago, Moffic and Paykel (1975) screened 150 medical inpatients using the Beck Depth of Depression Inventory. They found that 27.7 per cent were depressed at a level meriting clinical intervention. Following this, the *Lancet* (1979, 1: 478–9) ran an editorial comment noting various studies that indicated psychological disturbance or disorder at a level ranging between 30 and 60 per cent in certain categories of medical inpatients. Little has changed, as Johnston (1997) confirms.

Assisting with psychological care and psychological therapy

My aim in this chapter has been to describe a range of psychological reactions to illness and injury that you may well encounter as a health care practitioner. As explained, the list offered is, in part, based on my personal clinical observation and therefore makes no pretence of being a complete list. For additional reading on this general theme, Salmon (2000) serves as a useful complement to the material covered.

Discussion time

It could be a useful exercise if you now review and discuss the type of cases with which you are most familiar and investigate whether you are able to extend the range of reactions listed. You might also be able to add variations and detail to the list as it exists. Try giving some answers to the following questions:

- What type of cases are you most usually involved with?

- What are the more common psychological reactions and problems that your patients or their spouses, partners or caregivers experience?

- What are the early signs and symptoms that give an indication of the difficulties you have named?

- Do the features that you have listed fit in with those itemized above, or do they merit a separate category that can be added to the list?

- To what extent do the medical and nursing staff in your unit or centre collude to keep these reactions out of sight, as opposed to assisting patients and partners in working through them?

The next task is to specify how we should intervene and offer care and treatment.

PART 2
Skills and Strategies for Psychological Care in Medicine, Nursing and the Therapies

3 Monitoring psychological state and the organization of psychological care

If you are a doctor, nurse, therapist or health care practitioner in a hospital or health centre then I urge you to accept that you must be the 'psychological eyes and ears' for your patients. If *you* do not serve this function then there is usually no one else who can or will. In that case, the first that anyone will know about a patient or partner being in difficulties will usually be the attention attracted by some sort of breakdown. This means that the casualty model will have triumphed over the preventive model. Organized psychological care seeks to stop this happening. *In these terms, the most important item in the provision of psychological care is an arrangement for the systematic monitoring of your patients' psychological state.* The rest follows as a logical progression, as Figure 3.1 reveals. This diagram is a simplified version of Figure 1.2. It shows the relationship of monitoring skills to the other components of psychological care.

The import of the diagram links directly to the points made in the first two chapters. Any health care practitioner regularly involved with a patient will be in a position to monitor the psychological state of that patient and, on an as required basis, continue with psychological care. Should circumstances dictate, a referral to a clinical psychologist or similar professional psychological therapist can be made as part of that care. A health care practitioner with only one scheduled contact, say a diagnostic specialist, can still be a useful participant, as indicated in Chapter 1. A small amount of effort at inquiry will reveal sufficient concerning a patient's psychological state (including information and expectations) to allow a general impression. This may justify a brief intervention of a psychological care type, such as a short information-giving session. Alternatively, it allows the opportunity for some indication of the situation to be sent on to the health care practitioners

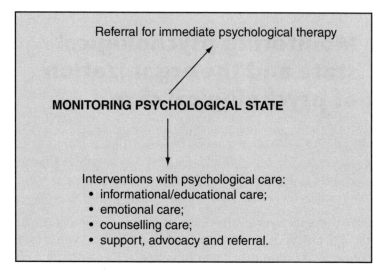

Figure 3.1 The relationship of monitoring skills to other components of psychological care.

regularly involved with the patient's care – that is, the GP, practice nurse, hospital ward manager etc. *Either way, the basic psychological state is noticed and something is done – should this be necessary.* That is what is important.

If the situation in which you work is fairly solitary or is one in which you find little sympathy towards psychological care from colleagues, you will have to provide psychological monitoring and care on an individual basis. This is far from ideal for you, of course, but far better than no provision at all, especially for the patient. A much better arrangement is one in which, as part of ward, clinic or health centre life, the body of staff involved agree to include and integrate basic psychological monitoring and intervention in their work. This was the approach developed and described by Nichols (1984) and Woodhams (1984) in a renal unit. It worked relatively successfully as a nurse-provided resource, although, sadly, without much active support from the nephrologists. The constraints of the 'internal market' introduced into the British health care system in the 1980s and financial prioritizing based on political objectives also proved less than helpful. However, it was a sufficient demonstration to show that such schemes can function effectively without too much time drain on staff, and to the positive benefit of patients, their partners and the staff. Incidentally, the nursing staff generally seemed to agree that the introduction of psychological care into their daily tasks in the renal unit increased job satisfaction by allowing a sense of completeness of care and professionalism.

There is more on the organization of a scheme of psychological care below. Next, though, I want to look at the actual tasks for you, personally, in monitoring psychological state, whether you have to work alone or as part of an organized team who all give psychological care.

Approaches to monitoring psychological state

This is not a task that you should regard with apprehension or diffidence. Nor should you give credence to a belief that special powers and advanced knowledge are necessary to monitor psychological state. The core requirement is for quite basic but essential interpersonal skills. These are the ability to put a person at ease and thus encourage them to talk to you, the ability to listen to what they are saying, the ability to note any evident emotionally driven bias in their manner and the ability very briefly to assess what they know and 'where they are at' with their diagnosis and treatment.

I do not believe in a set recipe for the exchanges that permit the assessment of basic psychological state because different people have different needs for communication. For example, one of my recent contacts with a patient started with him unlatching a briefcase, and taking out a typed recent history of problems and an attached list of questions. In the first instance he wanted the encounter to be business-like, directed by him and relatively distant in character, like meeting a solicitor. Our first 10 or 15 minutes were in this style but I gradually moved us into a less defended style of conversation, with more openness, although still meeting his need for information and predictability in the encounter. In general, I find that such a strong need in patients to control conversational encounters with staff is unusual and, therefore, as a basic guide to beginning the type of conversation that allows you some assessment of psychological state, I would say *keep it simple, keep it human, keep it short and keep the emphasis on listening*. Otherwise it can become a tiresome and laborious chore and it will be tempting to postpone or overlook the event, especially in a busier clinic setting or at the end of a day when energy is low. At the same time, since the observations need to be meaningful and systematic, a degree of direction from you is necessary, as otherwise it will all become rather random.

It is time for an illustration. Last week I met an individual patient, a 46-year-old man who had sustained a mild heart attack four months previously. He was attending a coronary rehabilitation programme and this was part of the programme routines – meeting the psychologist for (in the first instance) a brief review for the purpose of monitoring psychological state and information provision. The encounter was simply designed as a 10-minute 'screening' conversation with enough content to allow a basic psychological assessment. This is what you would have heard once the door had closed and the patient sat down (he knew who I was because I had given a talk to the group the previous week). Note the simplicity.

> KN: (with a brief but genuine smile and kindly, direct gaze) 'Hi, come on in. This is just a 15-minute review, Steve, nothing intense. Basically, it is so that I can ask you how you are getting on and ask what your outlook is for the next month or two.'
>
> Steve: 'How am I getting on? Well, there's a good question. Not as well as I had hoped, if I'm honest, in fact, not that well at all.'
>
> KN: 'What are we talking about, how you're doing physically or personally?'
>
> Steve: 'Well, both really, I suppose.'
>
> KN: 'OK . . . do you feel like taking me through it briefly?'
>
> Steve: 'Yes I do, I want to talk to someone about things a bit more. I wasn't so bad at first, when I joined and talked to Cheryl [cardiac nurse], but it's been over four months now since my heart attack. I was hoping to be back at work but it's all going a bit wobbly. What bothers me most is . . .'

Steve is settled and talking. He feels safe and that he is being listened to. He is aware that he is struggling with his rehabilitation and the aftermath of his heart attack. He recognizes that he needs support and assistance. He would probably talk for an hour or more, but this is a brief encounter to allow me to monitor his psychological state and assess needs, so it is disciplined. As it is already appearing likely that he will need some type of intervention for psychological care, this will be arranged at the end of this brief session. The objective now is to obtain a systematic picture. To do so I (and later, I hope, you) must be clear about what falls under the label of 'psychological state'.

Again, simplicity is an ally, so the list is short. Psychological state is used here to refer to a person's:

- emotional functioning – general bias, trends etc.;
- character and accuracy of knowledge concerning illness and recovery;
- expectations and outlook (positive/negative) concerning illness and recovery;
- related behaviour – compliance, stance to treatment and rehabilitation etc.

I expect that you are asking yourself 'How can this be made quick and simple?' One method is to use the discipline of a simple written record based on the schedule of items given in Figure 3.2. These 'observations

---

PATIENT..................................... DATE...............................

RECORD MADE BY............................. NOTES...........................

PREDOMINANT MOOD STATE? Anxious, tense, agitated, fraught, worried, stressed, tearful, low, guilty, depressed, negative, withdrawn, confused, frustrated, angry, aggrieved? Relaxed, cheerful, calm, positive, good morale? Other? Comments:

....

HOW WELL INFORMED/OUTLOOK AND EXPECTATIONS?

....

PSYCHOLOGICAL OR BEHAVIOURAL DIFFICULTIES?

....

ACTION TO BE TAKEN?

....

Figure 3.2 Observations for psychological care.

for psychological care' are suitable for use in any hospital or health centre setting. *I do not mean that you fill this in while talking with your patient.* Instead, use prompts from it as a guide and write out a few notes on the form later. A blank copy is given in Appendix 1. There is nothing sacred about the layout or content, by the way. You should feel free to modify it to suit your own needs and preferences, as long as the last item, 'Action to be taken', remains intact. It is important.

To illustrate the use of 'observations for psychological care' and show that it is something that any competent health care practitioner with good general interpersonal skills can readily use, I will continue

---

PATIENT: Steve P   **DATE:** 09.05.02

RECORD MADE BY: KN   **NOTES:** time since MI 4 months, conservative management

PREDOMINANT MOOD STATE? Anxious, tense, agitated, fraught, worried, stressed, tearful, low, guilty, depressed, negative, withdrawn, confused, frustrated, angry, aggrieved? Relaxed, cheerful, calm, positive, good morale? Other? Comments:

Is worried about lack of progress and failure to feel ready to return to work – very guilty about being off work, impatient to get back – feels he is letting colleagues down – generally pretty 'wound up' – wife troubled too. Neither of them sleeping well.

HOW WELL INFORMED/OUTLOOK AND EXPECTATIONS?

Seems confused about time-scale for recovery of energy, had not expected fatigue problems and further chest pains, thinks he should be more capable with the exercises. Unrealistic about predictable exhaustion. Does not think he can cope with full day at work yet – overly self-condemning.

PSYCHOLOGICAL OR BEHAVIOURAL DIFFICULTIES?

Restless at home, trying to push himself to do jobs and exercise but not resting during day – fighting against his own need for rest. Making himself irritable – gets cross with himself, then wife and children. Then feels guilty.

ACTION TO BE TAKEN?

Needs reorientation to aims of rehab and importance of combining rest and self-care with his exercise and work. Ask physio or OT to have session with him focusing on pacing and rest and time-scale for rehab. generally. Book in for one session with me to look at issues of guilt and self-condemnation plus general review of information and expectations – stress need for phased return to work with emphasis on pacing and compensatory rest.

Figure 3.3   An example observations form.

with some examples by first returning to the encounter with Steve. His opening remarks led on to a 15-minute exchange, with most of the talking coming from him. At that time I only had 15 minutes before another appointment, so it was not appropriate to do anything but listen and note. He was disappointed in his progress, mainly because his expectations were not very accurate and he thought that something was wrong. My entries on the observations form are shown in Figure 3.3.

A second example is given in Figure 3.4. This was supplied to me by a speech and language therapist who had been working with a 62-year-old woman who had had a stroke and was suffering significant speech impairment and paralysis of her right-sided muscular functions.

PATIENT: Evelyn H   **DATE:** 12.10.00

RECORD MADE BY: CT   **NOTES**: 4th session

PREDOMINANT MOOD STATE? Anxious, tense, agitated, fraught, worried, stressed, tearful, low, guilty, depressed, negative, withdrawn, confused, frustrated, angry, aggrieved? Relaxed, cheerful, calm, positive, good morale? Other? Comments:

Very low today, needed lots of comfort, but says that her moods are up and down, last week not so bad. Missing friends and residents at work very much – lonely? Gets very frustrated. She can't understand why she is so tearful. Guilty that she can't do domestics and cooking for her husband yet.

HOW WELL INFORMED/OUTLOOK AND EXPECTATIONS?

Understands reasonably well what has happened but too pessimistic in her outlook. Thinks she will never speak properly again, which is why she is so upset.

PSYCHOLOGICAL OR BEHAVIOURAL DIFFICULTIES?

Tending to sit at home rather than getting out with her husband. Withdrawn, doesn't want to meet friends with her facial paralysis – feels disfigured. So she misses friends and gets lonely and depressed.

ACTION TO BE TAKEN?

Give some time to support work and reassurance in next session. Go through info. on recovery and time-scale again. Encourage her to go out more into situations that do not require too much talking initially. Try and build up motivation and hope.

Figure 3.4   A second example observations form.

The key skills for monitoring psychological state: patient-centred communication and active listening

It used to be the case that conversations to do with communication and listening to patients had a degree of novelty for doctors and nurses. No more, it seems, because, these days, medical and nurse training schools include such issues as front rank items on the curriculum for professional development. Thus, it is appropriate that, as we talk about monitoring psychological state through the means of short, focused conversation based sessions, *only a reminder should be needed* on these most fundamental of skills for the health care practitioner – or so we might think. To be quite frank with you, though, I do find myself a little depressed at the deficiencies in communication and listening skills that I regularly encounter or hear of from patients that relate to events in a hospital or health centre. For example, let me report some comments made to me recently:

Patient 1: 'I have been feeling quite emotional and bad tempered lately, and very tired too. I've been wondering if it is menopause or hormones.'

KN: 'Have you discussed this with your GP?'

Patient 1: 'Not really, no. I mentioned it but he just went "mmm". You don't have a discussion with him. He gives the impression that he never really listens to what you are saying anyway.'

Patient 2: 'Actually it was like some sort of nightmare. I was both terrified and humiliated at once. One of the nurses was quite helpful and said not to worry about calling her. But the others seemed, I don't know, resentful and cross. They made me wait ages sometimes. It wasn't my fault. When I came round I had terrible, terrible stomach pain and cramps. I did not know what was going on. Nobody said anything to me. I still have nightmares about it.'

Patient 3: 'Well it was quite funny in a bizarre sort of way. I'd done the tests with the audiometer thing and she had said I needed hearing aids and was getting things ready to make impressions of my ear. So I said to her, "How bad are my ears?" and she said,

"Well, you have lost half your hearing." Just like that, nothing more. She did not even look at me.'

Of course, it is by no means all bad, there are many examples of excellent practice to be found and, quite possibly, the majority of the millions of acts of communication that go on daily in our health care system are adequate. At the same time, something seems to happen that erodes the motivation or opportunity to practise these skills in a proportion of patient–practitioner encounters, which then become a disaster. It is something that we should all be on the alert for. In Chapter 4 I include some research reports on problems with practitioner–patient communication, and will not go beyond these personal observations at present, since the issue of importance is communication and listening skills to monitor psychological state effectively. Meanwhile, let us move on to some reminders on the basic skills needed in monitoring the psychological state of our patients.

Reminder 1: what is meant by 'patient-centred communication'?

Weinman (1997) puts this very clearly. He writes:

> One of the broadest distinctions made has been between consultations which are described as patient centred and those which are described as doctor centred, reflecting the extent to which the doctor or patient determines what is discussed. Doctor centred consultations are ones in which closed questions are used more often and the direction is determined by the doctor, typically with a primary focus on medical problems. In contrast, patient centred encounters involve more open ended exchanges with greater scope for patients to raise their own concerns and agendas.

Much the same criteria apply to nurse–patient, physiotherapist–patient and radiologist–patient communications among many. As is fairly obvious, perhaps, some situations do require a high degree of doctor-centred communication, at the admission and assessment stage in an accident and emergency department, for example, and, similarly, educational briefings by a physiotherapist during recovery from spinal fusion surgery. In reality, there is often a need for *phases* in questioning and information exchange. Typically, these may involve a sequence in which a more practitioner-centred early phase is entertained that allows efficient information-gathering or information exchange. This is then followed by a progressively more patient-centred phase, which encourages the patient to explore issues, resolve doubts and gaps and then react to information or their situation generally.

Reminder 2: open versus closed questions

This distinction is useful to note and practise in everyday conversation with friends. 'How are you getting on?' or 'What kind of day have you had?' are open questions, because there is very little narrowing down by the questioner as to what can be thought about and included in the answer. 'Does your arm still hurt?' or 'Did you work late?' are closed questions, since the focus of attention is narrowed down by the questioner and the answer has to remain on this narrow basis, sometimes as a yes/no reply. *If you are wanting a person to talk with you in their own words and to explore and speak of the things that are on their mind and in their feelings (when monitoring psychological state), use open questions.* If you need precise information, sometimes on a yes/no basis, use a mix of closed and open questions as required. Thus, generally, in our quest to assess the psychological state of our patients, open questions are the more useful tool for the conversation.

Reminder 3: good listening skills

Another key feature of good patient-centred communication is good listening skills. This is really a composite of sub-skills or behaviours. They are easy enough for most health care practitioners to achieve and second nature to many people anyway, especially women, in my experience. The composite is built up by a combination of:

1 *The body language and behaviour of the listener.* The important sense of *attending* that draws a person on to talk is given by a relaxed stance on the part of the listener, ideally facing and looking at the person in an interested, easy way. There will be occasional nods or utterances that communicate that the listener *is* listening and following. It is about signalling full attention through body posture and signs from the face and voice. This is, of course, quite hard to do if one is simultaneously

typing material into a computer or engaged in some other task – although on occasions situations are not ideal and that is the way it has to be.

2 *Creating the sense that the listener is understanding, absorbing the information being given and sensing (empathizing) what the talker must be feeling.* This also communicates that there is an expectation for the talker to say more. Again, there is no magic needed here. Think, for a minute, of what you would need personally from a listener to facilitate the continuation of your own conversation. I will illustrate this with an example of ordinary 'coffee room' chat.

Compare:

A: 'I was really quite cross and said to the others, "She can be quite a prima donna at times." I thought she had left the room but as I turned round to go she was still standing there, listening.'

B: 'No, heavens, you must have felt awful. What then?' (Shows attention and empathy and expectation that she will continue.)

A: 'Yes, right, I did, I felt terrible. I was cross with her but I didn't want to hurt her. Anyway, half an hour later I thought I've got to go and explain, so . . .' (Conversation continues easily, good listening skills.)

with:

A: 'I was really quite cross and said to the others, "She can be quite a prima donna at times." I thought she had left the room but as I turned round to go she was still standing there, listening.'

B: 'I don't let things like that get to me, I don't think that it is worth worrying about. Actually, it happened to me once when I was in London. My flatmate had her friend round and I said something about her when I thought she was out of the room but she wasn't. It was awkward but she soon got over it.' (The conversation falters because the listener has not sensed that the talker is upset and needs to talk things through. Instead she diverts attention to her own advice and experience, so choking off the conversation – very poor listening skills.)

The key to this skill of listening is that you maintain your attention on what a person is saying and do not kill off the conversation by intruding with personal views and experiences, or 'throw in' disruptive questions that lead on to another theme. Think for a moment of a person in your life who you can talk to easily and then think of one who somehow makes it a struggle. The former will be a natural listener. They face you, look at you, nod, make an occasional utterance to show that you have their attention, allow you space and sense when you have reached a natural point where a comment from them is helpful. Often this will be of a questioning type that leads you on to say more. Think now of your example of a poor listener. Often these are people who simply vie for possession of the conversation and a reversal of attention on to themselves, as in the example above. As you speak your first few sentences you can see the word 'I' forming on their lips. They are not going to ask you more about yourself or listen, but will, predictably, break into what you are saying to start telling you something about themselves, blocking any need you might have to talk and thus converting you into the listener. (I find people with such deficient listening skills to be something of a bleak and frustrating experience and label them LSOs, which stands for 'listening service only'. That is, the conversation with them is one in which I inevitably do all the listening because they continually try to possess the conversation to talk of themselves or their own views.)

An additional ability that supplements the general sense of 'I'm listening, say more' is a skill that is referred to as *reflection*. This is the ability to catch in a few words the true meaning of what it is that a person is saying. If the story above had been told to a counsellor or psychologist in a therapy session then it is likely that the practitioner would have made the reflection: 'So you felt both guilty and acutely embarrassed having said that?' This brief utterance condenses down into a few words the central element in what has been spoken. It is said to have been 'reflected back', since the allusion is to a mirror. *One seeks only to produce an image of what has been said, not comment on it or question it at all.* The point of reflecting back is that it enables an accuracy check and serves as confirmation that the talker has been listened to. If the listener has got it right then a reply something like 'Yes, that's right' will follow. If the listener is off track then the reply will usually involve a natural correction: 'Well no, not exactly, I wouldn't say that I felt guilty.' Then the two people can work together to achieve full understanding.

Finally in this list of ingredients in the composite that we call good listening skills, it is very important to create the sense of safety and freedom that allows the person talking to set out his or her thoughts and feelings without anticipation of challenge, correction, gratuitous advice or critical comment (although this may be relevant to the talker and sought after later).

If you are already a good listener, and I believe that a good proportion of health care practitioners are, then you will have had the experience of patients or patients' relatives saying to you, 'I feel that I can talk to you.' In other words, they find you to be a good listener who makes talking about difficult issues much easier. Even so, we have to be on our guard and work at the provision of this skill. Poor communicators and listeners are not hard to find in the medical setting: the GP who is slightly ill at ease, does not make much eye contact and discourages any depth of conversation by writing at his computer; the practice nurse who is full of a blocking, jolly triviality as she takes blood pressure and blood samples; the rather remote radiologist performing an echocardiogram who makes no effort to find five minutes to relax a patient after the procedure and find out how they have coped and what they are thinking and feeling after the event. Most readers will have examples from their own experience of atrocious listening and communicating in the health centre or hospital, and I add a few more in Chapter 4, which is on the theme of caring by informing.

Having monitored psychological state, what then?

The final question on 'observations for psychological care' is 'Action taken?' It may be reassuring to hear that quite often very little action is actually needed. In fact, your inquiry into a person's emotional state, general coping and level of information can often be such an important experience of care and reassurance that it meets the needs of the average patient in itself. As repeated and explained in greater depth below, *the process can be as important as the content.* This is an important phrase that is derived from counselling theory. It conveys the message that your patient's experience of the caring concern that you communicate can provide an important and powerful boost. A combination of this with the knowledge that a relationship has been made and that you are there if things change and further support becomes necessary may be sufficient psychological care at the time. This assumes, of course, that the people involved have good and accurate information that generates realistic expectations (otherwise you need to do some informational care work).

But then, again, a proportion of people whose psychological status you assess may present as having significant needs. You may detect hints or, indeed, florid examples of some of the psychological reactions described in Chapter 2. You may find that your patient is struggling in various ways and failing to cope with the situation, as was the case in the many case examples given so far in this book. Similarly, you may find that their information is patchy, inadequate or just plain wrong, and that, consequently, their expectation and general outlook is inaccurate. Finally, you may find that they need ongoing general support or representation of their needs to other colleagues – for instance, scheduling admission for a procedure so that difficult domestic upheaval and stress are avoided.

How do we proceed?

At this point you must ask:

> Can I handle it myself by providing psychological care personally or do the needs of the person I have just assessed point to referral for psychological treatment or counselling as a more suitable option? Is this a case where there should be a mix of both?

The next two chapters deal with how to provide informational and emotional care and the issue of when and how to proceed with these. First, though, I want to make a general statement to those of you who are likely to be able to offer psychological care on level 2 – that is, certain types of doctor, most nurses, most occupational, speech and physiotherapists, most dieticians etc. *I can say that the provision of informational care will almost always fall to you – because there are no 'information specialists' to refer on to.* Otherwise, as a minimum alternative to personal delivery of information, it should be for you to initiate some arrangements for its provision or link with dedicated patient information services, if they exist in your organization.

Basic emotional care is also something that I hope the average health care practitioner will routinely provide, but you do have to feel comfortable with the task and be capable of the type of interaction described in Chapter 5. It is also important to be able to judge when a person has crossed a threshold and requires psychological treatment in addition to emotional care. This will usually be because they have become disabled in some way by adverse reactions or are in serious distress. The basis for this judgement is also talked through in Chapter 5. However, note one golden rule. Never refer a person for psychological therapy unless you have discussed it with them and you have confirmed that it is something that they understand, want and will use positively. I sometimes receive referrals from consultants who are, effectively, sending patients to me without discussion. This can be very difficult for the person involved, especially if they do not understand the function of a clinical psychologist and psychological therapy. This lack of understanding tends to leave them believing that their doctor is dumping them because he has decided that their problem is not physical but psychological. This results in the arrival of an angry, resentful patient who is in no way motivated for psychological therapy work – quite the opposite, in fact. When this happens the first session often has to be given over to dealing with the anger, assuring the person that they are not abandoned or seen as a 'head case' and then explaining the point of the referral and subsequent therapy. Not an ideal start.

In general, by far the majority of patients will respond very well to the process of monitoring psychological state, followed by a little gentle emotional care. They will usually want and be grateful for any additional clarification and information relating to their injury or illness that you are able to provide. If you have some basic training in counselling skills then most will settle easily into a basic, problem-solving style of counselling interaction, as described in Chapter 6.

In summary, psychological care proceeds along the following pathway. The brief screening task based on 'observations for psychological care' is carried out at a convenient point during clinic contacts with a patient. If you detect psychological needs related to information, try to deal with them there and then or make an arrangement to return and provide a brief information or education session later. Having gently explored the person's emotional state, if emotional needs exist and time permits, you might also spend a few minutes in emotional care and support work. Otherwise, again, make an arrangement for another contact for a little emotional care work with them. If there are associated problems or significant, adverse psychological reactions linked to the illness or injury, these might be dealt with by a more time expensive (but rewarding) counselling intervention, but failing this, discuss referral for further assistance by either a professional counsellor or a clinical psychologist.

Sometimes I am asked about using questionnaires like the Hospital Anxiety and Depression Scale for assessment. They can be helpful as a supplement but they should never be used as a substitute for talking with your patients, thus making personal, supportive contact. Moreover, if your unit is buying them they can prove expensive.

The organization of psychological care

I expect that you will have gathered by now that I am quite keen on there being some level of *organization* in the provision of psychological care, regardless of whether it is a resource in a health centre or in a hospital. In the same way that Chapter 1 presented involvement in psychological care as being on one of three levels (awareness, interventions and referral for psychological treatment), it is helpful to specify the organization as being on different levels. These can be loosely described as is shown in Box 3.1. On the whole it is all fairly obvious, but I will amplify the description with some examples and additional comment.

Box 3.1 The organization of psychological care

- *Solo, non-integrated*: individual staff working alone with no support or recipient organization.
- *Part integrated*: loosely embedded in a wider organization with informal links and procedures. Personal records only.
- *Fully organized and integrated*: an explicit organization with staff allocated duties and time for psychological care work, records kept and an agreed procedure.
- *Referral/expert dependent*: basic awareness of psychological care leading mainly to referral to a psychologist or counsellor; fewer 'in-house' interventions.

• Solo, non-integrated

The 'solo' situation refers to a health care practitioner who attempts to offer psychological care to patients but does so in a situation in which he or she tends to function fairly independently or in a situation where colleagues do not or cannot contribute and offer support. It used to be a common experience to meet hospital nurses who would complain that they were rebuked for breaking off routine duties to talk to patients. In other words, general communication of the type needed in psychological care was discouraged. Similarly, in the past, physio-therapists tended to be seen as brisk, efficient and pretty switched off to the emotional needs of their patients. Thus, the odd one or two who attempted some kind of psychological care were rather isolated indi-viduals. It is to be hoped that those days are long gone now. Even so, it is quite easy to find wards or departments in a hospital where the senior staff do not encourage psychological work, and it has to be undertaken as an individual initiative by staff. This 'solo' arrangement is the least preferable for psychological care work, since it is demotivat-ing for the member of staff and leads to patchy care.

> Wendy was a practice nurse in a small rural health centre. The GPs in the practice were mainly part-time and were all fairly pressed with basic duties. Although happy enough for Wendy to add a psychological component to her work and prepared to consider making referrals for psychological treatment if Wendy requested these, the doctors adopted a 'hands off' approach to preventive psychological care themselves. It was seen as a luxury for better days, when resources were improved and everyone in the practice had more time. Wendy was pretty much alone in her psychological care work.

It is hard to know just how commonplace the situation that Wendy found herself in might be these days. However, I can say that during the past few months I have been involved in training courses for practice nurses linked to the so-called National Service Framework in Coronary Heart Disease. This is a requirement by the British gov-ernment to upgrade and optimize care in the NHS for people with coronary heart disease. I met a total of about 40 practice nurses on these courses, and none seemed able to confirm that there already was an organized and well supported scheme of psychological care in their practice, although most were convinced of the importance of psychological care work for patients suffering a heart attack and felt it to be a priority to set something up soon. Several hinted that they would be working 'solo' if they did so, however. Thus, based on a small, local sample from primary care, the provision of psychological care on an individual, non-integrated basis might be common.

Sometimes the 'solo' mode of providing psychological care is a function of the situation itself, rather than a lack of involvement of other colleagues. In these terms it is the only sensible option.

> Darren, an occupational therapist with links to an orthopaedic department and pain clinic, developed a service for patients who had suffered injury to their hands or arms and appeared to be developing complex regional pain syndrome. Patients were referred to him as an individual clinician on an outpatient basis. He worked through a programme of assessment, graded exercise training and various palliative procedures, and also provided psychological care personally in terms of informational and emotional care, together with general support. Cases that needed special assistance psychologically he referred to the psychologist working with the pain clinic.

• Integrated and loosely embedded in a wider organization

This is the more familiar situation, I believe, especially in the hospital environment. Typically, a centre or ward will have an awareness of psychological care but no formal organization of resources under that name. If one approaches, say, the clinical nurse manager and asks, 'What happens about psychological care on the ward?', she will probably say something like, 'Looking after patients' psychological needs is important to the staff on our ward and so they do try to work with patients to keep them informed and deal with any emotional upheavals. The nurses are encouraged to be holistic in their general approach and therefore psychological care is seen to have value and credibility. When necessary someone or other will make a referral to the psychology department if things seem a bit difficult for the patient. However, no, there is not any actual organization of psychological care, records are not kept and the nurses have had no special training or supervision in psychological care.'

This type of situation is certainly more encouraging, because psychological issues are part of the daily life of the ward staff and not something that is occasional, exceptional or dependent on isolated members of staff. Obviously, if psychological care is part of the general working atmosphere more patients will benefit, even though the provision is informal. There are criticisms to be made, though. Probably the more significant shortcoming, in my view, is the lack of an organized, guaranteed procedure (as described in the next section). This suggests that the default position of the ward when, for example, it is busy and distracted, is that patients need the 'ticket' of some sort of evident distress or collapse to make certain that their psychological needs are noticed, assessed and responded to. *In other words, it drifts towards 'casualty-based' psychological care and not preventive psychological care, which is much more patient-centred and efficient.*

There is also the issue of standards and objectives. In an organized scheme these are explicit and stable, but in the type of situation being discussed here they are vague and variable. There is an open acknowledgement of the value of the holistic approach and psychological care but no 'operationalization' of the approach. That is, the good intent is not translated into specific procedures, objectives and occasional simple records.

• Fully organized and integrated

Some health care environments enjoy a relatively favourable staff–patient ratio and a working pattern that gives a more extended time of contact with patients – for example, oncology units, renal and cardiology units, diabetes centres, spinal injury and orthopaedic surgery units. It is in these settings that the stable and full organization of psychological care can be more readily created. This is in contrast to medical settings and health centres that function with a fast and full flow of patient intake and so deal with a perpetual stream of new people. There is no doubt that this can create overload problems. It also introduces limits to psychological care, in the sense that a patient may be making only one visit. Hence, adapted and rather more limited organization might be the only way forward in these situations (even so, it is still crucial to patient well-being that psychological care is developed and organized at *whatever* level circumstances dictate).

If we could walk into a unit that had a fully organized and integrated psychological care programme what would we find? Conversation would quickly reveal that the staff were aware that psychological care was an important component of their duties and that they were *expected* to commit a small proportion of their time to it. This would have been discussed at their selection interview, and their job description would include mention of psychological care duties. Those who needed it would have had training in basic skills, together with support and supervision from the clinical psychologist linked to the unit. The unit would provide something like the 'observations for psychological care' record sheet for routine use. In the case of the nurses there would be organization of the psychological care duties, based, perhaps, on the named nurse system. The named nurse for a new patient would be expected to establish a supportive talking relationship with the patient and partner and, within a reasonable time period, begin monitoring psychological state. Again, it has to be stressed that this is not an onerous and time consuming task that competes with the routines of physical care. It can be fitted in with those routines.

Another feature of such a unit will be that the information from this monitoring of psychological state is reported back to the other colleagues involved with day-to-day care, probably at 'handover' time at the end of a shift. Not rigidly, every day, but as and when required. This reporting back is important, because it has the effect of making the psychological component of nursing care expected, routine, scheduled and valued. At the same time, any significant issues for a particular patient are discussed with colleagues and the 'action to be taken' element is reviewed, which is supportive for the nurse giving the care. Arrangements are then confirmed for further informational, emotional or counselling care as required. If it appears that a referral for psychological treatment is needed, arrangements are made as to who will discuss this with the patient and who will make the referral.

I am describing the ideal version of a fully organized and *integrated* approach to providing psychological care. In discussion with the nursing staff on this unit we would now discover how the term integrated is used. The nurses provide the basic care but the doctors are also involved. They expect the care to be provided and, on rounds or case discussions, will support the staff by asking about issues and progress in psychological care for each patient at appropriate intervals during their stay in the unit. Similarly, the physiotherapists, speech and language therapists, dieticians, occupational therapists or whoever becomes involved with the patient will expect brief pointers concerning psychological care issues. All the medical and therapist staff will be aware of the effort that the nurses make in psychological care because the clinical nurse manager will have briefed them all and will regularly engage them in mention of the issues. The medical and therapist staff will support the effort with participation on level 1, at least. With some patients these staff may become actively involved in level 2 interventions with informational or emotional care work. All staff are aware of and involved in the notion of monitoring psychological state and dealing with any issues arising, because this is seen as an investment of effort that supports and underpins medical and nursing treatments. Finally, as mentioned, the unit has direct links with a clinical psychologist or professional counsellor who visits the unit on a regular basis to work with patients or give training and guidance to staff.

I wonder what your thoughts have been while you were reading this description. You think it is a happy fantasy, perhaps? I can see why but, at the same time, some units that I have been involved with or visited come close to it. Often the weak link is the true comprehension and involvement by the medical consultants. If they request and truly value this addition to routine physical care it makes it so much more likely to happen and so much easier for the staff involved.

> *Organized and integrated psychological care from the patient's vantage point.* Amy, a 49-year-old woman with diabetes, had been aware that her kidneys were failing for the past year. Outpatient visits to the consultant nephrologist had made the situation clear. She always appreciated these visits because the clinic was very supportive in atmosphere. The consultant would always inquire how she was personally and mentioned several times that the nurses would be looking after her in terms of information and emotional support. On these occasions she also met a dialysis nurse for a brief general discussion and question session. The nurse took her through some basic information concerning dialysis and, on one visit, took her to see the unit and watch a video explaining the basics of peritoneal dialysis. The nurse found 10 minutes or so on each occasion for an open talk about her thoughts and feelings as she approached dialysis start-up. She was not particularly distressed because she had learned from her long 'career' as a person with diabetes to deal with the inevitable deterioration that microvascular failure brought along. Even so, she found the supportive contact with the nurse valuable and a source of comfort.
>
> When the time came to insert the peritoneal catheter and commence dialysis she was admitted to the unit for several days. She already knew some of the nurses from the previous visit and was quickly introduced to her named nurse. It was a busy few days, with much information and instruction concerning the procedure for the catheter insertion

and then the bag change system. She coped, essentially, but became preoccupied to the point of occasional anxiety attacks concerning the risks of infection at bag change and subsequent peritonitis (since this might lead to her removal from the transplant list). Both her named nurse and another from the dialysis team spent a little time with her going through basic information and technique and working with her to reassure her and talk through preoccupying worries. She was told that she could see a clinical health psychologist if she felt that she needed more specialist help. However, with the psychological care from the nurses she recovered her composure and confidence quite quickly. Once she was competent in the bag change system she met the home dialysis nurse counsellor and they worked through plans for her return home. Several home visits were made and an extended support relationship set up, which allowed Amy to get in touch with the home dialysis nurse should she have problems to do with health, technique and equipment or personal issues that troubled her.

During these months Amy felt cared for and supported. She had her knowledge and expectations checked through several times. When she became a little 'wobbly' emotionally she had immediate help and the offer of more specialist help should it be needed. This preventive psychological care helped her to deal with a difficult phase in her struggle with diabetes and acted as a preparation for a kidney transplant later on.

• Referral-based or expert-dependent organization

As the last variant in the organization of psychological care, this particular approach is quite common these days. From the patient's point of view it can work quite well. From the purist's view (that's me, I guess) it represents a great step forward from a situation of no organized psychological care, but it does carry with it the potential for built-in weaknesses and that might lead to neglect. Two somewhat differing examples illustrate the emphasis in this type of organization.

1   A recent exhibition that I attended on the theme of developments in nursing provides the first example. This involved a maternity unit (thus, once more, a unit that enjoys a favourable staff–patient ratio). I asked the midwife attending a poster display what was done about psychological care on her maternity unit. She related with some enthusiasm and pride that

they had developed an excellent scheme for providing mothers with psychological care and that this was very effective, especially in helping mothers who had to deal with difficult births, premature births, genetically or physically damaged new born infants, miscarriages or stillbirths. The key to the scheme was that they had a unit counsellor who attended regularly for two days a week. She was exclusively available for individual case work with mothers who were in any degree of psychological reaction or difficulty. Furthermore, she was available directly to assist the midwives with guidance on how best to help the mothers at times when she was not present. Whenever possible she briefly met mothers to introduce herself, check on their well-being and let them know that she was available to help them if needed. The whole unit had an atmosphere of concern for the psychological well-being of the mothers but, in this instance, it was mainly focused on the resource of the expert counsellor.

2 The second example is of a health centre that had sessions from a clinical psychologist. This had come about because the doctors who were based at the centre were fairly psychologically minded and were weary of the negative effect of delays caused by long waiting lists whenever they referred patients for assistance with mental health problems. Although there was a general awareness of mental health issues, there was no specific psychological monitoring or screening system at the centre for people with physical illness or injury. Problems tended to be identified on a chance basis if the doctors or practice nurses happened to notice something untoward in a patient's conversation at routine clinics. This was responded to with supportive advice or information and internal referral to the psychologist. It was not a service specifically for psychological reactions to physical health issues but also dealt with mental health issues such as depression, anxiety, alcohol dependency and so on.

In both these examples weaknesses and potential risks are apparent. The maternity unit has a strong concern for psychological care and the mothers almost certainly receive an excellent service. A question arises, though, about the high level of dependency on the one expert. What happens if the counsellor is off sick for a couple of weeks or away for six months on maternity leave? Because the nurses depend on her and do not have routine involvement in emotional care in a self-sufficient way there could be a serious lapse in care. Furthermore, in the absence of an organized scheme for monitoring the psychological state of the mothers, might there be a proportion of needy cases who could go unnoticed while lacking information or needing emotional care? Even so, the scheme seemed to work and the quality of care appeared to be generally very good as long as the depended upon expert was present.

In the case of the health centre the same criticisms apply. However, in this case, detection of the need for psychological care interventions for the ill and injured was haphazard, in the sense that it relied on busy doctors and nurses noticing needs because the patient had said something – not because there was an established monitoring procedure. Again, if the psychologist was on leave or off sick the staff either put the case on the waiting list or dealt with it in an informal way themselves. This is better than nothing but a weaker arrangement than it need be.

Final words on the need to monitor psychological state and organize psychological care

Contrast the experiences of Amy, as described above, when she was being prepared for dialysis with the following.

After quite a struggle, Charlotte, aged 36 years, achieved her first, much longed for, pregnancy. She had been pregnant for four months when difficulties began. On a Sunday afternoon she was admitted to the local maternity unit. A day later she lost the baby. The miscarriage was dealt with efficiently and well by the staff, but other than a kindly word or two little was offered other than physical care. Charlotte was initially shocked. A great void had suddenly opened up in her life but she felt rather numb, so showed no actual reaction. She responded to the staff at the unit in a false, almost cheery manner. She hated being what she regarded as an emotional nuisance when she could see that the staff were busy. No one on the staff sat with her to talk, to find out how she was reacting to the miscarriage, to help her face the event or to offer support in her shock and loss. No one monitored her psychological state. No one made any referral for psychological assistance or sent word to her health centre that she needed monitoring and further support. The referral was not made because the need had not been identified. She was discharged and returned home with no psychological care and left to deal with the experience herself.

In fact, there were significant ramifications to this negligence of basic psychological care. Charlotte had a period of depression, was off work for a while and was eventually treated with anti-depressants by her GP. She never really found a true resolution for her grief. She found the emotional impact so difficult that she felt unable to contemplate pregnancy again for some while. Her sex life declined and a few years later she began to develop menorrhagia. This condition is sometimes associated with poor psychological state and it remains a possibility that Charlotte eventually developed a physical complication following her understandable but damaging psychological reaction.

Perhaps the use of such case descriptions is over-dramatic? I think not, and cite, in support, an article originating from the heart of the medical establishment in the UK, the *British Medical Journal*. McAvoy (1986) writes on death and bereavement. In a concise review he notes the strongly established link between loss of a close relative, in Charlotte's case her longed for child, and the increased rates of illness and subsequent death.

At this point it is appropriate to remind you of our 'mantra' expressed in Chapter 1:

> **In serious illness and injury good psychological care complements and underpins physical treatment regimes. Psychological care contributes to recovery. When there is no psychological care physical treatment plans may sometimes be undermined and thus the power of medical, nursing and therapist interventions will be reduced.**

I hope that I will, by now, have convinced you that the provision of psychological care for the ill and injured is an essential part of routine medical and nursing care. It must not be regarded as just an added luxury when time and circumstances permit. Nor is psychological care just a matter of being a little more caring, holistic and chatty to patients. It depends on the reliable monitoring of psychological state and organized, appropriate interventions. I also hope that if you find yourself working in a situation where there is no effort at psychological care you will feel disturbed by this and set about improving things.

Discussion time

- What are *your* views on the issue of monitoring patients' psychological state? Can it be dealt with successfully at an informal level or must there be organization and records?

- Can you suggest alternative approaches to that given in this chapter?

- What approaches have you encountered in your training and work experience for detecting whether patients or their partners need psychological care (including the provision of information). Do the approaches work?

- How would you describe the approach to monitoring psychological state and giving psychological care in your current work setting? Is there room for improvement?

- The strategy for hospital nurses in monitoring psychological state is fairly clear cut. It is less easy to be decisive about practice and community nurses, since there is much more variability in their situation. What are your views on monitoring psychological state in primary care?

- Practitioners such as occupational therapists, physiotherapists, dieticians and speech and language therapists (and many other types of health care practitioners) are often in a position to help with both monitoring psychological state and providing interventions of the level 2 type. From your own experience and observations what do you see as the best route for integrating these therapists into the effort to provide psychological care?

4 Providing informational and educational care

A glance through the literature to do with both acute and chronic pain confirms observations that are readily obtained in any pain clinic, namely that a person's experience of pain and, indeed, the extent to which it is perceived as noxious, frightening and intolerable are strongly influenced by that person's attitude to and knowledge of the problem. See, for example, Skevington (1995), who provides a useful overview of factors influencing the experience of pain, or Thomas and Clarke (1997), who discuss pain control. Combining such research-based knowledge with some 20 years of personal psychological work within a pain clinic, I can confidently say that people having to deal with pain generally do better if:

- they have an understanding of the cause of their pain;

- they do not associate the pain with a potential threat (e.g. cancer onset);

- their expectations are similar to the likely outcome of their problem;

- they feel a degree of control;

- they do not feel forgotten, abandoned or angry;

- they have ready access to information, support and understanding;

- they are not ashamed of any disability and consequently 'at war' with their body;

- they can move beyond focusing their attention on the pain;

- the psychosocial context is relatively benign (e.g. there is no threat to financial security).

Having made this statement, we can now ask an important question: to what extent are pain patients likely to be helped by a high level of good quality communication, information and education? It will be obvious to us all that the answer is 'considerably', since the first six of these items are issues dealt with by communication, information and education. The import of this conclusion is equally obvious. Caring by informing should be high on the list of treatment priorities for people encountering pain problems. Naturally, this does not apply exclusively to people with pain problems but fits across the spectrum of illness, injury and developing disability.

To keep people informed when they are receiving health care and to communicate with them on a regular basis should be a straightforward task. Yet it appears that the users of our hospitals and health centres still experience mixed fortunes. Patient reports include 'They were excellent. They really took their time and explained everything to us. Then they answered all of our questions. We could not fault them at all.' This was said to me recently by the relatives of a patient in an intensive care unit. Then there is 'My biggest complaint was the lack of information and the lack of time to ask proper questions. I came away feeling that I had been bullied and knew little more than when I went in.' This comment was made to me by a patient shortly after he had experienced a somewhat rushed surgical outpatient appointment.

This observed diversity in terms of the quality of communication and the provision of information to patients in hospitals and health centres is also noted by Thomas and Clarke (1997: 299):

> Over the same period there has been a greatly increased emphasis on the development of communication skills during nurse education . . . However, in spite of this clear recognition of the importance of this issue, the Ombudsman Annual Review . . . in the UK continues to demonstrate that a significant proportion of patients' complaints focus on deficits in communication.

The recognition that good information and communication are important in health care is not particularly new, it has to be said. For example, over twenty years ago *Nursing* (number 27, July 1981) published 12 articles all written to teach the importance of communication with the ill and injured and to discuss the basic skills involved. These articles focused on several guiding principles, in particular that in order to achieve good communication one must convey a feeling of having time, patience and involvement. The language used must suit the patient and a basis of trust must be established. The communicator must be familiar with patients' abilities and able to pick up cues indicating (for example) overload, confusion or distress. The right kind of information needs to be given at the right kind of pace. Ideally, the communicator will use the conversational skills of reflection and clarification. Listening skills need to be well developed, such that feelings on the part of the patient are allowed expression without blocking or interruption. Then there is the important non-verbal component. The way one touches another, looks at them, the posture and position adopted and the gestures made all contribute to the skill of communication.

Why did these authors place so much stress on efforts at communication? Because they saw good communication and information as a buffer against fear and confusion in situations of illness and injury. Thus, good communication was seen as a way of enabling a person to collaborate and follow treatment through in a more relaxed manner. In other words, effective communication is a positive contribution to recovery. The series of articles ends with an overview that may be summarized as follows:

- Each patient is unique, bringing different needs and abilities and, therefore, requiring an individual approach by the health care practitioner.

- Communication skills are equally necessary for the 'average patient' and for those receiving highly specialized health care.

- The type of communication given must be assessed in relation to a person's particular state, needs and communicating style.

- Essential communication skills should be taught to health care practitioners.

- Communication makes demands on the professional. The primary demand is involvement and, because of this, there must be support for the practitioner.

Perhaps this will seem a bit on the idealistic side, especially for those of you in a pressured work environment. To be fair, though, I should comment on the context in which these authors wrote – that is, to point out the atmosphere of concern over apparent deficiencies in medical communication that clearly existed in 1981. What these authors were reacting to was a public debate centred on the common belief that consultants and doctors in general were often remote and incommunicative. A related problem was that nurses seemed passive in the situation (perhaps too anxious about upsetting doctors to take matters into their own hands and improve communication and information for patients as a unilateral initiative?). Thus, there was, at that time, a search for a new approach. Here, for example, is an extract from a typical newspaper feature article that appeared in *The Sunday Times* in June 1983. It catches the atmosphere of public concern. A woman is describing her recent experiences of childbirth:

> 'I never wanted to be treated like a VIP but it was the most important and frightening thing that had ever happened to me and I felt that they just couldn't be bothered.'
> At each of her dozen or so antenatal checks, she was prodded by a different pair of hands. Finally, on the basis of an estimated date, doctors concluded that she was overdue. An induction was recommended and she was told that she was risking her baby's life if she refused.
> 'I was flat on my back for 20 hours with electronic monitors, drips and then emergency oxygen because the speed of contractions was causing distress. It terrified the life out of me.'
> After a difficult forceps delivery performed, says Beverley, by a nervous junior doctor, 'My baby was cleaned up, wrapped and handed to me briefly. Then everyone just filed out of the room without a word. The drip was turned up so high that I was still contracting after the delivery. I found out after that they couldn't just turn it off, it had to be turned down gradually, but no-one would explain why I was in such terrible pain.' The bruising was dismissed by midwives as 'what motherhood is about.'

Richards (1981), one of the authors of the set of articles whose contents were summarized above, pressed home his complaints concerning poor communication in an orthopaedic ward with the following narrative. This was from a woman patient who recounts her experiences after an accident in the home:

> 'A brief visit from the surgeon dismissed the idea of an operation but revealed that I was to be admitted and I finally reached the ward six and a half hours after entering casualty. By this time I was unable to take in what was said to me. I was put on complete bed rest and eventually gathered that I had broken the first lumbar vertebra. But it was not until the consultant appeared a week later that the injury itself and some of the possible consequences were explained. I was told that it was a serious injury – the vertebra was completely smashed and I was lucky not to have any nerve damage. I was also told it would be about six weeks before the fracture was sufficiently consolidated for me to move. Three weeks after admission, more X-rays were taken of my back. The registrar showed them to me shortly before the consultant arrived and explained that, although the bones were starting to knit together, it would be another two or three weeks before I could be moved.'

> 'When the consultant arrived late that afternoon, my first impression was that he had enjoyed a good lunch! He glanced at the X-rays, decided that they were too dark to see and then announced that I should get up the next day. Having arrived late, he was in a hurry and unwilling to be engaged in discussion. It is, in any case, extremely difficult for a patient lying flat on her back to initiate a conversation when she is separated by a blanket cage from the group of doctors and nurses talking among themselves at the foot of the bed. As common sense and reason, as well as all my earlier information, were against the possibility that my recovery time should suddenly be reduced by half, I decided not to take it seriously.'

> 'The next morning I was distressed at the arrival of a brisk physiotherapist announcing that she had come to get me up. Suddenly all the pent-up anxiety about the possible consequences of things not properly explained focused on what I felt sure was an ill-considered decision. I wept profusely and refused to move until the decision was explained. I was left alone for some time but, later, when I tried to explain my anxiety to the staff nurse on duty, she reproached me as if I were a five year old, at the same time accusing me of childish behaviour.'

Well, that is the way it was, it seems. The key question is, though, **'what is it like now?'** There is no doubt in my mind that there have been significant improvements *in awareness* over recent years. This is readily apparent from casual conversation with doctors, nurses and allied professionals. While collecting views and material for this book, I have had some very encouraging conversations with health care practitioners in current practice. For example:

- *The nurse.* 'Nursing has moved on a great deal. Probably the biggest gains have been in the areas of patient information and education. It has become very systematic with quite a lot of effort put into providing written aids and structured verbal information. We also use video instruction as a basic educational tool. But, to be honest, I think there has been less progress in recognising and dealing with the general psychological and emotional effects of illness' (P. Woodhams, personal communication, 2002).

- *The dietician.* 'At our conferences and training schools, you find a tremendous emphasis on the theme of good communication, good information and even counselling these days. It is part of the job now' (G. Slade, personal communication, 2002).

- *The occupational therapist.* 'One third of our training time as occupational therapists is given over to psychological issues. Key skills such as communication and information are to the forefront. The work of the occupational therapist depends on good communication' (C. Penny, personal communication, 2002).

As a further encouragement Weinman (1997: 286) writes of the current situation in medical schools:

> In medical school, communication skills training is now regarded as a fundamental part of the curriculum . . . Typically, students are provided with an overview of the basic skills of 'active' listening, which facilitate patient communication. At a basic level these include the importance of developing good rapport and the use of open-ended questions early in the consultation, appropriate eye contact and other facilitatory responses to help the patient talk, together with the ability to

summarise and arrive at a shared understanding of the patient's problems. These skills can be taught in a number of ways, but the successful courses inevitably involve active learning, using role-plays with simulated patients as well as real patient interviews . . . In addition to these basic packages, it is also necessary for students to learn how to communicate about sensitive or difficult areas of medical practice, including dealing with distressed patients or relatives and giving 'bad news'.

Such statements from those involved in medical training are very encouraging indeed. Things do seem to be well set on a path of improvement. Having said that, let us apply the 'ward visit' test (go to the nearest general hospital, take the second ward on the right and go and speak to the patient in the third bed on the left). Alternatively, try the 'health centre exit interview test' (stop and interview any 10 patients leaving a health centre after an appointment with a GP or practice nurse). What is the probability of finding the patients or accompanying relatives to be satisfied with their information and able to give a reasonable account of their situation and its likely outcome? Answers will vary a lot from place to place but one thing is certain: we will find that there is still much work to be done to bring standards up to a basic satisfactory level. I regularly meet patients and their partners who have been very well informed and are full of compliments to the staff. But then again, I also regularly meet terribly under-informed patients and partners. It is a familiar experience for me to have to refer patients and partners to our hospital information service because their general practice staff, or their hospital doctors, nurses and other health care practitioners, have either not attempted or not succeeded in the task of basic communication and information provision.

A national audit of performance in informational care would, obviously, be ruinously expensive, so we must rely on local observations (yours are as valid as mine) and occasional indicators in the research journals or newspapers. As a very last example of such indictors I want to include extracts from a little report that recently took my attention:

Arthritis victims are suffering in silence
The Arthritis Research Survey (AAG), carried out for the Arthritis Action Group, revealed that more than 40 percent of arthritis sufferers believe that nothing can be done to improve their condition and are unaware of other options.

The survey was carried out in eight European countries.

The survey showed that 76 percent of GPs did not provide patients with leaflets and 82 percent did not provide patients with information on the treatment options.

(The Times 17 June 2002)

What do we conclude from this survey and the title of the article? That a very large proportion of a very large group of patients who suffer chronic pain and disability go without even the most basic provision of informational care. The article blames the GPs but many of these patients will have also attended facilities at both primary and secondary care levels. They will have met nursing staff and some will also have met physiotherapists and possibly occupational therapists. Somehow they emerge from this contact ill-informed about treatment options. Clearly there has been no monitoring of information levels and little by way of information-providing interventions.

The current position, therefore, seems to be that much is now known about the importance of information and communication in health care. Much training effort now goes into producing graduates versed in the skills of informational care and communication. Yet, given this higher profile for information provision and communication in training, professional practice, research and even government edict, *we can still find large groups of patients who have little information concerning critical issues and who have been the victims of very poor communication.* Before turning to the everyday, practical business of giving informational care, we must try to understand what goes wrong and also ask 'is it always the health care practitioners' fault or might some of the responsibility belong with the patients?'

Information provision: how it can go wrong and why it is sometimes a waste of time

Let us imagine, for a moment, that we will spend a while observing a hospital department where the whole range of the staff do concern themselves with good communication and do believe that information is important. They go about their work in the usual way but make an additional effort at communication with their patients. Would we discover that their positive motivation alone achieves the objective of well informed patients? Probably not; there are practical issues to be understood and dealt with before efforts at communication reliably yield well informed patients as the status quo. These must be appreciated if a good system of informational care is to be successfully established. In Nichols (1993) I presented a list of likely pitfalls for sincerely meant efforts at information exchange. Some of the key points still stand as, I believe, important issues to be kept in mind and I am, therefore, going to re-run them together with some additional points blended in from Weinman (1997) and other sources. These points are summarised in Box 4.1:

Box 4.1   Pitfalls that wait for us when giving information
• **Inappropriateness:** the recipients' needs are ignored. • **Distraction:** an adverse social or emotional context exists. • **Egocentricity:** it is incomprehensible. • **Overloading:** there is too much of it. • **Minimalizing:** there is too little given, in a rushed style. • **Non-retrievability:** no accompanying aids to memory. • **Uncoordinated:** disorganized, no one person coordinating. • **Passivity/intimidation:** no demand for information. • **Selective listening and forgetting:** accuracy fades. • **Conflicting health beliefs:** cause problems. • **Reliance on videos:** tempting but not a substitute.

Unfortunately this has turned into a longer list than I expected, so apologies for that. The truth is that there has been a great deal of research and exploration into the business of information exchange and so there is a strong knowledge base. I would commend to you the work of Ley (1988, 1997; Ley and Llewelyn 1995) for a full account of research and findings. Add to this my many years of talking with physically ill and injured people, a proportion of whom have angry complaints about the poor communication that they have experienced since starting to receive health care, and there ends up being quite a lot to say. Now I would like to take a look at these items in a little more detail. I will combine some of them where they are closely related in theme.

Pitfalls 1: inappropriate emotional and social context, and distraction

Put succinctly, it is quite common to find that efforts at communication with a patient have been a partial failure because we chose the wrong time and wrong place. Information may be well presented and comprehensible but that in itself does not guarantee that a person will be able to register it at the time or recount it the next day. The nature of the situation chosen for information exchange is an important factor that can degrade attempts at information provision, sometimes making it a waste of time, because there will inevitably be a poor outcome in terms of keeping a patient or relative well informed. For example, anxious people are often poor listeners. The anxiety, especially if they are nervous at the time, reduces the capacity to attend to and take in information. It can also reduce 'presence of mind' and levels of assertion, so that requests for explanation, repetition, consolidation and discussion are harder to make and therefore less frequent.

A nurse briefing a patient just before going into a procedure room for an angiogram will probably be surprised to learn how little some patients take in because they are so anxious and distracted. Relatives visiting an intensive care unit after the admission of a seriously injured patient may be similarly disadvantaged in terms of their shocked emotional state impeding their capacity to take in information. Similarly, anger or tearful emotional states make a poor context for information exchange (although good communication to do with support and emotional care is very valid).

In addition to emotional context there is the issue of social context. As noted in the two case stories reproduced above, hospital environments create an unusual social situation, one that is often parodied in comedy films. In particular, the sometimes terse, socially awkward atmosphere of the ward round or an outpatient clinic with a panel of doctors present make fine examples of raised social tension, which can intrude on the information exchange, if there is any. In such circumstances we know in advance that patients' capability to deal with an information-giving session to their own satisfaction is reduced and the likelihood of them retaining much is lowered. Like myself, no doubt, those of you reading this who have been in the inpatient situation will probably confirm this from personal experience.

Thus, information exchange may fail to achieve its objective if the patient is experiencing adverse emotional states or if the situation itself is inducing an adverse emotional state or distraction effect. In these terms some of the customary settings for interaction between staff and patients in a hospital carry the risk of reducing the ability of people to make use of the communication content, and this must be kept in mind by the health care practitioners involved. Usually, a visit to a health centre is less likely to be vulnerable to this disadvantage, unless the doctor or nurse is evidently very rushed or attends more to the computer than the patient – so inducing a distracting anger in the patient (might one of the author's top irritations be on display here?).

Allied to this theme, there is the issue of establishing our patients' actual needs in relation to information. I have been quite consistent throughout this book so far in stating that part of good psychological care is keeping patients and their partners properly informed. Now is the moment to confess that there is a catch to this. That is, *not all patients want to be kept informed.* Some adopt a rather passive stance, preferring to stay 'switched off' to the medical details and thus handing themselves over entirely to the staff. Occasionally one does meet the patient who says 'Just do what you have to do and leave me out of it, doctor.' Weinman (1997) picks up on this point and draws attention to a dimension of difference in the needs and coping styles of people when they are ill or injured. Some people cope by confrontation and mastery – that is, by accumulating as much information as possible so that they have more of a feeling of control by following a known pathway. Others avoid information entirely because they find it threatening. My own clinical contacts over the years suggest that the greater proportion of people do prefer good, basic information and feel upset and wary if they do not get it. A smaller proportion of people collect information about their case in an almost obsessive way, but I have met very few who truly do not want to know more than the absolute minimum. However, cultural difference may be important here. Attitudes to handling illness and relating to health care staff differ in different cultures. In your part of the world there may be differing trends.

In conclusion, a key act for 'professionalizing' information provision is to establish that:

1   *The place and timing is right.*

2   *The patient is ready for information and is 'feeling right'.*

3   *The patient actually wants information.*

Without these checks it can all go horribly wrong and we can end up walking away feeling that we have done a fine job when in fact it has been a failed attempt at information exchange.

Pitfalls 2: egocentricity and overload

Egocentricity is a term used to indicate a communication that is obscure because the content of the conversation means a lot to the communicator but very little to the recipient. This mismatch is sometimes referred to as *egocentric communication*. Health care practitioners often give information to patients that is, effectively, unusable. This is because it is not in a form and language that the individual can readily understand or (importantly) remember. Various factors influence the chances of good understanding being achieved. Given that the communication is often about medical issues, levels of prior knowledge of medical terminology and concepts is clearly important, as well as general intelligence and awareness of language differences. When there are major discrepancies in these assets between the practitioner and patient difficulties can arise, especially where there is a combination of a lack of assertiveness on the patient's part at getting usable information and a lack of effort on the communicator's part to make meaning clear. In such situations, despite attempts to give information, the patient can end up little better off. This is clearly going to be more likely if the practitioner giving information makes no effort to establish the patient's linguistic and intellectual capabilities and then moderate content, language, visual aids and pace to cater for these. Hence, a few hours after receiving information, a patient may be ruled by confusion. It is so familiar to me to hear people saying something like 'Well, I didn't really grasp all that he said. Something about injections in the nerves, or was it the joints, I'm not sure that I really understood, to be honest.'

These differences between patients and their doctors in terms of their knowledge and language skills explains why early investigations revealed such unimpressive outcomes in medical communication. For example, Ley (1982) reports from some of his own well conducted surveys that approximately 50 per cent of patients or relatives interviewed after being given medical information did not understand what they had just been told concerning the diagnosis, cause and likely outcome of their complaint.

A related obstacle to good communication is the problem of *overload*. Overload will be an experience familiar to us all from having attended rushed lectures with too much information and no opportunity for clarification and consolidation of the information. It is easy for us to cause this to happen in the clinic too. There are few reliable hard rules to help us but, as a very rough guide, unsupported, hearsay-based 'knowledge' allows me to say that the average person struggles to remember much more than four or so significant clusters of information over a 24-hour period. Motivation, rehearsal, written records and so on will alter this dramatically, but it probably does apply to the average patient at, say, outpatient clinics. Worse, if we overload people with information, especially concerning unfamiliar topics, it may have the effect of leaving them confused and actually remembering even less. The enthusiastic and helpful communicator, therefore, needs to be cautious and keep the reins tight on amounts of information on any one occasion. Otherwise, that same enthusiasm may result in the patient being overloaded and, thus, in another failed attempt at communication.

One further point relates to the needs of the people that we work with. Allen and Brock (2000) offer a book with the interesting title *Health Care Communication Using Personality Type*. Their basic point is that people differ and tend to fall into various categories in terms of preferred styles and type of communication. They introduce an approach called FLEX care, which has, as its focus, the effort to assess one's own and other people's preferences in communication and receiving information. The intention is to use this material to enhance health care communication. It is certainly worth looking at this approach for further insight and depth in communication awareness. It extends the quest to make our communications optimally suited to our patients' needs. There is too much detail involved for me to do justice to their work here, though, and in some respects it would be impractical for the average health care practitioner in the average clinic setting. But it is certainly worth the effort of familiarizing yourself with the approach.

Pitfalls 3: minimalizing and rushing

A rather indignant 71-year-old lady who had developed non-insulin-dependent diabetes recently complained to me:

> 'It was like getting blood out of a stone. He just didn't seem to want to be bothered talking to me and answering questions in any detail. I felt quite angry. I know that they tell you all about it at the diabetes clinic but he might have tried a bit himself. They are supposed to talk to you these days aren't they?'

I do not think that an explanation is necessary for this one. Errors of this type are easily avoided by asking the person that you are working with, 'Am I going at the right pace?' and 'Is that enough information for you at the moment or would you like more?' In this instance I suspect that the GP was running way behind schedule and was desperate to get on with his list. As noted below, a little coordination on information provision goes a long way, and this lady would have felt well dealt with if, after an apology about his unavoidable rush, the GP had said that the practice nurse would meet her and explain things more fully.

Pitfalls 4: non-retrievability of information

Distracting situations and emotions, egocentric communication and overload are woes enough, it might be said, but unfortunately there are more to come. An additional factor, a lack of *comprehensible reminders*, can further reduce the likelihood of successful recall. I will present a little more information on factors that affect retention of information below, but here, as we examine how well motivated attempts at information provision can fail, our attention should turn to the need for assistance in helping recall.

In many non-medical settings important information is recorded in various ways, possibly on paper, perhaps on a computer or on either audio or video tape. The proceedings of a court or a committee, a pilot obtaining airways clearance from air traffic controllers over the aircraft radio, ambulance controllers taking details of a call out etc. – all receive information verbally and back it up with a written or recorded form. The information is written down or recorded because it is vital to retain accuracy and it is recognized that the 'vehicle' of the spoken and then remembered word alone is inadequate. However, may I ask you to look back to your last visit to a doctor, physiotherapist or practice nurse. Was the information given to you backed up by any written notes, diagram or closely related leaflets? Perhaps it seemed unnecessary? Perhaps a diagnosis of 'flu with a secondary throat infection, the latter to be attacked by amoxycillin, does not need explanation and written notes (although some patients may be left a bit confused about why there is not a drug for the 'flu itself). However, a patient attending for consultation with a cardiologist, after, say, an echocardiogram has just revealed a significant leak from her mitral valve, will have a huge amount of information to absorb, much of it related to things of which she knows very little. In such a situation, prepared notes together with diagrams that can be amplified and personalized to fit the individual case are essential. Ideally, there will also be a tape recording of the conversation with the cardiologist to take home and play over again to relatives. However, as you and I know, such practice is unusual at present. Often the consultant will give a short, efficient, kindly, verbal briefing and that is the business done. The risks of the patient being confused, or just not knowing much of the detail in a day or so, are thus very high.

All this would not matter so much if the patient, after the meeting with the consultant, then immediately met a cardiac nurse (who, ideally, would have been present at the consultation) who gave a properly designed induction to the world of valve repair or replacement. This would include diagrams, notes and personal details of the case and either a tape recording of the session or a prepared video to take home. Without this rehearsal of the information and aids to assist retrieval of information, no one at that clinic should fall into the belief that they are doing a good job of communicating. For one thing, our lady patient is likely to be in some shock, especially because of the need for cardiac surgery. With a leaking mitral valve to be fixed she is likely to need many 'bits' of information if she is to achieve some level of understanding. There will be some information to do with anatomy, some to do with the vascular system and fluid on her lungs, some to do with recommended drugs and their effect on blood pressure and heart performance and some to do with surgery options, recovery and prospects. Yet, as we have discussed, people do not usually do well taking in information in large doses, especially in these circumstances. Thus, overload comes quickly and, consequently, a failure to absorb information fully. This predictable effect has to be headed off with additional aids to information delivery and retrieval.

Pitfalls 5: lack of coordination

In an institutional culture that fails to foster good communication and information provision the allocation of responsibility to keep patients informed is often haphazard. In fact the failure to coordinate and organize information provision can be the basic cause of the problem, not, as is often believed, a lack of motivation on the part of the staff. In such a culture information is presented piecemeal, if at all. Sometimes this is by doctors, sometimes by nurses or other practitioners. There may be confusion about whose job it is or, even, 'who is allowed to tell what'. If there is no one person who has a responsibility to check how communication is going, what the patient knows and what needs to be done to achieve reasonable levels of information for a patient, then disorganization rules. It will all be left to the 'luck of the draw' whether there is effective communication by one of the staff or not. What proportion of our health centres and hospital departments fit this description? I truly do not know, but it is quite clear to me that the percentage is *not* zero. There is more on organization in the following sections.

Pitfalls 6: passivity and feelings of intimidation

This concerns what the *patient* does or does not contribute to the information-giving session. In the preceding few pages we have been looking at why, even with good intent to communicate and give good information to patients and their partners, it can sometimes go wrong. I hope that I have kept away from an atmosphere of general blame and shown, instead, how various factors, some of which are not readily apparent in the situation, can fool us into thinking that we have done well at communicating when, in fact, the opposite is the case. But it is not just we, as communicators in health care, who have to make an effort in the business of information exchange. A contribution from the people we are communicating with is another important factor. Ideally, we will find our own motivation to communicate in depth and give good, usable information complemented by a parallel motivation on the part of our patients to obtain information from us.

Weinman (1997) writes of *inputs* (i.e. the attitudes, beliefs, expectations etc. that patient and doctor bring to the consultation), *process* (the nature of the encounter) and *outcome* (the short- and longer-term effects on the patient). In these terms, the overall success of an information-giving session can be influenced by the inputs from the patient and their contribution to the process in the session, in particular the active involvement of the patient in seeking understanding and information.

Bennett (2000) illustrates the issue. He describes studies that reveal how a significant proportion of patients can leave their consultations with doctors feeling angry and ill-informed. Yet, he writes, 'between half and three quarters of patients who want more information during a medical consultation ***do not ask for it.*** Possibly as a consequence of such a failure, between 7 and 52 per cent of people report not having fully understood the information they were given.'

The reasons for this failure to intervene and seek information are important for us to understand, because, somehow, we need to motivate the people to whom we offer health care to engage more actively with us in the process of obtaining information (those that want it, that is). Bennett observes, 'Some people may not prepare questions to ask the doctor or may not be able to develop and articulate them during the consultation. They may not ask questions because it is only later that they realise they need more information. Health professionals may actively inhibit questions by the use of closed questions and other non-verbal cues. This may be facilitated by some patients' reluctance to ask questions of a busy doctor: a frequent claim in hospital wards.'

It is easy to empathize with much of this because, in general, few of us have much induction into the role of patient, other than the stereotypes that are generated on television. If school education included life skills such as role-playing practice in dealing with doctor and nurse consultations it would be easier. Many people do feel intimidated and non-assertive in the consultation situation. This produces a quiet passivity and the behaviour of getting up and leaving an information-giving exchange with a doctor, nurse, physiotherapist etc. despite not understanding or not feeling well informed. Intimidation and passivity might be less likely during home visits from a community nurse or health visitor but, even so, the need for prepared questions and active involvement by patients is not well recognized.

One solution that I have adopted to deal with this problem is the technique of *guided questioning*. This is explained below.

Pitfalls 7: selective listening and forgetting – information drift

Something told does not mean something heard
and likely to be remembered.

This is an effect of unexpected power at times. If we become ill or injured it is very difficult not to harbour a sense of threat that is accompanied by a sense of urgency to return to health and a normal existence. Listening to and remembering information about our condition is, therefore, vulnerable to 'corruption' by the hopes, fears, fantasies and the strong personal needs that come with the state of being ill or disabled.

I have had frequent experiences through the years that illustrate how some information is easier to listen to and retain than other types. People can hear what they hope to hear; then, later, they will have a convincing memory of information received that will be inaccurate. Added to this, in a hospital environment particularly, information can arrive from different sources. A hospital doctor, a day shift nurse, a night shift nurse or other patients in a unit may all make comments to a person that may contain slightly different biases. For example, recently a registrar had been passing information to a patient during the day about tests and future outlook. She made an effort to be accurate and give realistic expectations. Some hours later a nurse on her night shift, sensing the patient's anxiety, made reassuring statements that differed somewhat in bias by giving a 'best scenario' version of expectations. A day later it was the latter that was remembered and caused some conflict of versions. An example of an incident in a kidney unit catches the problem. This was a case that had been referred to me some years ago. I use it because, although educational approaches have changed somewhat now, the case serves as a classic example of this obstacle to the retention of accurate information. The referral was because the patient had become angry and difficult with the staff and they were not sure why:

Tony was a self-employed, industrious electrician aged 34. He had two children. He was very self-sufficient and prided himself in his ability to deal with problems, usually other people's. Unfortunately, after an infection he developed health problems that resulted in rapid onset renal failure and treatment by dialysis. Initially, Tony was treated at the renal unit with haemodialysis but, being otherwise fit and capable, was quickly prepared for CAPD, the bag change system of peritoneal dialysis. Although very shaken by this completely unexpected event in his life, he held to an optimistic outlook and was impatient to try getting back to work at the earliest. He met with nurses for the standard preparatory education and information briefing sessions prior to the insertion of a catheter and the start-up on CAPD. The staff avoided giving exact time schedules for eventual discharge home because various technical and health obstacles could slow down progress. In general terms the expectation was encouraged that he ought be home and self-sufficient for dialysis in five or six weeks from the date of the briefing sessions. However, a week later, as one of the dialysis nurses giving CAPD training was chatting to Tony, it emerged that he had made plans on the basis of being definitely discharged home in two weeks after his catheter was fitted. The nurse commented that this seemed a little unrealistic. At this point Tony exploded in rage and said, 'But Sue told me it would be two weeks. You people just change things to suit yourselves. The organization here is hopeless. Why can't you get your act together?' Naturally the nurse was somewhat taken aback. She 'knew' that no one had actually told him a definite time of two weeks. At the same time Tony 'knew' that he *had* been told two weeks. At least, that is what his memory conveyed.

In retrospect the ingredients of the incident were clear. Tony found that his continued presence at the renal unit and the powerlessness that he felt there were very hard to tolerate. It felt like being in a cage. He was used to solving problems himself and doing things at his maximum rate, not at other people's rate. He could not bring to bear the self-reliant skills and problem-solving powers that were his primary defence against threat and anxiety. He was, understandably, profoundly ill at ease and desperate to get back to an independent life. He drove himself to this end, learning all that he could by talking with the doctors, nurses and fellow patients. He learned that one patient had recently made the start-up with CAPD in just over two weeks and decided that he should be able to manage this too. In fact, this other patient was very experienced in surviving by dialysis and so needed less instruction on general issues such as diet and good technique, whereas Tony was a novice. Other patients had encouraged him. Then, regrettably, a conversation with a young nurse had, unwittingly, led to an inaccurate version of events being remembered. As she helped him with a bag change the following conversation took place.

Tony: 'Can people finish their training and go home after two weeks?'

Nurse: 'Well, I think some do it in nearly that time if they get on very quickly and know what they are doing.'

Tony: 'How am I getting on, do you think?'

Nurse: (sensing both Tony's anxiety and the pressure he was exerting) 'I think that you are doing very well. You are a quick learner and the catheter is fine.'

Tony: 'I must get back to work soon or I'll start losing my customers. Do you think finishing in two weeks is possible?'

Nurse: 'I'm not sure when your discharge is planned but I should think you might make it if you keep up like this. You should ask sister or the doctors tomorrow.'

Unfortunately, Tony did not really register the hesitancy or qualifications in this exchange and, later that day, told his wife, 'The nurse said I will probably be finished in two weeks.' He fixed this objective in his mind and a day later 'knew' that he had been told it would take two weeks to finish training and get back to relatively normal life. He blocked out the more tentative information concerning time schedules given to him just before he started training.

It is easy to see what was happening. It is a classic case of selective listening and remembering with information drift. Some of Tony's questions to the young nurse were manipulative in the sense that he signalled that he was anxious and made clear a way to reduce his anxiety, namely by the nurse conceding that his hopes of completing training in two weeks might be met if things went well. He then heard the bits of information that fed his hopes and soothed his agitation. The selected out material was remembered rather more easily than the more cautious 'it might take longer' communications.

This event illustrates two very important principles that I really want to emphasize to you and hope that you will always carry with you in your work:

1   Because you have given a patient or a relative some information or advice this does not mean that they have registered what you have said and will remember it accurately – thus, *something told does not mean something heard, understood and remembered*. To survive intact, your information must run the gauntlet of the active processes described above, such

as searching for reassurance and blocking out information with threatening implications.

2   If you are involved with information provision in the health care setting then it is a mistake to believe that once a person has been informed the knowledge that they have received will endure as a stable and reliable memory. Informational care is a little like wound care. In wound care you need to return to the patient every so often to change the dressing. *In informational care you need to return to the patient to check what has happened to the information that he or she has been given because the likelihood is that it will have drifted off from your original version and so will need to be checked and reinforced*. In the ideal setting, therefore, information delivery is not a one contact only event.

Pitfalls 8: conflicting health beliefs

Allied to these concerns there is the issue of the attitudes and beliefs that people hold as they take up the role of patient. In short, what is referred to by the term 'health beliefs' is the composite of knowledge, experience, outlook and bias in view that a person has accumulated concerning health care and health care practitioners during their life. It is the reason why some patients and partners hold on to what you say as a matter of life-saving importance, while others may regard it to be of dubious value or low in the ordering of priorities in life, and so reject it. For example, some people with diabetes are very exact in the management of their insulin regime and diet. Others are sloppy with their regime or actually negligent to the point of risking their long-term health. A woman in late middle age with a family history of osteoporosis would not go on HRT because her male GP had a rather negative attitude to the preventive use of oestrogen. She in turn had an absolute faith in the judgement of her GP.

Rutter (1989) wrote on the health belief model of Becker (1974) in relation to breast self-examination for the early detection of breast cancer and also the practice of safe sex as a defence against AIDS. He describes the health belief–behaviour relationship as having 'two principle variables: the value an individual places on a particular goal; and the individual's estimate of how likely it is that a given action will achieve that goal. For preventive health behaviour, the model suggests that there are three specific dimensions: perceived susceptibility, perceived severity and perceived benefits and barriers.' This adds up to saying that people may react to what you tell them with an immediate judgement of its payoff and the personal cost of following or not following advice. Similarly, Rutter goes on, Fishbein and Ajzen (1975), with their theory of reasoned action, argue that a person's behaviour is influenced by an intermix of their private attitude to performing the behaviour and perceptions of how people who are important to us believe we ought to behave.

> Becky was 15 and had been diabetic for about six months. Although able to inject herself with insulin, Becky steadfastly refused to do so unless it was absolutely unavoidable. This meant that her parents had to arrange to meet her or accompany her throughout the day to make sure her blood sugar was controlled. Becky accepted an invitation to go to a summer camp for young people with diabetes. This was at an activity centre in Scotland. Her parents, naturally, had to go along too and stay in a nearby hotel. On the day of arrival her parents were on hand before lunch and dinner to administer the insulin injection. They discreetly disappeared after that to leave Becky to join in with the evening activities and discussion group. The sleeping accommodation was dormitory style and so, when Becky's parents arrived next morning to give the pre-breakfast injection, she was happily mixing in with the other girls getting ready for breakfast and the day to come. On being called by her parents for her injection Becky rather brusquely told her parents not to fuss since she was quite capable of doing her own injections. She continued to be self-sufficient for the rest of the week. I lost track of her after that but my suspicion is that she continued in her new self-sufficient manner because her beliefs had changed and, importantly, because her perception of what the peer group of young people with diabetes thought and did had also changed.

Pitfalls 9: reliance on videos for informational care

Finally (and it is nice to be able to say finally because it has been a rather long list), there is the problem of communication and information provision through video material. Watching an instructional video can be a very helpful and informative event. Not the least among the benefits of this type of information provision is that the video can be watched through several times if necessary and is usually professionally produced and so refined for best clarity, pace and content to suit an average audience. However, the video approach should be regarded an aid rather than a substitute for face-to-face informational care in cases of significant injury or illness. I emphasize this because the material in an instructional video will not be specific to the individual patient's case features. More importantly, perhaps, in the next section, on techniques for information provision, you will find that I stress the importance of matching communication to the patient's needs and, above all else, checking the accuracy of what information they have actually absorbed. The temptation with video material in a pressured clinical situation is to drift into the convenient delusion that the video material is self-sufficient for information provision. In most cases it isn't. The work of informational care is supplemented by the video but not replaced by it, added to which, *good informational care blends into emotional care*. Thus, after a major briefing with key information, the effective health care practitioner will encourage a patient to express their reactions to the information that they have just received. This expression of reaction should include their immediate thoughts and perceptions and, importantly, emotional reactions to the information, since these may determine what people do with information and how accurately they are able to remember it. Thus, we should be on our guard with 'convenient' video tapes. I learned recently that the Germans sometimes use the very helpful phrase 'worse betterment'. This is a wonderful way of commenting on the acts of politicians and civil servants when they introduce 'improvements' that actually make things worse for the rest of us – like introducing the internal market into the health care system, dare I suggest. *Thus, communicating by video alone can lead to cases of 'worse betterment'.*

> Nurse 1: 'Has Mrs Evans been brought up to speed on having her bypass yet?'
> Nurse 2: 'Yes, all done. I gave her the video to watch this afternoon. She's gone home now.'
> Nurse 1: 'Is she OK with it?'
> Nurse 2: 'Not sure. She disappeared off somewhere and then I went up to the ward. Haven't spoken to her.'
> Nurse 1: 'By the way, Jenny said she saw her crying in the day room.'
> Nurse 2: 'Oh really?'

Not what we actually had in mind, I think you will agree.

Putting it all together

Caring for patients and their partners by informing and communicating is an important contribution to overall care and well-being. Not only that, it has implications in terms of workload and the basic costs of health care. For example, Ley (1989) refers to studies which reveal that 20 per cent of *readmissions* to hospitals are correlated with poor adherence (non-compliance with recommended treatments). I can also confirm that the poorly informed patient or relative is a much bigger potential time drain on staff, particularly where lack of information leads to a misinterpretation of symptoms, body sensations or pains and, consequently, an unnecessary consultation with a GP or hospital specialist. Good informational care can save money and time. Finally, for the vast majority of patients, good communication from health care practitioners and high availability of information is much preferred. Two studies from some years back will serve as a last exhortation and final example of what we absolutely must get away from.

Elian and Dean (1985) interviewed 167 patients with a recent diagnosis of multiple sclerosis: 18 per cent were ignorant of the nature of their illness; 24 per cent had been informed by a doctor other than the diagnosing consultant; 19 per cent had relied on guessing what the diagnosis was themselves; 6 per cent (incredibly) had found out by accident (e.g. ancillary staff); 7 per cent had been spontaneously informed by their consultant; 83 per cent preferred to be properly informed.

Picking up on the last item from this list it is of note that Reynolds *et al.* (1981) interviewed 67 people with advanced cancer and discovered that: 91 per cent wanted full information on the diagnosis; 92 per cent wanted information on the symptoms; 88 per cent wanted information on the prognosis; 97 per cent wanted information on treatment and side-effects. If we are serious about quality of care for the ill and injured then the work of communicating and caring by informing is central among our obligations.

> **Box 4.2**   A key statement for informational care
>
> The work of 'caring by informing' is the platform on which psycho-logical care is built. This is because a person's psychological state and psychological reactions are very much influenced by what that person knows and believes and, consequently, the expectations generated from this knowledge.

Informational and educational care in practice

What is the real objective of informational and educational care? It is to provide and maintain our patients' information at a level that:

- produces realistic expectations;
- reduces the fright, stress and confusion of 'not knowing';
- leads to effective participation in treatment and self-care.

There is no real hard borderline between informing and educating, but I will make a practical distinction by regarding educational care as concerned with larger quantities of information organized into courses of instruction. Such interventions are often related to teaching technique. There is a separate section on this below.

Practical techniques in informational care

We move now into a 'how to do it' mode. This will take me into a rather different style of presentation, more like that of an instructor. I hope that you will find this efficient and helpful rather than irritating. It means that I will no longer be presenting a mix of theory together with clinical and research findings, but will be passing on my own views, based on first-hand experience, concerning the best approach to informational care. I will be telling you in quite definite terms how I believe we should all go about organizing and providing information to patients in our health care system. This is also the way that I like to be kept informed when I take on the role of patient. Because of this change in style please maintain your own evaluative perspective. Discuss the ideas, clarify what you find acceptable and add anything that you deem to be important but missing. *What follows, therefore, should not be mistaken for the one and only way to go about informational care. Instead, it is my personal outlook.*

There is one warning. I know that the majority of you will not work in the ideal environment for optimal communication and informational care. Some of you will be managing high case loads and facing various time pressures. I recognize that. But to outline the optimum for organization and information provision I have to assume an ideal environment. For the purposes of clear teaching I will be using examples from somewhat idealized settings where the staff have time to think and the resources to organize good care.

There is no great mystique to the approach. **Communication and information provision flows naturally if certain basic principles are always observed. These are the key principles:**

1 There needs to be ongoing encouragement from the clinical lead in your unit that fosters *a culture emphasizing communication and information provision to patients and relatives.* This applies equally in a hospital unit, therapy department or community practice. How does your current work situation answer up to this feature? If your situation is not ideal then the next best alternative is that you and immediate colleagues foster a more 'local' culture emphasizing communication and information provision, with mutual support for one another. At the same time you have to work patiently and diplomatically at developing good information resources for your unit and apply your effort to shifting the convictions of your clinical lead. Yours will be the evidence-based and user-preferred stance. Never forget that. **Question: what is your current work culture like? Does it encourage** *good* **communication and information provision?**

2 It is necessary to have an underlying level of organization such that *an identified person is responsible for overseeing the provision of information to a particular patient.* This does not mean that one member of staff rigidly monopolizes information work with a patient. Instead they hold the responsibility for making sure that the work gets done. They need to check that patients have been and remain adequately informed in relation to their needs and capabilities. In the past days of primary nurses and then named nurses this type of organization was rather more

easily provided. **Question: does anyone in your unit organize information provision – or is it just hoped that, somehow, it gets done?**

3   There is no set level of information required. Instead the target adopted is that of maintaining levels of information that allow: (a) *a basic understanding*; (b) *realistic expectations*; and (c) *an understanding that encourages good adherence.* The patient's need for information should play a part in adjusting the levels of information provided and, in most circumstances, patients should be encouraged to be active in seeking information. **Question: would a random inquiry reveal that your patients are kept informed at a level that gives them a basic understanding and generates realistic expectations?**

4   *The task of communicating information has to be made thoroughly professional* in the same way that other skills – for example, venepuncture – are made professional. At the same time it must in no way be dehumanized, but remain a supportive encounter. This means that there is a right way and a wrong way (in my view) to go about the task of giving information. Thus, staff likely to be involved in information exchange (which is a large proportion) should have received training in their approach to information provision and educational interventions in order that they are practised as a professional skill. It is unacceptable that it be left as an uncoordinated, amateurish, free for all conducted by staff who, although trained and competent in their own special field, are actually untrained in the basic skills of communication and information provision. It is to be hoped that most people now entering the health care professions receive this type of training in their basic training course. The core content of this professional skill is set out in the next section. As with most skills it is a help if there is an occasional check and feedback session with a colleague to ensure that basic skill levels are maintained. **Question: how professional do you see your own information work and that of your regular colleagues?**

5   In many situations the 'professionalization' of information provision has implications for the care team as a whole. This is because we cannot achieve reliable information provision unless *the separate members of the team cooperate to keep one*

another informed about the care plan for individual patients and update one another on changes to this. Thus, nurses and therapists who are aware of an original care plan for a patient cannot offer good, up-to-date informational care unless the medical colleagues involved with the case keep the nurses informed of recent medical decisions to alter the plan. Of course, this is fairly obvious stuff but, nevertheless, lack of coordination and the complaint that 'they never tell you anything here' remain familiar. The same applies in a general practice. Community and practice nurses cannot do a reasonable job of informational care with their patients unless medical colleagues have introduced a means of conveying the essentials of the case and recent changes to these colleagues. Before long, 'integrated care plans' may be at the peak of fashion. These should include a built-in device to ensure the updating of colleagues and then, subsequently, patients and partners on changes in plans. **Question: do you have the luxury of being kept up-to-date on the care plan for the patients that you work with?**

In summary, the foundations for informational care are:

- a culture emphasizing communication;
- identified staff with a responsibility to organize informational care;
- patients kept informed at level that allows basic understanding and realistic expectations;
- informational and educational interventions made a professional skill;
- coordination of information provision for colleagues and then patients.

An approach to informational care: working with the IIFAR scheme

IIFAR stands for:

- Initial check.
- Information exchange.

- **F**inal **A**ccuracy check.

- **R**eactions.

The IIFAR sequence set out above denotes a routine that will provide a backbone for the professional skill of giving information. Each element will be expanded briefly to give an overall picture and then repeated in fuller form using a clinical example. At this point I am really thinking of a situation in which the patient and partner are facing quite a lot of new information. This might be someone starting up treatment following the diagnosis of insulin-dependent diabetes or people who have sustained injuries such as serious burns or spinal cord injury. It is inevitable that more than one information session will be needed in these situations. Ongoing contacts and little bits of updating information later on will still need careful, professional practice but are less exacting, since you will already know the person and will have covered some of the ground. So, to the routine.

I: initial check

(a) Before beginning to give information, check the general emotional and cognitive state of the person that you are working with. Make a decision as to whether or not it is a *suitable time* for them to receive information.

(b) Check that they actually *want information* at this juncture.

(c) Now check what information they have already and establish what has to be provided. Most importantly, **do not just ask people if they have been told about key issues, but have them tell you in their own words** what they know so that you actually establish what they remember and how accurate it is.

(d) Make a judgement about their basic needs, the language to be used, the level of complexity and the quantity of information.

A true incident. Being quite keen on meeting his patients and explaining things to them personally, the surgeon looked in for a brief visit to talk with Molly, a nursing sister, as it happened. He was to strip out some troublesome varicose veins that afternoon. He gave a brief review of the procedure and mentioned that he had changed the actual plan since their meeting some weeks before. He then gave some instruction on the care of the leg following the surgery. After the surgery, which went well,

Molly had only the haziest memory of him being in the room and no memory at all of what he had said. The problem was that she had received her premedication drug half an hour before his visit and was (to quote her) 'off with the fairies'. It was a shame that he did not check her general state and the suitability of the situation for giving information.

I: information exchange

Where there is some knowledge, correct and extend this as necessary in order to achieve what you judge to be an adequate level of information. Where there is no knowledge, start at the beginning. Give your information in a form that is divided up into 'packages' comprising up to a maximum of about four or five short sets. Take 'mini breaks' between packages, using these for questions, repetition and discussion if needed. *Support your verbal delivery with the use of diagrams or written notes to aid memory.* You should make the notes yourself because if your patients feel under pressure they may be more concerned with placating you and not wasting your time than keeping full and accurate notes. If you are presenting prepared leaflets as well as verbal information do not just hand over a leaflet and consider things done. Instead, look through the leaflet with the patient and write personalized notes to assure accuracy of information. **Consider using a tape recording if it is an important session involving lots of detail. Encourage the patient to play back the session after you have gone.** Keep the session efficient and do not clutter the exchange with unnecessary detail. During the session regularly check (by asking) that you are not stretching your patient with too much information and detail and be prepared to declare 'enough for now' and arrange to continue at a later date.

FA: final accuracy check

You have delivered the information that you needed to deliver or, at least, you have delivered as much information as is suitable in one sitting. It is not yet, though, time to voice the phrase 'all right then' and slip away. There are two more tasks to complete with information-based interventions that will allow you to leave feeling that it was a thoroughly professional job. The first of these is the accuracy check.

Now you must ask your patient to give you, in their own words, a quick summary of the key points from the information that has

been exchanged. This can be done in the guise of rehearsing what they will be saying to their partner later on, rather than having the atmosphere of a test. Listen carefully and check for errors or gaps, and rework these parts of the information. This is one of the more important parts of the information process, so try not to skip out on it or rush through it in a superficial way. If you do, it is quite likely that, later in the day, your patient will be heard to say, 'I did not really understand all of it.' In that case your information session will have partly failed because you did not keep to the professional disciplines and run a final accuracy check.

R: reactions

This final phase of IIFAR intervention blends into the topic of the next chapter, namely emotional care. It is to do with checking what cognitive and emotional reactions a person has had to our information. This is another vital addition to routine tasks in the 'professionalization' of information provision. In fact, it is the basic reason why I use the phrase informational *care*. Put simply, it is not professional and caring just to confront a patient or relative with a quantity of information and then walk away from the situation, no matter how well the rest of it was done.

Most of us will have received information from a nurse, doctor or physiotherapist in our lives. I suspect, though, that few of us will have had the experience of the health care practitioner that we were listening to saying to us, 'OK, sit back a minute and tell me what has been in your thoughts and feelings while I was giving you all this information.' It matters. For one thing, informational care is a component of psychological care and, therefore, we need to check what our patient is feeling, identify whether the patient is in distress and, as a minimum, give support through listening to them and helping them to make an expression of feeling. Care is about promoting well-being. Leaving people alone with information that might have considerable consequences in their life rarely promotes well-being. We need to give that little bit of extra time to be with them and help them explore their first reactions. We must also check that their immediate thoughts and beliefs are not causing them distress through being overly threat-laden or provoking conflict.

Thus, after the final accuracy check, change the atmosphere away from information-dominated communication, make sure that your patient is at ease and *briefly explore with them how they are react-ing to the information and what thoughts and feelings it has evoked in them.*

It is worth a reminder here that I am stating this scheme with reference to major events in information-giving, like the induction to beginning life as a diabetic or information after the diagnosis of multiple sclerosis. Naturally, judgement has to be used with the reaction check because it is not always necessary or appropriate in quick follow-up encounters or brief factual additions to ongoing situations. It is a matter for your judgement, and not rigid routine. But try not to forget to ask yourself, 'Should I now spend a few more minutes checking her reactions?' Two things ought to be in your mind: first, the possibility of adverse conceptual reactions; second, emotional responses. For example:

Lindy had listened intently to a description of different options in pain management for her severe neck pain. These options included referral to the pain management service acupuncturist. It was emphasized that this was an accepted and often helpful Western style of acupuncture based on our current understanding of the pain system. It would be given by a well trained female doctor. At the end of the review I asked her, 'So, what are your immediate thoughts and feelings about the way you would like things to go?' She said, 'I know one thing, I don't want acupuncture. I have beliefs against sticking needles into our bodies.' It was something unexpected in terms of health beliefs that we had to discuss further.

Mike had noticed a lump forming on his left testicle. He worried about it for a while but did nothing. Eventually he felt he had to go to his GP and have it checked. The GP said, 'It is not the best of news, Mike. It might be a cyst but it could also be a tumour. I don't know at this stage. We'll have to get you to a specialist as soon as possible.' Telephone calls were made there and then and arrangements set in motion. But then the GP said, 'Don't rush off, Mike. This is not everyday news. How are you feeling at this moment?' Mike replied, 'I'm not sure, a bit numb. I sort of expected it but it is still a shock. It's going to be a big worry, quite frightening really. Marion is a bit wound up already.' Then the GP added, 'Then why don't the two of you come back at the end of my evening clinic and we can talk it through a bit more?'

The inquiry about reactions to information is a true act of care and professionalism. After giving information, a check on the patient's reactions can reveal important needs. Unless these needs are attended to, it will leave the care incomplete and possibly leave the health care practitioner open to the accusation of being negligent in relation to the patient's basic well-being.

Many routines are helped by a *checklist*. As a final way of emphasizing the importance of the routines necessary to make information exchange an act of professional care, the IIFAR checklist is presented in Box 4.3.

Box 4.3   The IIFAR checklist

Initial check

- Cognitive and emotional condition of patient?
- Appropriate to give information?
- What is known already?
- Language and complexity levels needed?

Information exchange

- Give packages of information with breaks for questions.
- Use diagrams and write notes for the patient.
- Check for overload and problems in understanding.

Final accuracy check

- Request patient summarizes information in own words.
- Check accuracy, rework as required.

Reactions

- Check patient's cognitive and emotional reactions to information.

A working example using IIFAR

Bearing in mind our wish to avoid some of the pitfalls listed above, it is essential for us to stop and think for a minute or two before attempting information work with a patient. Perhaps one of the more important questions in our mind should be 'Where am I at with this patient?' If you are a physiotherapist giving treatment sessions you will know the person quite well. Similarly, if you are a speech and language therapist in the middle of speech rehabilitation work after a stroke, or a dialysis nurse running regular haemodialysis sessions for a patient, then you will be starting any new information work from the position of an *established rapport*. However, a large proportion of encounters between health care practitioners and patients are from a 'cold start'; in other words, there will have been no prior contact. Thus, even before we think of working with a patient to give information in the style of the IIFAR scheme, there is a brief task that we may need to perform to get the 'cold' out of the start. *This task is to establish a general, supportive rapport with good, relaxed communication.*

I will go through the stages of an important information session in the context of a 'cold start'. As an example, I will describe the situation involving a person attending a cardiac department as a day patient in order to have an angiogram. This is a typical case of a person struggling with angina who has seen a GP several times and then had an out-patient appointment with a consultant cardiologist. He is reattending now for an angiogram procedure conducted by the same cardiologist. He is to be received into the catheterization unit by Jane, a cardiac nurse. Jane has four patients to deal with and prepare for the procedure during the morning, roughly at intervals of three-quarters of an hour. She has to settle the patients, manage the basic nursing tasks, record blood pressures etc., and have the patients ready to walk into the 'cath lab' for an immediate start. Later, she must receive them back and monitor them in recovery. I will sketch out a typical set of interactions as she makes the effort to include good preparatory informational care into her duties. These are not meant to be perfect examples, but the sort of relaxed, everyday exchanges that life inevitably settles into when there is a routine to follow and time is fairly short.

(I should emphasize before beginning this example that the following is *not* meant to be an accurate script for use in angiogram preparation. Since I have never been trained as a technical specialist in catheterization there are bound to be technical inadequacies and elements that are out of date in what follows. The content is based on my own experiences of an angiogram and what I would have liked by way of pre-procedure preparation. The real point is to give an example of the style of presenting information based on the IIFAR scheme and to indicate the sort of depth and language that information work in busy clinics might be pitched at. So do not take the procedural details in this example as reliable.)

Establishing rapport and basic communication

Jane collects John Edwards from reception. He is 47, happily married with three children and works as an IT expert in an electronics company. Jane begins contact with a friendly greeting and personal introduction:

> 'Hi, it's Mr Edwards isn't it? I'm Jane, your cardiac nurse for this morning. Thanks for getting here nice and early. By the way, we are all on first name terms here so are you happy if I call you John? That's good. Come through with me and I will take you to your bed area, where you can change and then rest after the angiogram. I will just have a quick preliminary chat with you to start the ball rolling.'

Once he is established in a chair by his bed, Jane fetches herself a chair and sits opposite him. There is no pen and pad. She looks at him, smiles and continues:

> 'I'll just have a short talk with you to say hello at the moment, then I'll be back a little later to do some observations like blood pressure and to go through some detail about the angiogram itself. Maybe you would like to tell me how you have been physically in the last week or so and how you are feeling this morning . . .
>
> 'OK, and just briefly on a more personal note how are you feeling about the angiogram?'

In reality Jane has little time but she asks one or two more general unrushed questions of this type in order to give John a chance to talk a little. She hopes that he will feel listened to and cared for right from the start. She can also crudely assess his general emotional and cognitive state. She carries on with a little more background.

> 'One of my responsibilities this morning is to give you an outline of the experiences you will have during the angiogram and try to set your mind at rest so that nothing comes as a surprise. But I just need to check that you do like to have this sort of information because not everybody does . . . Fine. Now

firstly I need you to change into this gown and then either sit in the chair or get into the bed so that I can come back and do blood pressures. Tea will probably arrive in a minute or two. After that I will talk you through the procedure.'

I: initial check

It *is* important not to start talking at and questioning people straight away; instead, make their first experience of you be that of you listening to them for a short while. This establishes a balance and pace and deals with the common complaint, 'She just didn't listen to me.' Jane did this well. Now she moves on to part of her initial check. Only part of the initial check is now necessary because in her first little conversation she covered some of the ground for the initial check. She now knows that John is intelligent and has a good command of language. She expects that he is quick to take in information. She also knows that he does want full information on the events to come and is in a perfectly good state to receive it. He is, though, understandably and noticeably nervous. He had expected his wife to be present for the whole time but problems with her mother means that she will come a little later. Jane returns and carries out her observations. Tea also arrives. Jane now has a few minutes to get on with her informational care work. She completes the initial check by assessing John's current knowledge about the angiogram.

> 'The next thing, John, is that I just want to find out what you have been told about the angiogram and what you know about how the procedure is carried out. So can you tell me briefly in your own words what you know please.'

He has a good grasp of the basic problem of coronary artery disease and understands why an angiogram is necessary. But he has a hazy picture of what the procedure actually is and what he will experience. Jane knows that this is an important area for her to make clear because if she intervenes with good informational care she might save him quite an amount of needless anxiety and tension. Box 4.4 amplifies this as a general point.

I: information exchange

Having completed her initial check, Jane now begins her main work of preparing John for the procedure:

Box 4.4   Preparing people for difficult procedures

In general most of us tend to worry when it is not clear if a procedure will be very uncomfortable or painful and whether or not we will be able to tolerate it. Cataract replacement surgery is an obvious example. Most of us will feel pretty nervous when it is time to have ours done, I expect. Thus, providing in advance a probable pathway of experiences and guidance as to what will be seen and felt helps to avoid the likelihood of our being taken off guard by the actual experiences in a procedure. Experiences that are *expected and known to be tolerable* are less frightening than those that are unknown. Good prior information reduces the risk of our being made agitated and frightened. Thus, information about places, people, actions, physical sensations, noise, smell and how to assert a little control in the situation (should that be necessary) can be as good as a sedative for many people. Such informational care would be applicable before, say, an MRI scan. Scans have proved to be very alarming for some patients. Catheterization for an angiogram is another example. An expanded review of the problem of patients needing to cope with stressful medical procedures is given by Benyamini and Leventhal (1997).

'As you have told me, John, the point of the angiogram is to obtain some X-ray pictures of your coronary arteries so that your cardiologist, Russell May, can see where they have narrowed and work out the best way of dealing with the narrowing. What happens today is that a small catheter, which is a very fine flexible tube, is placed into one of your arteries, either in your arm or your leg, and fed up through the artery until it enters the heart. This diagram shows what happens. Russell has not decided yet whether to use the artery in your arm or the leg. He will decide after he has had a look at your vessels. Once the catheter has been fed through to your heart Russell injects a dye through the tube and the dye is released into your heart. This dye immediately spreads into the blood and quickly starts running through the coronary arteries of your heart. They then take the sequence of X-ray videos that you might be able to see on the monitor. The dye makes the outline of the arteries in the heart stand out really clearly on the X-rays. It is all recorded so that Russell can study it later. After that the catheter is slowly withdrawn and you are brought back here where I will be waiting.'

There is a short break. Then:

'Next I am going to go through the sequence of events that you will actually experience but I'll stop for a moment to see if you have questions about the general procedure so far.'

Jane continues:

'OK, now, the big question is what is this going to be like for you? It may help to know that we do hundreds of these a year and the team is very well practised. Very few patients have any great difficulties. I have written down the sequence of events on this card with a diagram so keep your eye on that while I talk you through it. I will take you to the cath lab, as it is called, and as you go in you will see Russell and the technicians and nurse for the session. They all have to wear X-ray protection clothing by the way. There is a surgical couch and quite a lot of high tech X-ray equipment buzzing away in there. Once you are settled in lying on your back on the couch the **usual ECG and blood pressure monitors will be fitted up**. Then Russell will do a quick examination to choose a site for the catheter. When he has chosen an artery a local anaesthetic will be given at the sight for the catheter to be inserted. This is usually the only part which can be noticeably uncomfortable because **it stings for a few seconds before going numb. It is not excessive pain and only lasts a few seconds.** After this Russell makes an incision in the skin. You might feel pressure but you should not feel any pain with this. Then the catheter is slowly inserted into the artery and worked back through the artery up to the heart. It can take some minutes. Most people do not feel much as the catheter is fed through the artery but one thing that you may notice is that when it arrives at the heart it can **make the heart put in extra or irregular beats.** You might hear the irregular beat on the audio monitor. Relax with this if you can because it will stop once the catheter is withdrawn and is not dangerous. Lastly, one thing worth remembering is that as Russell injects the dye it can give **a curious hot flush type of feeling through your body**. It doesn't last long and is not distressing, just odd. You will probably be able to see the screen and watch the dye appear then. The videos of the X-ray pictures are recorded for a few minutes then, after that, they reverse the procedure, withdraw the catheter and put stitches in to seal the wound and that's it done – about half to three-quarters of an hour in total. You may find that you have a tendency to brace yourself in a tense way during the procedure. Try and consciously work against that by concentrating on relaxing your body. Shut your eyes if it is helpful. Don't feel that you have to keep absolutely quiet. If there is anything that troubles you or something that you need or need to know just speak out. They are a caring team and will help you in any way that they can.'

There is another short break.

'Nearly done. I'll pause there to see if there is anything else that you can think of that would be helpful to have explained, or any questions generally that you have.'

Jane rounds off:

'Right. Now, all that's left to say is that when Russell has finished you will be brought back through here. You might feel a bit tired or wobbly after the procedure but should not feel ill. I'll get you to have a rest for a couple of hours while I monitor your blood pressure regularly. You can have some lunch and Russell will come through at some point and have a word about the findings. By the way, I'll keep an eye out for your wife and keep her up to date with what is happening. Keep my notes and diagram until you go in.'

The information exchange is complete.

FA: final accuracy check
'Now just briefly tell me back the main items from this briefing in your own words. Use my note sequence and diagram as a prompt if you like.'

R: reactions

> 'Very good. You have grasped all of that very quickly. We should be ready to start in about quarter of an hour. I have finished my briefing now so as a very last thing I wonder if you would like to give me a hint as to what is in your thoughts and feelings at the moment.'

You can see that this is an adapted information exchange that allows Jane to use the same material with all her patients. Because of the time pressure she uses prepared notes and a diagram but makes the odd personalized jottings on them as required. She is concise, stops twice for questions and remembers to do a final accuracy check. John has plenty of opportunity for questions and Jane also gives him the opportunity to say how he is feeling and what he is thinking about the event. Naturally, she responds to his replies in a supportive way. Unless there is an unexpected problem in the procedure he now knows what is likely to happen and what he is likely to experience. This is caring by informing. Jane's work will have taken away the fears of the unknown to a large extent and acted as a buffer against needless anxiety and tension. The likelihood is that he will be an easier patient to work with for the team too.

Set against this example, where everything went well, I must let you in on a conversation I had in a recent clinic. This concerned a 47-year-old lady who is a regular visitor to the clinic. She was telling me how she was facing the prospect of surgery to repair a hiatus hernia (she does interact with a degree of assertion, you will understand). She was relaying the outcome of a visit to her GP:

> Patient: 'I saw her on Tuesday and just for once she wasn't useless. She said she thinks it probably will need surgery and I should accept what Mr M says next month.'
> KN: 'How will you feel if Mr M says he thinks that it does have to be surgery?'
> Patient: 'Terrible. I'll be that worried. The trouble is surgery and me don't mix. My back pain got worse after the back surgery and I'm nearly crippled with it some days now – you know that. And the hysterectomy nearly killed me. I had six weeks in hospital with that. They said that this hernia thing is heavy surgery. I'm terrified, I can't do with any more surgery. Wouldn't you be?'

KN: 'Would you like me to help by getting some preliminary information about what they do in the surgery for hiatus hernia and how you will feel after it?'

Patient: '*No I wouldn't*, thank you very much. I don't want to know anything about it. *Nothing*. They can tell me after if they want. I'll be worried enough as it is. Let him get on with it and the less I know the better. And he better hadn't muck it up. I've had nothing but pain for the last few years, I want my life back.'

KN: 'Then how can I help?'

Patient: 'You have helped, you listen to me. It always makes me feel better for a bit. You're my lifeline – but I don't want anybody going on about that surgery. I won't sleep – right?'

She did say exactly all of that, I promise you.

> The moral is listen, communicate, show sympathy, solidarity and support and take things further with informational care when it is truly caring so to do, which will be in most cases. But if information is not in accord with the person's needs and wishes then 'don't push it'.

Physical contact during informational care

This is an issue that most of you will have discussed in training, no doubt. Different professions tend to have slightly different perspectives though. I do not have particularly strong views but it is relevant to raise the issue for discussion as a lead-in to our next topic. A hand upon a hand, a hand on a shoulder, a brief arm around a shoulder can be appropriate and helpful in some situations with certain types of patient and relative. It should not be contrived and should have the feel about it wherein both people, practitioner and patient, stay relaxed, feeling that it is right for the moment. This especially will be where a move towards comforting of some sort is relevant. That is, the information given has been of the type that may well cause some worry or apprehension. Alternatively, this sort of physical contact may help when information is of the type that requires strong encouragement or reinforcement because it announces demands on the patient: the dietician introducing a dietary plan to a person newly diagnosed as diabetic, the physiotherapist outlining an exercise programme to a person recovering from very recent back injury and so on. Subtle differences in physical contact mean that it can be an act of comfort, a pseudo-parental interaction or a means of asserting the 'authority' of what you are saying. But only you, as the one who knows the individual patient and the character of your relationship, is in a position to judge whether physical contact is likely to be appropriate and helpful or not. It is worth discussing the issue from time to time with colleagues when in supervision or CPD sessions.

Informational care when the information is bad news

The task of imparting bad news to the people that we work with in health care is often given separate attention. There is special consideration for, say, the intensive care nurse who has to face a patient's wife and tell her that her husband has just died. It is similar for the neurologist who must convey the news that her patient has a tumour developing in his brain or the care team in a spinal unit helping a patient to grasp that she may never walk again. It all makes for a tough situation for the staff and a very tough situation for the patient. One of the burdens of this kind of intervention is that health care practitioners are essentially healers by disposition. Our natural inclination is to relieve suffering and, therefore, there is special stress in giving news that is about suffering to come or news of the failure of our healing efforts. It is stressing because it causes rather than relieves distress in the patients and partners that we work with. Thus, our key question for the moment is: are there special ways of handling this type of situation?

Faulkner (1998) wrote under the title *When the News Is Bad* and addresses this issue. Her basic approach to communication and information delivery reflects many of the elements of informational care presented above. But she does add in one or two items that apply especially to the task of giving difficult information. These include:

- Making sure that the intervention is in an appropriate place, with privacy and quiet.

- Adding early statements in the conversation that leads up to bad news as some kind of preparatory warning. Faulkner refers to this as a 'warning shot', a curiously harsh metaphor but one that conveys the meaning to us well enough, e.g. 'Please come in and sit down, Mrs Harris. I do have some difficult news for you I'm afraid.'

- Providing some space to absorb the news. This is meant literally, in the sense of providing a quiet place where the recipient of bad news may have a short period to absorb what it is that they have heard, and also in terms of freedom from 'cognitive demand' – that is, no questions or distractions, just some personal space to come to terms with the information.

- Being able to recognize and deal with shock. News such as the diagnosis of cancer or a recent death can easily cause shock, both psychological shock and, sometimes, physical shock. The latter involves a drop in blood pressure, sharp rise in heart rate and loss of concentration at one level or another. It may involve actual fainting. If it occurs it will usually result in the person you are working with going a little blank or becoming oddly uncooperative for a spell. In any event, stopping for a while, perhaps a little physical contact as support and the usual care such as a cup of tea should be considered, followed by a check on how the person is feeling. This allows you to assess reactions and, therefore, the appropriateness of carrying on with any further information at the time.

- Faulkner adds to this the effort to encourage an initial reaction on the part of the recipient of the bad news. This takes us into emotional care. I deal with this in the next chapter.

- Finally, on the practical side, some effort to mobilize support by way of contacting relatives or friends to assist the person home and take over the effort of support is a very helpful contribution.

Your personal psychology and informational care: withholding information, giving best scenarios only or being overly blunt

We health care practitioners deal with the difficult task of giving bad news in differing ways. This is because our own psychology comes into play in the situation. In particular, our identification with the potential distress of our patients (that is, the degree to which we can predict and sense the feelings that they will experience) may interact with our own acquired reactions to the distress of others. This explains why some colleagues will volunteer to do this kind of difficult work and why others will feel uneasy and seek to minimize it. We also differ in our acceptance of and relaxation with the emotions of others in general and, indeed, our own emotions. There is a wide disparity in tolerance to emotion (again, discussed in the next chapter), with some people being really quite ill at ease with any significant expression of emotion.

Once the issue of our personal tolerances and needs in information-giving has been made open and included in training it can be discussed from time to time in supervision. By this means it should become easier to work out where we stand and what our personal characteristics in information work are. One thing that we have to watch out for very carefully is the risk of our own needs and projections (seeing in others what is actually within us) playing a covert part and influencing the way we go about giving, or not giving, information. There can be some powerful and destructive effects on informational provision. For example, not long ago, talking to one of the nursing sisters running a cardiac surgery unit, I commented to her that the level of information that patients were given on discharge from her unit was rather minimalist, to say the least. There was no pre-discharge briefing, and little information regarding possible effects, complications, discomforts or pains during the recovery phase from cardiac surgery was offered. The sister replied, rather indignantly:

> 'If we told the patients half of the effects that they might have after surgery most of them would never leave here until we forced them out.'

There is both thinking and feeling behind this statement but I suspect both were 'reflex' or automatic in character, enhanced perhaps by a few formative experiences. Certainly she had no obvious awareness that her suspicious stance to information provision could be a feature of *her own* psychology. *She seemed to have an apprehension linked to giving bad news and information and, consequently, there was a mistrust of her own and her patients' capability to cope with it.* In addition, perhaps, there was a mistrust of the capability of the staff to help the patients into positive coping. Without talking to her further, which I did not, I can only surmise that some experiences in her past led her to project her own discomfort with receiving frightening news on to her patients. She 'knew', through the psychodynamic of projection, that the patients would be disturbed and difficult if they were properly informed. She felt that she had to minimize information exchange to protect them and also to protect her unit from the anticipated demands from frightened patients. It is true, as described in the early chapters on the psychological effects of heart problems, that cardiac patients can lose confidence and become anxious. However, in most cases, this can readily be dealt with by an appropriate information, education and support scheme run by the staff. *Informational care rarely makes things worse if it is done properly.* In this instance, my own judgement was that it was the sister who had the problem and not the patients.

To balance the history I should recount that, in contrast, a nurse running an associated cardiac rehabilitation scheme was quite open, forthcoming and relaxed about talking of after effects. Talking to one patient who had recently had mitral valve surgery and was asking if there were likely to be any after effects of open-heart surgery, she was heard to say:

> 'Yes, of course there will be, it's very heavy surgery and a lot of chemicals had to be pumped into you. You had a five or six hour general anaesthetic and your heart was stopped. The next few months will be quite interesting for you. You will get all sorts of effects and pains for a while. They will start, reach a peak for a week or two and slowly go away again. You've just got to relax with them, ride them out and talk to us about anything that you think is serious. What's troubling you at the moment?'

The point of these anecdotes is to highlight the notion that ***our own approach to informational care will be heavily influenced by our own psychology***. If you have acquired an anxiety about other people becoming upset, this can influence you and lead to hesitancy. If you have a need to deny your own emotion and have a distaste for the emotion of other people, it may make you seem brash and uncaring as a source of information. This may be especially so if this feature is accompanied by beliefs that you, personally, can handle whatever life throws at you without much emotion. Thus, we can encounter various extremes in general medicine. There are some doctors and nurses who are evasive and tell patients little, perhaps even actively withholding information. Others may present difficult information with a directness and bluntness that suggests little sensitivity towards the feelings of the people being cared for. In fact, it used to be the norm for senior medics to be rather remote and apparently unfeeling, since a style of relating known as 'detached concern' was actively favoured and modelled. This fitted in with and complemented the British cultural leaning towards repressed emotional expressiveness.

On the other hand, there are doctors and nurses who are very sensitive and, consequently, sometimes rather frightened of giving bad news because they feel protective to their patients. The effect is that they tend to give 'best scenario' communications. These are not always reliable communications because they break the basic principle of informational care – that is, to help our patients towards *realistic expectations*.

Efforts to work against this 'best scenario only' effect are worth discussing and illustrating a little further. It is very common, and most of us do get caught up with it from time to time, to feel a need to protect patients and partners from bad news. We are looking for a balance though. It is counterproductive to frighten people and leave them in a state of raised anxiety. At the same time it is also unhelpful and potentially quite destructive deliberately to leave patients in a state of helpless ignorance about things to come that are fairly predictable. *Patients and their partners should not be left to find out for themselves through first-hand experience.*

I will give an example of an informational care intervention designed to 'head off' frightening experiences and help patients relax with the possibility of the complications that can and do occur in renal medicine. It is the kind of work that helps to avoid the 'best scenario effect', with a nurse doing her best to achieve realistic expectations in her patient. The example is to do with the run-up to the insertion of a peritoneal dialysis catheter. It was supplied by a dialysis nurse a few years ago (note again, this is not a recommended script because procedures at this unit have altered now, but is given solely as an example of style). We join the nurse and her patient, Carol. The nurse works with the IIFAR scheme. Initial checks have been completed earlier and information on the procedure itself dealt with. However, as she turns to a new section of the information the nurse does add in an additional check:

Nurse: 'Lastly, Carol, now that we have gone through the procedure, let me just check to see if anyone has told you about possible complications.'

Carol: 'Not much, I did hear something about someone getting peritonitis but I have not had anything formal. I didn't know there were many complications, to be honest.'

Nurse: 'Well, to be equally honest, it would be unrealistic to see any part of medicine as a problem-free zone and, as you know, we have our fair share of problems in renal treatments. I truly do not think that there is any reason for you to be frightened because the procedure is very routine. But, at the same time, it is probably best if I just sketch out some of the possible problems just in case something comes up and it all takes a bit longer. This will give you more of a sense of the maximum time that it might take to get things working properly – if you are happy with that and feel that you can cope with it today.'

Carol: 'Yes, that's fine, but just give me the important bits for now.'

At this point the nurse can readily admit to a mild feeling of unease. It would be so easy to say that most people do not have any problems with catheter insertion, so, not to worry, it will all be fine. This approach will not do though, since, to protect Carol from unexpected difficulties and a disruption of plans because a longer stay in hospital is needed, she does need to have some basic information about possible complications. Unless, that is, she specifically declines it.

Nurse: 'Right. Here we go then, I'll write these down in note form as we go. Number one, the end of the catheter that is put into your abdomen may become obstructed because it has ended up in a poor position or because it becomes clogged with tissue that forms around its end. This is not at all dangerous and neither will you feel anything, but it is a nuisance because the dialysate fluid will not flow properly through it and so the catheter has to be repositioned with another small operation. The chances of this happening are about one in ten at worst. Number two involves the other end of the catheter where the dacron collar forms a joint with the skin. Occasionally this can be a bad seal and so it leaks. Again, this means that it has to be redone by the surgeon. Number three. Occasionally an infection can form at the site – if so it will be treated with antibiotics. Lastly, number four of the common problems, is the one you already mentioned, peritonitis. This can happen if, despite best sterile technique, some bacteria or fungal organisms get into the abdomen during insertion or in the days after. Then the lining of the abdomen, the peritoneum, becomes infected. It makes your abdomen feel very painful and tender and you will run a temperature. It means having strong antibiotics run in with the dialysate. Fortunately, we do not get that many cases of peritonitis but it does happen. By the way, in a worst case situation, if it is a resistant infection you may have to have a temporary spell back on haemodialysis while we sort it out, but that is unusual. This is why I am a little bit evasive about the time it all takes. Many of our patients go straight through without any problems but then some do get delayed by one or more of these complications. So, think of a time band. If it goes well think of about four weeks to get self-sufficient and be doing bag changes happily at home. But, do not assume this to be the case because if you get a complication it could be double that. OK, enough for today, except, as always, just briefly tell me in your own words the main points about complication and timing and how you are feeling about it all.'

We cannot all be the same. Nor is it an enviable prospect to see a future in which we are all trained into a bland sameness. However, there are minimum requirements in communicating with patients and providing informational care, especially when this involves bad news. Thus, as professional people, we do need to get to know our own psychology a little and so explore our reactions when giving information. A little insight can go a long way in helping to refine personal technique.

Box 4.5   Résumé

- **Care by informing.**
- **Use the IIFAR scheme or something similar.**
- **Give information that leaves a person with realistic expectations.**
- **Inform caringly but do not 'cop out with best scenario' evasiveness.**
- **Review and discuss your own feelings and psychology with respect to giving bad news.**

One psychologist has made a particularly important contribution to the business of information provision when the news is bad, both in unequivocally establishing that most people with cancer want to be properly informed and in specifying the damage that can occur when doctors or nurses withhold or distort information linked to the diagnosis of cancer. Fallowfield *et al.* (1995, 2002) are essential reading in this area.

The potential of preventive informational care: two cases where informational care would have made a big difference

(1) At an eye hospital

Mrs N had developed shingles on her face. This had spread to affect her left eye. Unfortunately her early care was inadequate and the eye became seriously damaged and very badly ulcerated. She finally saw a specialist who discovered that the eye was effectively destroyed. He said to Mrs N, 'I will admit you to see if there is anything that I can do to save the eye, but please do not hold out too much hope. It may be best to get rid of it for you since it is no good and is causing so much pain.' While he talked at length about the condition of the eye, he gave no information at all (that she could remember) on the actual events to come in the hospital. Mrs N was inclined to anxious fantasy and worry and, left in the state of not knowing what she would experience, *she suffered two days of near terror.* On admission her nurses knew little more and made no attempt to find anything out for her about what was to happen. One did say that it might be an injection in the eye or surgery. On the strength of this she spent another sleepless night churning with anxiety and when visited by her husband next morning was very shaky. *No one meant her any harm but they caused her harm. The staff were, quite frankly, quite clueless about how to care by informing in general and seemed ignorant of the critical importance of preventive informational care in particular.*

(2) At a cardiac surgery unit:
discharge after mitral valve surgery

The patient had suffered a sudden rupture of his mitral valve and, three weeks later, was admitted for surgery to repair the valve. The preliminaries included an immediate, 'surprise', trans-oesophageal echocardiogram. This had gone well enough, although no information about this procedure had been offered at all other than that, on signing a consent form, he had been told that the procedure could damage his oesophagus. The surgery to repair his mitral valve had also gone well, although, once again, none of the staff offered preparatory informational care concerning the events of the surgery. *He found out about events as they took place.* Recovery in the first few days after the open heart surgery was trouble-free, other than a raised temperature that caused some antibiotics to be produced and a mild physical shock reaction when he first stood and walked a few steps. On day six he managed a flight of 20 stairs under the supervision of his physiotherapist. At that point both his surgeon and cardiologist said that he could go home when he chose. There was no formal pre-discharge briefing or information session, although a leaflet covering general issues concerning rehabilitation was provided. If he initiated questions these were answered in a clear manner, but any information had to be actively sought through his own initiatives.

His wife took him home from the unit at the end of day six after the surgery. The leaflet he received stated that one of the staff from his own health centre would be in touch a couple of days after discharge. Nothing was heard, probably because they did not know he was back home. A close friend who was a clinical nurse manager in another speciality visited on day nine and was visibly staggered at the pace at which he had been discharged and the poor level of informational care that he had received on discharge. He and his wife managed the next two weeks but experienced one real fright. After several days his pulse had episodes when it became rapid and unstable. It was frightening because the heart felt rather like it had before the mitral valve was repaired, so the worry was that the repair was failing in some way. A GP was consulted by phone and was kind enough to call by at his home. It was atrial fibrillation, the GP explained. Apparently, there was a 40 per cent chance of it developing after heart surgery in a man of his age. Medication to control the instability was introduced and the problem receded. The medication was stopped four weeks later. At that point he attended a cardiac rehabilitation group and was pleased to be back in an environment where information was readily available if requested from specialist staff. His preference was for as much information as possible. He had found it quite difficult and needlessly stressful muddling through and finding things out in retrospect either by personal experience or through indirect sources. As a record he composed the diagram shown in Figure 4.1, which illustrates what he was left to find out on his own during rehabilitation but would have preferred to have been told in advance to reduce the tension and inevitable worry for both him and his wife. Certainly some of these effects were predictable enough to be given in an informational care session – *if there had ever been one.*

This case illustrates the point that 'the less they know the less they

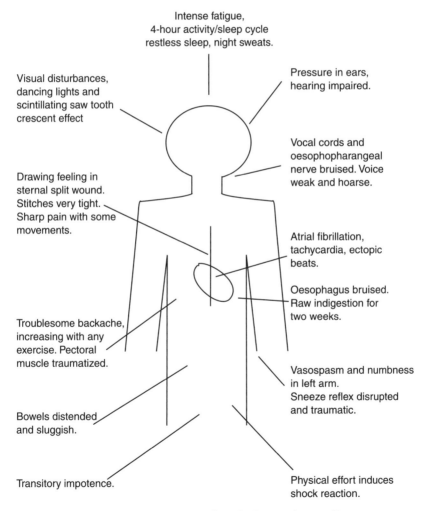

Intense fatigue,
4-hour activity/sleep cycle
restless sleep, night sweats.

Visual disturbances,
dancing lights and
scintillating saw tooth
crescent effect

Pressure in ears,
hearing impaired.

Vocal cords and
oesophopharangeal
nerve bruised. Voice
weak and hoarse.

Drawing feeling in
sternal split wound.
Stitches very tight.
Sharp pain with some
movements.

Atrial fibrillation,
tachycardia, ectopic
beats.

Oesophagus bruised.
Raw indigestion for
two weeks.

Troublesome backache,
increasing with any
exercise. Pectoral
muscle traumatized.

Vasospasm and numbness
in left arm.
Sneeze reflex disrupted
and traumatic.

Bowels distended
and sluggish.

Transitory impotence.

Physical effort induces
shock reaction.

Figure 4.1 Some things not mentioned on discharge after cardiac surgery.

worry' is, in fact, a dangerous myth. Most people worry *more* when things happen that they are not expecting and do not know anything about. This is especially so if the events are not clear in meaning and can imply a possible threat to health. Clinical experience reveals that the partners of patients being discharged after cardiac surgery or a heart attack worry enough as it is without the stress of encountering *unexpected* side-effects or complications. If given advance information they may still worry, of course, but it is usually productive worry, preparing for and maintaining vigilance in relation to known possibilities. This is a lot less frightening than, as described above, encountering an unknown effect such as atrial fibrillation and wondering if it means that the surgery has failed. *It is best gently to share your knowledge with your patients and their partners in order that they are prepared for eventualities and will then not find them so alarming if they occur.* Thus:

> Nurse: 'Sometimes in the first few days people can develop what is called atrial fibrillation. This is where a false electrical signal, possibly from the scar on your heart, interferes with the main pulse and sets the heart into episodes of a faster, unstable beat. Don't confuse this with ectopic beats, which is where the heart misses a beat and puts in a big compensatory beat just after. Most of us have these from time to time. They can go in runs of several at a time and then the heart goes back to normal. Atrial fibrillation will be a more extended period of fast unstable beating. It is not anything to panic about but, if it does happen, do let us or your doctor know because there are some good medications which control this instability and you will be a lot more comfortable with them. The effect can fade after a few days or be around for some while. Any questions about that?'

A positive example of the power of information to help and heal

Jackie, a young nurse, had been knocked over by a car 14 months before we met. She had sustained head injuries and minor brain damage and now, although back at work, was struggling to cope with 20 hours a week, part-time, low-key nursing duties. She was desperate to get back to her full-time work in respiratory disorders but it was still too much for her to cope with. She was cross with herself, demoralized, frightened and confused about why she could not recover full health. I met her informally and, since we only had a very rushed 15 minutes, I briefly listened to her story and then went straight on to caring by informing. Information seemed to be her primary need.

After quick initial checks on what she had been told I gave her a copy of my standard letter to people that I meet who have either undiagnosed or insufficiently recognized brain damage following a head injury (which includes severe whiplash injury). I sat beside her as we read it through together, with pauses for her to question, comment and have bits of discussion. The letter is set out in the Box 4.6.

At a second even briefer meeting a week or so later Jackie said to me:

> 'That information was so helpful, it has made such a difference. I feel much more settled. It is getting on for a year and a half now and I couldn't understand what was going on and why I was feeling so awful. They hadn't told me anything that I can remember when I was discharged after the accident and my own doctor just said it will all clear up in a few months of its own accord. I was starting to think that it must be me losing it. It was becoming a real nightmare. It has been so reassuring. The funny thing is that, after our talk, I thought about how I was pushing myself and getting headaches all the time and feeling so whacked out. So I talked to myself about self-care and started easing back a bit and resting in a more positive frame of mind, rather than feeling guilty, like you said. It has helped. I actually do more, although I still get the headaches and tiredness every day. But best of all it has given me some hope and I don't feel so desperate.'

Guided questioning: another approach in informational care

You might work in a practice or unit where time really is tight and the kind of organized, prepared, information-giving interventions seem like a distant luxury. It is still possible to provide basic information that is efficient and individualized, involves limited but definite

Box 4.6   A letter to a patient

Dear . . .

The impact of your head injury

At our meeting today we discussed your recent head injury and how this may affect you for the next year or two. I have listed some general points below that summarize the situation for the average case. Each case is different, though, so this should be taken as a rough guide only. It will be helpful if you discuss these points through with your partner and bring him or her to our next meeting.

In the recovery phase following your head injury, you may find yourself troubled by some of the following difficulties:

- Persistent headaches
- Nausea and/or dizziness
- Visual disturbances and problems
- Poor concentration
- Difficulties with memory
- Difficulties with speech
- Sensitivity to noise
- Lassitude (finding it hard to get up and get on with things)
- Proneness to severe fatigue
- Lack of resilience and inability to cope with demands and stress
- Irritability
- Emotional fragility and depression
- An increased need for rest and retreat

With time these effects fade but it is not possible to say how long they will last in the individual case – they may be gone in three months or still trouble you several years later. The way you go about life is important and we will discuss this at our next meeting. This time can also be a great strain on your partner or caregiver so do, please, bring them along to our next meeting.

Best wishes in your efforts at recovery

Keith Nichols
Consultant Clinical Psychologist

face-to-face contact and will meet your (I hope) felt need, as a health care practitioner, to care by informing. This approach I refer to as *guided questioning*. You need a prepared, printed set of standard questions that cover relevant areas of your patients' information needs. This written set of questions is given to the patient or partner with an invitation to look through them and then book a little time with one of the staff to obtain replies to the questions as applied to their case. It then becomes the responsibility of the patient or partner to take up this offer. Most will choose to do so. The patient whose story of discharge from cardiac surgery is given above would have loved such an opportunity.

A short example is necessary, so I will return to Carol, the CAPD patient, whom we met in the example of informational care. If she had been in her kidney unit when there was a surge of staff sickness and staff time became in short supply, the following approach might have been used.

Carol is now stable on her peritoneal dialysis and ready to go home. Certain elements of additional information need to be exchanged pre-discharge. One of these is a very basic briefing on *kidney transplantation*, which is a future possible treatment. To make sure that Carol does not leave uninformed about transplantation her nurse drops in with a guided questioning sheet. The sheet reads:

Dear Carol

Before you are discharged home we would like to tell you some basic things about kidney transplants. Will you look through the questions below, add any others that you might think of and then book a little time with your dialysis nurse or sister and ask them to supply you with the answers as they apply to your own case.

1   *Am I suitable for a kidney transplant?*

2   *Am I on the waiting list?*

3   *Do I need preparatory surgery?*

4   *How long will I have to wait?*

5   *What is the procedure if a kidney becomes available?*

6   *Where will I have the surgery and be cared for?*

7   *What is immunosuppression and how is it done?*

8   *What are the common problems with kidney transplants?*
9   *What is life like with a transplanted kidney?*

The very rushed member of staff will have to settle for just straight answers to the questions but, ideally, there will be enough time for elements of the IIFAR schedule, including a brief discussion of reactions at the end. Blended in with normal informational care, guided questioning can prove to be quite a powerful aid.

Educational care

As noted above, there is no sharp boundary between informational care and educational care. The latter refers to larger quantities of information that form part of the training schemes sometimes necessary in health care training, e.g. in lifestyle changes and medical treatment techniques such as those required in insulin-dependent diabetes. In educational care the same strategy is needed as in informational care, with the same effort to be 'patient-centred' and engage in listening and dialogue as part of the general approach. Where contact by several members of staff is involved (and this is often the case) there needs to be a great effort at coordination and consistency, as otherwise confusion in the patient can result.

Sometimes life serves up helpful coincidences. One of these occurred around the time that I began to work clinical sessions in the renal unit at Exeter, in 1978. The coincidence was that I also began flying lessons. The relevant part of the story for us here is that, at this time, I had already begun laying the foundations to the research work that eventually led to Nichols and Springford (1984). This research report, entitled 'Psychosocial difficulties associated with survival by dialysis', involved a series of interviews aimed at identifying issues that troubled patients and their partners during their training for home haemodialysis. One of the more prominent issues that emerged early on was the inconsistency in the content of the training sessions between one dialysis nurse and another. In comparison, my training to fly an aircraft was a model of consistency, despite my having various instructors. This was achieved by means of a tightly specified syllabus and a careful record of what had been taught in the previous lesson. This attracted my attention. I thought that patients at the renal unit could well benefit from a similar approach that maximized consistency in communication during their training. Accordingly, the issue was discussed with the sister in charge, who set about revising and improving the training schedule and records of educational/training work at the unit. Since that time she and her staff have continued to improve and develop these.

An excellent example, 'Outline of the kidney unit and learning plan for CAPD users' (by P. Woodhams) is given as an appendix in Nichols (1993). The syllabus comprises a sequence of learning experiences, involving a coordinated blend of face-to-face instruction, demonstrations, short educational videos and readings. Each event in the education/training sequence is 'signed off' as completed satisfactorily by the particular dialysis nurse undertaking the instruction. Each nurse will check previous progress and comments before beginning the next session. This allows for the necessary interchangeability of nurses (a fact of life with the shift system, duty rota, days off, annual leave etc.) but provides maximum consistency in content of the information and training given to patients. A caring approach to education.

Information after care: creating information 'hotlines'

In the UK the importance of easy access to advice and information is increasingly recognized. The government-inspired NHS Direct provides a good example of an immediately available, telephone-based, medical information inquiry service. However, while it may stand in quite good stead as a first port of call for people with health-related queries who might otherwise need to go and visit their family doctor, it is no substitute for people who have been discharged from hospital after some specialist treatment who still need access to advice from specialist staff: patients returning home after their first treatment by radiotherapy or chemotherapy, patients discharged after a stroke or colostomy, patients discharged after head injury or spinal damage or the partners of all of these, for example. Many such people will receive a friendly invitation from the staff, such as 'phone us if any problems arise'. But many will hesitate to do so, fearing that the issue troubling them is too trivial to take the time of busy staff. Or they may fear that they will be thought a nuisance, interrupting the routines of the staff. The easiest way to deal with this and provide an effective information after care service is to create a dedicated 'hotline' that is specifically for the patients' use. It need not be too onerous. A couple of separate hours in a week when it is known that, say, a ward sister will be doing administration can be combined with a scheduled 'hotline hour'. It can be made known to patients by means of a note on discharge that the sister is expecting calls, since time has been set aside for that purpose. This makes the act of calling in for information feel rather more like a legitimate function of the patients' role and, in my experience, makes it more likely that people will use the facility.

The last word to Ley

I do hope that this chapter will have convinced you of the importance of information provision in your work as a health care practitioner and that you will examine what you provide at present and assess any need for improvements. I am conscious that many of my examples come from a hospital setting and involve nurse–patient interactions. Reminding you, though, of my very first few pages in this book, it should be clear that my concern is for all the health care professions to make an effort towards reliable information provision for patients and their partners, either within the hospital or within the community health care services. If you have felt moved to introduce any of the approaches described above, such as the IIFAR routine or guided questioning, then it is relevant to end by summarizing for you research work that helps to specify the general characteristics of successful information-giving. Successful, that is, in terms of the people involved being able to recall the information. Ley (1988, 1997; Ley and Llewelyn 1995) has been a prominent contributor to our knowledge in this field. It is certainly worth looking at some of his original research and very useful reviews. For now, though, I can say that all of us involved in information provision should remain mindful of some of his main recommendations. To maximize the chances of effective recall:

- Be aware of the primacy effect (that is, people recall best the first few items that they are told at any one time).

- Stress the importance of particular items of information (that is, the items that you regard as important and especially want your patient to remember).

- Keep things simple – shorter words and sentences.

- Label categories of information ('now I am going to tell you about your drugs and after that I will tell you about washing the wound').

- Repetition helps – so repeat key elements.

- Specific rather than general information is best for people to recall.

- Schedule further interviews to check understanding and retention.

To be honest, I should have said 'very nearly the last word to Ley'. Truly to conclude, let me say that our motivation and opportunity to make the effort to provide really high quality informational care will vary from time to time. There will be good phases and bad phases, as in any other human activity. Events in the place of work, pressure of work or personal issues may have an influence. At times we might need to step back from this intensely interpersonal task a little. That is only realistic. It is important, though, that we do not step back from the obligation of seeing that informational and educational care continues for each patient. In a similar vein, it is both useful and professional to have a colleague listen in once in a while as we give an information session for a patient. Feedback is always helpful and the event of someone else listening in tends to make us examine what we do, usually to good effect.

Discussion time

Should you end up in a discussion group reflecting on these issues, or should you just be musing on it alone or with colleagues, you might want to address some of these points:

- How many marks out of ten does your ward, unit, department or centre achieve for its general delivery of informational care to patients and their partners?

- What is the attitude to informational care in your place of work?

- Think of a recent case that you know of in which informational or educational care was done well – in what way was it done well?

- Think of a recent case that you know of in which informational or educational care was done badly – in what way was it done badly, and what can be learnt?

- What opportunity do you get personally for informational care work? Does this allow you to meet your responsibilities in keeping patients and partners properly informed?

- How effective are your own information provision and related skills? Are changes and developments needed?

- Do you have criticisms of the approach described in this chapter?

- Do you have suggestions for improving on or adapting the approach described in this chapter to suit your own situation?

5 Emotional care for ill and injured people (with notes on psychological therapy and counselling)

You will have realized by now, I am sure, that providing psychological care is an approach within health care that is as much about attitude as practice. By this I mean that you cannot have a positive, informed attitude towards psychological care without it taking you into interactions with a patient that inevitably lead to the practice of one or more of the psychological care skills. This in turn may reveal other psychological needs in your patient that also require psychological intervention. Thus, monitoring psychological state or giving informational care may well suggest a need for emotional care. Conversely, an early brief intervention with emotional care may reveal the need for prompt informational care, with reliable monitoring of psychological state thereafter.

You will recall that the final phase of informational care using the IIFAR scheme is the check on the patient's reactions to the information received. These reactions involve both cognitive issues, such as the beliefs and views taken by the patient, and their immediate emotional reaction. What if, during contact with a patient for informational care work, you ended with a brief check on reactions and the patient said to you something like:

> 'It is a shock. A terrible shock. At this moment I feel deeply frightened and very emotional.'

Or:

> 'I just feel incredibly bitter. I feel like, in a way, they have broken my body, sort of broken my soul too. I keep seeing their faces. They have not even said sorry to me. That really hurts me, especially the surgeon. Was he cheerful the day after it

happened? What did he think about it a week later? I don't know if he will have thought much about it at all. And I'm left like this. It feels so unfair.'

The good thing about working with health care practitioners in the current era is that, when in conversation with members of your professions – that is, physiotherapists, young doctors, radiotherapists, community nurses, hospital nurses (it does not matter who) – almost all of you will now say, 'These two patients should not be left like this. Someone should talk with them.' Better, many of you will feel it perfectly appropriate if that 'someone' is yourself in the first instance. As an example of this current climate of growing psychological awareness, Box 5.1 reproduces much of the contents of a letter that I received (C. Enderby *et al.*, personal communication, 2002).

Box 5.1   Letter from C. Enderby *et al.*

Intensive Care Unit

Dear Keith

We are writing to inform you of a new bereavement service that the intensive care unit will be setting up in the next couple of months. Several members of the ICU team have felt that when patients die our unit doors close. This has led to some of us feeling that our care is incomplete. In response to this, it is proposed that we set up a simple service as set out below:

- Card of condolence sent to the next of kin approximately 10 days after the death with details of the bereavement clinic.
- Bereavement follow-up clinic run on first Friday of every month, sessions open to any relatives, appointment based.

The bereavement follow-up clinic will be nurse led . . . reduce the risk of psychological morbidity and depressive illness and, importantly, help staff to feel their care is more complete.

It really was very pleasing to receive this note because it does add to the impression of a growing concern for psychological issues in the health care professions. I know that there are other examples locally and many hundreds to be found nationally, which is a great encouragement.

But, on the other side of the coin, time and time again during recent years I have also met patients or their relatives who are in great turmoil or emotional distress *and discovered that no one has talked with them at all*. The two little bits of script from patients given above were not made up but actually said to me, quite recently. Tragically, though, they were said to me weeks after the original situation that troubled the patient in the first place. Emotional care was needed then, on the spot, at that time. It was not to be, though. Worse, my personal observation and belief, which has recently been corroborated by senior colleagues in clinical psychology, nursing, occupational therapy, practice nursing and by many, many users of the health care service, is that emotional care is not routinely provided in our hospitals and health centres, other than in units where special efforts are made, such as the example of the ICU given in Box 5.1.

This is a strong statement to make and, risking being repetitious, I do want again to stress my recognition of the fact that there are 'hotspots' where there is, say, a stroke counsellor or where a team has formed to provide some kind of emotional care. There are also many individual practitioners in the primary care services and hospitals who do offer good emotional care on an individual basis. It would be biased and unjust not to make this recognition. In these situations there *is* reliable emotional care. However, going back to our 'average patient in an average ward' test or 'average patient leaving an average health centre' test, how much confidence can we have that these average patients will have been cared for in a place that does have some resource for and regular practice of emotional care?

Understanding emotional care

As originally conceived in Nichols (1984), emotional care is not quite the same as counselling, although it is a very closely related intervention and can readily lead on to counselling or psychological therapy. There is a contrast with counselling that holds implications for all health care practitioners. *At the heart of the contrast is the concept of emotional care as part of a care routine. That is, emotional care is blended in and scheduled within the overall care plan, as with informational care.* Initial emotional care interventions are also preventive in nature, in the sense that patients and partners are given an opportunity to identify, express and progress with the ***normal*** emotional processes provoked by their situation. Emotional care is not, therefore, specifically concerned with personal problems, psychological distress or the range of issues that take people to counsellors or psychological therapists. It is concerned with giving our patients support and companionship as they deal with the thoughts and feelings evoked by their situation and facilitating an expression of those feelings where it is helpful to the patient. An outline of objectives in emotional care work is shown in Box 5.2.

Box 5.2   Emotional care

Objectives

- To support and assist people with the emotional reactions provoked by their illness, injury or disability.

Skills

- Creating a safe situation for a person and giving them 'permission' for emotional expression.
- Helping the person to relax with their emotions and move beyond inhibition and shame to free emotional expression.
- Enabling a gentle exploration and discussion of emotional reactions.
- Communicating back understanding and acceptance.
- Giving support by showing that the person's feelings are respected and valued.

Attitude

- Being free of a need to stop tears and banish grief, anxiety and anger. Being able to relax with and respect the person's emotion.

Our own reactions to emotion in others

Naturally I will deal with each of the objectives in Box 5.2 in more detail, with plenty of examples. However, one task should come before this. We need to talk about our own reactions to other people's emotions, since these have a tremendous influence on our general presence with patients and our attentiveness to issues of emotional care. We also need to understand our own attitude to emotional reactions in a medical setting and what this makes us want to do when they occur. To begin with, I will quote three statements that I have heard recently in order to illustrate certain outlooks that, I believe, still live on and exert an influence.

> 'Yes, she was upset but I didn't say much because I was worried about saying the wrong thing and making it worse.'

> 'Well, I think that it is important to talk to patients who are upset. You can't leave them to it if they are upset. Anyway, if you talk with them you can find out what the problem is and try to help them with it. I always say to patients – if you've got any problems call me.'

> 'I am against stirring things up. If it's not broke don't fix it. OK, if a patient is in florid distress then do what you can to comfort them, otherwise, leave well alone.'

These views allow me to name some *unhelpful assumptions* that can hinder or block the provision of emotional care.

Unhelpful assumption 1. Emotional reaction by patients inevitably means something is wrong and has to be put right as soon as possible. In my early days of working within a general hospital as a clinical psychologist, I was regularly treated as if I was a kind of 'emotion-damping fire brigade'. Typically, there would be a telephone call of the type 'Oh, Keith, could you look in today and have a chat with Peggy M. She's been very upset and quite angry with everybody.' It was not quite a case of 'the best patient is a smiling patient'. Even so, the urgency of these calls indicated a view that if emotion on the part of a patient disturbed the equable atmosphere of the clinic setting then something was wrong and something needed to be done quickly to restore the previous safe calm. In fact, a significant emotional reaction in a patient seemed to alarm some staff, as if, somehow, they were failing in their job.

Thus, this unhelpful assumption is about emotion in our patients being seen as an adverse state – something that has to be 'fixed'. It follows from this that there will be a secondary assumption that it is the duty of the staff involved to 'do battle' with those emotions, to diminish and calm them one way or another. *In other words, emotional reaction is treated as a brief illness.* Occasionally this might be true in the sense that cases of psychological disturbance and breakdown obviously do occur in a hospital or community practice. But in the majority of cases that you and I are likely to meet it is not the case. As will be argued below, emotion is part of a natural process of adjustment. Attempts at the rapid suppression of emotion in patients by staff, which suggest that they, the staff, are uncomfortable with a patient's emotion, lead to poor quality care.

Unhelpful assumption 2. Involvement with emotional reactions is 'expert territory'. In the first quote (which was something said to me by a nurse), the belief is expressed that special things need to be said to people who react with an expression of emotion. Since she did not believe that she knew about special things to say, it felt to her that she could readily do harm. The assumption here is that supporting people in emotional reaction leans heavily on health care practitioners who have special skills and ought to know the 'right thing to say'. The result of this is a hesitancy and an inclination to call in 'experts'. In reality, intervention is about listening and giving support and does not usually need advanced training, as will be shown below.

Unhelpful assumption 3. Involvement with emotional reaction in a medical setting is inviting trouble – the Pandora's box notion. This kind of apprehension is usually based on a fear of, or embarrassment with, emotion in others and, often, in oneself. It steers the practitioner into keeping a degree of distance in relations with patients. Emotions have to be quite evident before such a practitioner will even register them in conversation. Often there will be a denial of the importance and value of emotional process. Sometimes this denial is expressed with some vehemence and unwitting comedy. Outbursts that I have heard over the years include, 'I haven't got the time to deal with patients moping around the place. I've got a clinic to run diagnosing and treating heart disease. They'll have to sort themselves out' and (rather spectacularly, at a conference) 'Counselling, emotional care, psychological care – I'm sick of it. We've got counselling coming out of our ears. We'll have counselling for constipation soon.' Well, that was kind of wearing his psychology on his sleeve – a robust defence against a basic fear of feelings and emotions, it seems. I did not discuss it further to find out.

To be fair, it can be the case in very busy clinics or health centres that, say, a doctor who is already running late fears emotional reactions not for the emotion itself but for the burden of further time demand. This does not excuse an indifference to emotional reaction, although it might lead to arrangements for emotional care at another time or from another practitioner.

Unhelpful assumption 4. Emotional care is only relevant when a person is seen to be in distress, thus being an unscheduled activity limited to 'emotional casualties' and not a specific task routinely undertaken with all seriously ill or injured people.

Unhelpful assumption 5. Similarly, emotional care is something undertaken only when people have 'problems'. In fact, the opposite can apply. Emotional care is relevant when, other than the illness or injury itself, there are no immediately pressing problems.

Helpful assumptions

My promotion of emotional care as an essential part of our care for the ill and injured is based on alternative assumptions.

Helpful assumption 1. Emotional care involves assisting people with normal emotional processes. As shown in Chapter 2, serious illness and injury can trigger a wide variety of emotional reactions. Many of these are *normal emotional processes* that will be worked through in the course of time. However, if it is our intention to offer complete care, with a holistic emphasis, then there is no way that we can distance ourselves from our patients and leave them to deal with emotional reactions and processes on their own. There is also an important preventive element, since, although the concern is often with normal processes, sometimes these can become protracted and then disabling, as with the grieving process that can become 'stuck'. In giving emotional care we become better acquainted with where our patients have got to in their reactions and whether assistance might be needed in terms of therapy.

Helpful assumption 2. Emotional care can assist recovery. Patients and their partners who are given an opportunity for emotional expression that is combined with support and companionship in their situation almost always appreciate this greatly. They tend to manage their situation rather better, are less distressed and often come to terms with the changes resulting from illness or injury that are necessary in their lives rather more quickly. It can help them to rehabilitate more effectively. I have seen this scenario played out with many, many cases in cardiac rehabilitation and also in the treatment of renal failure and diabetes.

Helpful assumption 3. Emotional care is to be seen as an investment of effort that helps with adjustment and adherence to treatment, and might even protect general health to a degree. In relation to the last point, a powerful justification of the claim is to be found in the writing of Paul Martin (1997). He demonstrates, most graphically, the adverse effect of stress and distress on general health. Emotional care helps to reduce stress and distress.

Helpful assumption 4. Emotional care is a simple, non-demanding routine that should be on offer *to all patients with significant illness or injury;* similarly for their partners. Emotional care is not a treatment intervention as such but an intervention designed to facilitate normal emotional process and adjustment to circumstances. It is a form of support and care. Where a person has become very distressed or actually disturbed psychologically and is struggling to achieve adjustment, counselling or psychological therapy is indicated. In other words, the requirements go beyond emotional care.

Proof?

Do I need to prove the importance of emotional care to you? With the present generation of health care practitioners and trainees who are likely to read this book it is probably a redundant exercise. There is noticeably more emphasis on psychological issues in the present care culture in medicine, nursing and the therapies, that is certain. Moreover, there does seem to be a clear need these days on the part of many health care practitioners to give more complete care – that is, to include a psychosocial component. This is as a result of 'user pressure' and the recognition that, without an effort towards psychological care, damaging negligence in relation to many of our patients' overall well-being is likely. The key point is that it is impossible to give complete care and maintain a psychosocial emphasis without including emotional care as a component of the overall care package. However, some readers might want evidence of tangible benefits. Fortunately, such evidence is beginning to build. Davison and Petrie (1997) offer a useful review of research that includes studies yielding empirical evidence to show that emotional expression correlates with enhanced immune function and other health benefits. For example, Pennebaker *et al.* (1988) demonstrated that people who regularly expressed feelings about upsetting events in written form exhibited a stronger immune function than a control group who wrote only about trivial issues.

Perhaps my most important task, though, is to 'embolden' you to be more assertive in the provision of emotional care and to urge you to make sure that *your* patients do not go without it being on offer. As for the users of our service, the general plea for years has been 'please listen to us, please communicate with us'. These two behaviours are, of course, the core ingredients of emotional care.

Perhaps I should now emphasize this final point with a little case material. The following events, for whose authenticity I can vouch personally, illustrate my basic position.

The fantasy (how it should have been)

It is 9.30 at night. A new admission is in room 7, having arrived earlier that day for observation, an echocardiogram, the start-up of treatment with ACE inhibitors and diuretics to pull down very high blood pressure and preparation for an angiogram the next morning. Sudden, severe mitral valve failure is the diagnosis. He is outwardly very coping but inwardly rather shocked and unexpectedly emotional. The implications race through his mind. His named nurse comes in to take a last blood pressure measurement. She says,

'That's much better, 153 over 92. The lisinopril must be kicking in. We can relax a bit now. It really was very high earlier.'

She gets rid of the sphygmomanometer and sits on the edge of his bed and then briefly takes his hand.

'Quite a complicated day for you, I guess. It was all quite sudden, wasn't it. There is no need to be on your own with it though, unless you prefer it that way. If you feel like sharing with me what is in your thoughts and feelings then I'm here for the next 10 minutes at least.'

The reality (how it actually was)

It is 9.30 at night. A new admission is in room 7, having arrived earlier that day for observation, an echocardiogram, the start-up of treatment with ACE inhibitors and diuretics to pull down very high blood pressure and preparation for an angiogram the next morning. Sudden, severe mitral valve failure is the diagnosis. He is outwardly very coping but inwardly rather shocked and unexpectedly emotional. The implications race through his mind. His named nurse comes in to take a last blood pressure measurement. She says,

'That's much better, 153 over 92. The lisinopril must be kicking in. We can relax a bit now. It really was very high earlier.'

She gets rid of the sphygmomanometer, then walks briskly through the doorway, saying over her shoulder,

'Right then, try and get some sleep. Any problems, just call me.'

She is gone, and he is alone. That's a pity. He really could have used a bit of support and companionship with his shock and the looming thoughts of heart surgery to come. The past two days had all been rather distressing. Ten minutes of emotional care would have been much valued. But it was not to be.

Personal preparation for emotional care work

Are all people who function in a clinical role suitable for emotional care work? It is an important question. Reverting back to one of the themes in Chapter 4 – that is, the section to do with breaking bad news – it is of note that Maguire (1997) describes research that reveals how doctors will often actively avoid exploring their patients' concerns and feelings on giving them bad medical news. Sometimes the doctors will use immediate full information delivery as a device for blocking the patients' expression of concern and emotional reactions. This troubles Maguire, who has been a long time advocate of improved doctor–patient communication, particularly in relation to the experiences associated with cancer. Thus, he asks, '*Why* are doctors so loath to explore patients' concerns and feelings before moving into information giving and advice mode?' He gives a four-part answer to his own question:

- *Lack of training.* Few have had any formal training in strategies that would help them to break bad news in a way that facilitated psychological adaption.

- *Fear of damaging the patient.* They fear that they may unleash strong emotions like despair and anger and will not be able to contain these. Exploring patients' concerns and feelings will also take too much time.

- *Lack of support.* If doctors and nurses are to break bad news effectively, they need to feel that they are working in an environment that will be supportive of their efforts, especially when they encounter difficulties as a result of breaking bad news.

- *Personal survival.* Breaking bad news is a hard and unpleasant task. Once patients assimilate the truth they usually become very upset. If patients are then encouraged to talk about their concerns and feelings, this brings doctors face-to-face with the reality of their patients' predicament and suffering. Doctors question whether they can afford to do this frequently, since they have to survive emotionally.

In short, Maguire's position in relation to doctors giving emotional care is that they often find it too threatening, especially if they have little organized support. Support is easy enough to arrange and it should be regarded as a professional requirement to secure a support arrangement if heavily involved with this type of work (see the sections on support in Chapter 6). What about the other issue, though, to do with suitability and training? This has much to do with our own relationship with our own emotions.

Our reactions to emotion: important self-knowledge

This is something more personal. It concerns our own psychology. A person who is very wary of emotion, uncomfortable in its presence and who struggles to withhold his or her own emotion is not suitable for emotional care work – for obvious reasons. Nor, for that matter, is a person at the other end of that extreme – that is, someone with a background that makes them excessively focused on emotion and, perhaps, resolving issues of their own through identifying with and experiencing the emotional reactions of patients. Fortunately, both these are extremes and one does not often meet worrying examples in the caring professions. *Nevertheless, as one moves to include emotional care work in daily practice, it is a useful time to reflect on one's own emotional characteristics and one's own relationship with emotion. A little self-knowledge is important.*

In the normal course of our education we are not usually taught much about emotional functioning in the sense of formal instruction, either at home or at school. Most 'instruction' is achieved through modelling and arbitrary correction. Much the same has applied to training courses for the health care professions, although, it must be said, things are improving rapidly, with some training courses including mandatory modules in personal development in their curriculum. The result is that understanding of emotional functioning, sensitivity to emotion and the facility to deal with emotion vary greatly from person to person. A significant proportion of people are quite ill at ease with emotion and have poorly developed skills in recognizing their own true emotional reactions. They may also feel perturbed by the emotion of others and be grateful to distance themselves from it. Some upbringings and experiences in life result in an adult personality that has the characteristic of a robust defensive denial of personal emotional reactions. In other words, emotional reactions are repressed and

Reactions to your own emotions?

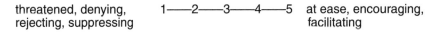

inhibited, shameful,   1——2——3——4——5   open, allowing,
blocking, lacking insight   accepting insightful

Your reactions to the emotions of others?

threatened, denying,   1——2——3——4——5   at ease, encouraging,
rejecting, suppressing   facilitating

Figure 5.1   Scales for assessing your reactions to emotions.

not freely available to fully conscious recognition, and certainly not to full expression. Compounding this effect is the fact that the British culture is noted as one that values reservation in emotional expression.

Where is all this leading? Each of us has our own, characteristic pattern of reactions to our own emotions. These range from *inhibited, shameful and blocking through to open, allowing and accepting*. Similarly, we all have our own characteristic reactions to the emotions expression by other people, ranging from *threatened, denying, rejecting and suppressing through to at ease, encouraging and facilitating*. These can be seen as personality dimensions, somewhere along whose lengths each and every one of us can be located, see Figure 5.1. Why don't you assess your position and also ask someone close to you to say what position they think you lie on? Do this in relation to different emotions separately. Try anger and then anxiety, for example.

Why do such differences occur between us? There is probably some involvement of genetics but childhood experiences account for much of the difference, I believe. A colleague who struggled somewhat with emotional expressiveness in both himself and his patients told me how, as a child, he was shamed and punished by his father for emotional outbursts. He was taught to strive for emotional inertness. Another mentioned that her mother had been a victim of lifelong depression and eventually took her own life. Before this, though, the mother leaned heavily on my colleague who, as a teenager, had to cope with her depressions and support her through their duration. She grew to hate the expression of depressed feelings or anxiety in anyone and both feared and despised them in herself.

Guidelines for understanding personal feeling and emotion

Our behaviour is primarily determined by what we perceive and how we react to what we perceive. We are in a continual state of reaction. It is a complex process involving our whole body reacting to our appraisal of a composite of past, current and future situations. Most prominent in our usual daily awareness, though, are our endocrine, cardiovascular, gastrointestinal and musculoskeletal systems, whose reactive changes we usually notice more easily. Picture yourself as you would be five minutes before an important interview or a couple of minutes after you have had a difference with a colleague. It is the sensing of our body state in relation to these major systems that provides our basis for what is called *personal feeling.*

The concept of feeling is rather broader than that of emotion, although the two terms are close in meaning and are often interchanged. This leads to a confusion. It is quite common for people to confuse the constant, ever changing flow of personal feeling with major emotional reactions. Thus, in group sessions, I have sometimes asked members what their feeling was at a particular moment in a conversation. Sometimes the reply is given, 'I'm not feeling anything.' What they actually meant was, 'I don't feel any strong emotion, I'm not anxious, tearful, angry or depressed.' *In reality it is impossible to be without feeling,* although we spend much of our time without major emotional experiences. Feeling refers to our continuing experience of our body state and its reactive stance to the events of the moment. Think of it as a sort of printout. So, let me ask you, what is your feeling at this moment? This is your psychological/whole-body stance to your current situation. To give it full meaning requires an act of interpretation that is linked to what you are seeing, thinking and the judgements you are making. One has to stop, reflect, look and *sense* within. Let me use myself as an example:

> It is 7.30 on a sunny Saturday morning in August and I am sitting at my computer composing these paragraphs. What do I feel? No major emotions, that is certain. But there is an underlying physical restlessness and a sense of needing to break away from this in about 10 minutes. My back is not aching but it is tired of the posture and my eyes are a little tired from focusing on the screen. I have been here for an hour. It feels like that is long enough. Something to do with feeling a bit trapped. I would not normally work at this sort of time on a Saturday but the

publishers are expecting this book in three months and there is a feeling of urgency. So I feel quite good to have got a little more done but I'm running out of patience with the business of writing now as it begins to feel like being trapped indoors when I want to get out to my yacht on such a nice sailing day. Overall, definitely restless because I feel a bit trapped. I can feel the conflict and know that the 'outdoors' will win soon but I can also feel a confidence that I will get the section finished by coming back tonight. So I feel relaxed and have a feeling of enthusiasm about my next move (out). I'm also quietly pleased with myself for having achieved some work this morning.

So, have another go – what are *you* feeling at the moment?

Am I suited to emotional care work and counselling type interventions?

Do not be alarmed: most people in the caring professions are suitable and most of those that are not could become so with a little personal development work (arranging just a few sessions with a counsellor, for example). But this is an instructive question to explore because, in so doing, one learns about oneself and also about the task of emotional care. In the two examples given above of people who had experienced damaging childhood experiences that left them wary and inhibited with regard to emotional expression, it is reasonable to say that, without further personal development work, they should not be involved in emotional care. This is because their own needs and anxieties in situations involving emotional expression by others will intrude and hamper their efforts to give true care. It must now be obvious that, in my judgement, practitioners involved in this work do need to have a relaxed stance to emotional expression. They ought to have developed a reasonable capacity to identify their own personal feelings and emotions and be able to express them to others without inhibition, shame or anxiety (when it is appropriate and only in safe and suitable situations, that is). Practitioners need to be able to 'own' their feelings to others rather than have a proneness to deny them while 'acting them out'. Without this level of emotional development the emotions of others are likely to make you feel uncomfortable and you will be inhibited and ineffective in emotional care work. There is a richness of opportunity to work on personal development these days. Introductory counselling courses, personal development courses or personal sessions with counsellors are readily available. The key question is: do I need them? Some more detailed notes on emotional development that will give you a basis for personal inquiry and comparison are as follows.

Notes on the personal emotional development needed for those engaged in emotional care work: the ideal profile

Attitude

A positive attitude is held towards emotion and emotional process. It is respected as a significant and inherent part of human functioning. Personal feeling and emotion are valued and the ability to express these to suitable others is seen as mature functioning that is advantageous for well-being.

Awareness

There is an awareness of the flow of personal feeling and emotional reactions within oneself. There is a capability for expressing personal feeling and emotion to suitable others without shame, inhibition or tension.

Understanding

Emotional reaction is seen as a normal part of our overall reaction to life events and, particularly, to illness and injury. It is seen as an important process and not as an intrusion that has to be battled with.

Self-awareness

There is an awareness of one's own characteristic emotional patterns and 'trouble spots' – that is, the personal feelings and emotions that are easy for each of us to identify, accept and express, as opposed to those that are not.

Reactions to emotional expression by other people

There will be an absence of negative reactions to normal expressions of emotion. For example, when patients reveal emotion there will be an ability to accept the situation:

- without horror and a need to escape;

- without a need to produce an immediate emotional calm;

- without the feeling that the patient's emotional reaction needs to be diverted or 'treated' and replaced with smiles;

- without a feeling of guilt, blame or failure;

- without a need to encourage the patient to suppress reactions;

- without the need to get away in case one's own reactions are stirred up.

Instead there will be positive and relaxed acceptance based on the understanding that the need is for an unrushed, accepting, supportive, sharing atmosphere that enables a patient to express emotion without any judgemental or 'curative' endeavours on the part of the practitioner. There will, though, be a concern for immediate comfort in terms of making the situation safe and helping the patient relax with their own emotion. The practitioner will be able to empathize and communicate about the particular feelings openly and easily.

Admittedly, these are all a little on the idealistic side. I do not know many people who are so tuned to perfection, added to which, perfectly groomed and faultless personalities can be a bit nauseating at times. However, Box 5.3 gives us some sense of direction and some reference points. I can't say that on *every* working day I manage to conform to the ideal that well myself, nor would I expect anyone else to. *We have to accept a day-to-day variation of tolerance to the emotion of others as part of our own emotional processes.* The features in the notes listed on pages 190–191 are something that we strive towards and discuss from time to time in supervision events or with like minded peers. Having said that, if on reading the notes you judge that you do have some work to do to gain confidence and development with your own emotional material and that of your patients, then that insight alone shows that you are off to a good start. Take it further with your local clinical psychologists or with colleagues who have counselling training.

Have things changed since 1984?

'The concept of "feelings" is often used disparagingly in our culture, the inference being that they are an indecent sideshow within us that is rather embarrassing and, for men particularly, something to be grown out of. Quite closely related to this is the aseptic atmosphere of the typical hospital ward wherein personal feelings are greeted like bacteria – something to take up immediate battle with. Thus, anti-depressants and anxiety inhibitors are handed out with the same sense of urgency as antibiotics.'

(Nichols 1984: 106)

Emotional process

I will be describing how you can provide emotional care for your patients and their partners in the next section. Since, though, I have used the phrase 'emotional process' several times it is important not to leave its meaning vague.

On first consideration, emotional reactions seem cumbersome obstacles to efficient human functioning. Sometimes they are a burden, and an uncomfortable one at that. We might argue that they do not actually do anything of real use for us. Or do they? The obvious reply is that personal feeling – that is, the sensing of the flow of psychophysiological activity in our bodies – is a *device that allows motivation, preparation and adaptation to the needs of perceived circumstances.* This in turn allows a combination of physical and psychological resources to be energized and directed to provide the most appropriate and effective response. In the broader sense this applies to situations of threat, caring opportunity, sexual opportunity, fatigue etc. At the same time it also applies to ever changing situations of everyday life. The flow of feeling directs, in part, how we conduct a conversation. You will certainly have observed that there is much feeling to be found in the health centre and the hospital clinic, but it is usually tightly held in, not usually referred to or noticed. In some instances, though, the everyday flow of feeling becomes engulfed by very strong emotional states – for example, anxious worrying or evident grieving. How should we regard these? The answer is 'judge with caution', because sometimes these emotional states are part of an important and continuing *functional* process that has a beginning, middle and end. I should stress again at this point that these emotional processes are normal and often have a function. I will illustrate this point with two examples.

(1) Productive anxiety: the work of worrying

Barbara, a 37-year-old medical receptionist, was divorced and due to marry again in three months' time when, to her great distress, her GP advised her that she thought Barbara had breast cancer and that it was moderately advanced. This was confirmed at a breast cancer clinic and the alarming news given to her that a mastectomy was necessary. The surgeon involved was kindly and reassured her that he would minimize surgery to what was truly necessary. Surgery was scheduled for two weeks later. During these two weeks Barbara was in a state of considerable anxiety. Her normal work and social routines became difficult and social interaction was an ordeal. At night she was restless and lay awake for many hours with her heart thumping and an alert tension denying her sleep. She spent a considerable amount of time contacting women who had undergone mastectomy through the Internet. She also visited a breast cancer nurse counsellor. Barbara became a little stronger and coping as the day for surgery approached, although she remained anxious and worried up to admission. Her worries had centred on the risk of the cancer continuing to advance and the personal impact of the partial loss of a breast. This troubled her a lot because she sensed the damage that this would do to her self-image (she had always had a strong sense of physical presentation, with her shapely breasts forming a central part of her self-image). This linked to worries for her impending marriage. The relationship had been built around Barbara's physical attractiveness and she worried that the disfiguring effect of the mastectomy would introduce strains that could finish the marriage before it started. She dreaded her first look at the breast after surgery and dreaded revealing it to her fiancé. Her worst fantasies were of being left alone and going through the rest of life without a partner.

It is pointless saying to a person in Barbara's position, 'Don't worry and don't be anxious.' We are designed to be anxious when we perceive threat. It is part of an important emotional process. Although her anxieties and worries were very uncomfortable and she truly wished that they would leave her alone, they did have a useful function. For example, her anxiety gave her a raised vigilance and an increased energy to tackle the threats she faced. It led her to strive to become much more informed, link with support networks, contact others who had had the experience and learn from them. She had visited a counsellor to seek help and advice. The product of the worry and anxious fantasies was that she adopted a confrontational approach to her problem – she became more prepared, more informed and more coping. Thinking about problems and losses that might arise and how to deal with them is often a help in Barbara's type of situation. She was, thus, less likely to be overwhelmed by events, unless it was the surprise of things going better than she had thought. *In other words, her anxious worrying had been a form of preparation*. It had been painful but it had a function. It is in this sense that some psychologists talk of the 'work of worrying', regarding it as a form of mental rehearsal (Janis and Leventhal 1965). Barbara's anxiety was part of a functional emotional process. As for her health care practitioners, they would be unwise to try to block out the process. It would be better to give her full support and emotional care, help her with information and planning and do what they can to help the process along to a point where she feels better prepared and ready to face the situation to come.

(2) Grief as an emotional process

Les had worked as a welder all his working life. He loved the work. It was, he claimed, all he knew. Surprisingly, abandoning his usual caution, he made an unbalanced move on an unsecured ladder while doing a little evening job on a neighbour's horse box. He fell and injured two lumbar vertebrae. The vertebrae never really recovered and, after being off sick for a year with continual back pain, he had to give up work and live on state benefits. Twelve months after this decision Les was still very down. He was quite emotionally fragile and would sometimes be found by his wife quietly weeping. This was more likely if he had been out and passed the docks where the welding company that had employed him was based. It was another year or two before he moved beyond his grief.

After a significant loss in life of something that is highly valued, or, similarly, after a bereavement, most of us will normally have some sort of grieving experience, as did Les. People differ greatly in the time it takes to complete this grieving process and then re-engage in an undisturbed life once more. During this period an emotional process has been taking place in which the strong attachments (or bonds) that have been disrupted (often unexpectedly) slowly weaken in power. The weakening in power and eventual freedom from these attachments is achieved by a process in which the memories and awarenesses of what has been lost are repeatedly re-experienced, often with much emotional distress. Eventually, this re-experiencing process leads to a weakening of the reaction to a point that new attachments can successfully be made once more. Some people get through the grieving process in a matter of months; for others it may take a year or two. A small number are troubled by extended grief, in which the process does not progress to completion and becomes an enduring pathological state.

Emotional reaction and issues of gender, race and culture

As is emphasized below, the provision of emotional care begins with a brief exploratory act on the part of the practitioner. The exploration is around the question: does this person need and want a brief intervention providing support and an opportunity to talk through emotionally laden issues? What seems simple can transform itself into something more complicated when thinking through some of the aspects linked to this question. Perhaps, in the patient's value system, communication concerning emotional issues might well take place in the presence of a female practitioner but never in the presence of a male practitioner. Perhaps the particular patient feels diffident or averse to the closer type of relationship that emotional care work produces with a relative stranger of a different racial background. Perhaps there are cultural issues that have to be discussed before a patient can relax with you and accept an invitation to talk about reactions to their illness or injury. These are not issues that I plan to take on in depth here. Obviously, one has to be sensitive to the needs of the patient and partner involved. For example, I will usually check on the gender issue at some early point and ask if the person that I am caring for is happy talking with a man. I try to offer the option of a female colleague if that is their preference. Similarly, if working with someone from a different cultural background I remain alert to the possibilities of significant cultural differences. Try to make it easy for your patient to voice these and do your best to have them taken into account. Sometimes checking with the partner or members of the family involved will be a helpful source of information. Being under less personal stress, they may have useful knowledge to impart concerning how things are talked about, to whom and when within their culture.

THE PRACTICE OF EMOTIONAL CARE

You are a dietician, occupational therapist, radiotherapist, nurse, it does not matter what. The question of the moment is: *why would I offer emotional care and does the patient in front of me have a need for it?*

The 'why' is easily dealt with. Emotional care is concerned with facilitating the emotional processes that we know, in advance, are likely to be active in many of our patients. It is about supporting them through a period of time when they may experience many differing feelings, some to do with threat and anxiety, some to do with anger, some to do with loss and sadness. It is about giving emotional care and support during times of difficult experiences. In simple terms, emotional care is an endeavour aimed at helping our patients to feel more comfortable, to experience a basic caring companionship. It is not directly concerned with solving problems or getting rid of troublesome emotional reactions – it is about *facilitating emotional process*. Thus, to the second part of the question: does the patient in front of me actually need it? That is something to be established in the individual case. Much will depend on the setting in which you work. If you work in oncology, there cannot be many of your patients who do not need emotional care. If you work as a physiotherapist in fractures and trauma, it will be mixed. If you work as a practice nurse, I suspect that it will again be a mixed picture. A good number of your patients will not have high needs for emotional care because they will be looking in to see you for routine contact concerning fairly minor health troubles. In short, the question is answered by your own inquiry and experience of your own patients. Again, do not forget the issues of gender, race and culture as a 'complication'.

Now it is time to turn to the business of giving emotional care. My thoughts will be centred on Figure 5.2.

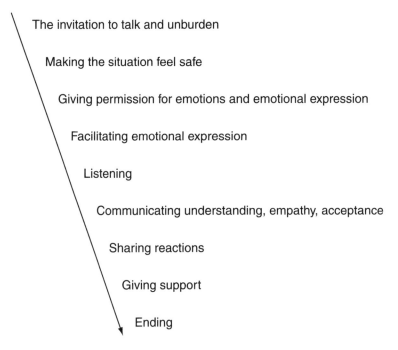

The invitation to talk and unburden

Making the situation feel safe

Giving permission for emotions and emotional expression

Facilitating emotional expression

Listening

Communicating understanding, empathy, acceptance

Sharing reactions

Giving support

Ending

Figure 5.2   Good practice in emotional care.

• Initiating emotional care: the invitation

It has been established that emotional care is for those of your patients and their partners who actually want it. It is not something to be forced on people. Because of this, emotional care work always begins with an invitation and continues only if the person involved recognizes a need and accepts the invitation. There should be no persuasion involved. In the case of patients with whom you will have an ongoing relationship, say as a cardiac nurse dealing with a recent admission after a heart attack or a physiotherapist with regular treatment contacts, the invitation and exploration of response can be made in advance, as in the example below.

Emotional care: an invitation in advance. John D, a 48-year-old computer specialist who runs his own computer repair business, was admitted to the cardiac ward for assessment and observation late one afternoon. He had suffered a moderate heart attack but did not need resuscitation or defibrillation. As part of the routines towards the end of the next morning, Debbie, one of the cardiac nurses, calls by for further observations and when these are complete puts the equipment to one side, sits with John for a moment and says:

> 'Part of my work is helping our patients with the personal and emotional side of their heart attack. This is because quite a few of our patients do find it very stressful at first and, naturally, they have lots of feelings about it. At this point in your treatment, I normally arrange to put aside 20 minutes or so to meet with you in private and talk through how this has affected you personally. This is just a bit of extra care and support for you if it is something that you would like. So I'm checking now if you would like to talk with me a little later today or would prefer to leave it for now.'

(I should note that in the above and following examples I again refer to typical situations in cardiac medicine. Although, as I have emphasized, psychological care and its component of emotional care are relevant in all areas of health care, it is better if I use examples from areas with which I am personally a little more familiar. I hope that you do not find this bias disagreeable and that you will find it easy to convert the examples so that they apply to your own circumstances.)

> *Emotional care: an invitation on the spot.* Two days later Debbie runs into Gail, John's wife. She is waiting for John to come back from having an angiogram. It is expected that John may need coronary artery bypass surgery. They exchange a few words and Gail is immediately tearful. She apologizes to Debbie for having broken down. Debbie replies:
>
> > 'Gail, please don't apologize for feeling upset. It is a very upsetting and frightening thing for any couple. Would you like to talk it over with me for a few minutes?'

• Beginning the encounter: making the situation safe and giving permission for emotions and emotional expression

Ideally, an encounter for emotional care work is something that you set up with thought, planning and care. You must take responsibility for it and design it so that it is a caring and helpful experience for your patient. The last thing that you want is for your patient to feel ill at ease or for there to be some jarring intrusion that disrupts the flow. This planning falls under the label of 'making the situation safe'.

We must now consider what is needed to make a safe situation. I have listed below the kinds of things that you need to take into consideration. I hope that you are happy for me to express these fairly directly as if we were in a tutorial together.

(a) Choose an appropriate environment

If there is an emotionally laden situation that you want to talk about yourself, with a colleague, what are your own preferences for the best environment in which to do this? Your own preferences could be a useful guide to the ingredient of a safe situation. This is because most people prefer somewhere to talk that is private and where they are not on open display to the passing world. It also helps if it is a smallish, comfortable place where a telephone is not likely to ring any minute and where there is an engaged sign on the door. The engaged sign means that there is protection from people knocking on the door or just walking in. British people in particular tend to be shy about emotional expression and often want to hide it away and apologize for it, especially if tears are involved. *In short, the ideal environment for emotional care is one that feels safe from scrutiny and intrusion.* Typically, an interview or consulting room makes a good place in a hospital, and similarly in a health centre. If you work in the community then a home visit should offer ideal circumstances, unless there are young or insensitive members of the family crashing in and out of the room disrupting the conversation, or the television is a competitor for attention.

Having said this, in reality you have to work with what you have got. I am often asked to visit people in a hospital ward situation, for example. The staff usually make every effort to provide privacy and often some kind of 'make do, borrow a room' compromise can be arranged. But at other times the patient cannot be moved and it is a matter of visiting them in an open ward situation – 'take it or leave it'. I do not care for this much at all: even with curtains drawn around us and conversing in hushed voices there is often constant distraction with noise from the rest of the ward and the general sense of an uncomfortable arrangement. In these circumstances I will often begin by discussing the problem openly with the patient, initially limiting things to talks about talks. It gives the person involved a chance to consider their wish for emotional care in such circumstances. If they are untroubled and wish to talk then we proceed, but if it feels too uncomfortable for them we plan another visit very soon when there is a better opportunity for privacy. Sometimes, people have a need to talk then and there, despite the lack of safety, but it is not ideal because it lacks the safety described above. Recently, while engaged in just such a conversation and despite messages left to the contrary, the curtains around us were suddenly swept open and in strode a registrar to check and adjust a drip. The conversation was disrupted, I was angry, the patient was embarrassed and the registrar became flustered.

(b) Who should be present?

Ideally just you and the patient should be present, although the patient may prefer to have their partner or a family companion with them on occasions (something to check on). It does not, in my view, make for a good, safe situation to have other health care practitioners present. The GP with a trainee doctor, the consultant with a registrar, a senior nurse with a trainee nurse – these are not ideal situations. The presence of an observer tends to be an inhibiting factor, so, in such situations, try to set up your emotional care work by arranging a meeting later on or by asking the third person (or persons) present to leave for a short while.

(c) Maintain a safe 'persona': narrow the social divide

> Nurse: 'I find that the best time to talk to patients is when you are bathing them.'

This will not do – not if you are serious about emotional care work. Like it or not there is a social divide between health care practitioners and their patients. I do not need to spell it out in detail because you live it. You have status as a health care practitioner. Access to you may be through a receptionist. You may have a title and a uniform. You will be fully mobile. You will be standing, perhaps, while your patient may be prone, weakened, disabled or, if in a bath, naked. *There needs to be an effort on your part to narrow this social divide, to make the encounter more 'person to person' and supportively human in atmosphere, as opposed to a distant professional engaging with a statusless patient.* It is all fairly obvious material, most of which you may well be practised in. Nevertheless, it merits reaffirmation. The following recommendations are for you to reflect upon. At the very least they can form a basis for discussion between yourself and your tutor or colleagues as to how best to set up emotional care encounters that have the quality of a reduced social divide.

It is impractical to shed uniforms in most circumstances, but there are plenty of ways of narrowing the social gap. One of the best signals is that of reducing literal social distance and physical barriers between yourself and the person involved. Sit with them rather than with a desk between the pair of you – perhaps side by side at a comfortable angle. Do not overdo the closeness at first but be close enough that you could take one of their hands if you felt it appropriate. Be relaxed yourself and try to be free of a sense of pace and clock watching. Be free of any clutter, such as mobile phones and pagers. Do not, of course, sit with a pen and notepad; keep your hands free. Give your patient full attention, with a gentle gaze rather than an intense regard.

Changing the terms of address is a major adjustment that is available to provide better social symmetry – that is, less of a social divide. It seems common practice already for physiotherapists, speech therapists, occupational therapists and junior nurses to introduce themselves with their first name and invite their patients to use this name, putting them on more equal terms of address. However, my personal experience is that specialists (e.g. audiologists), medical staff and senior nurses are less likely to do so spontaneously, if at all. In emotional care work, with its person-to-person approach, it is usually helpful if the terms of address are equivalent in form. In other words, establish the familiar, first name form of address early on, rather than you being referred to in a distant form with a title, perhaps, and the patient referred to by you in the familiar form (first name). I often use the following invitation if I am meeting a person for the first time and it looks like we will be involved in emotional care work:

Psychologist: 'Incidentally, we tend to be informal here and use first names because it makes it easier to talk together. So please use my first name, which is Keith, as long as you feel comfortable with that.'

By the way, to go back to the issue of conversations at bath time or its equivalent, yes, important supportive conversations may well take place in this or similar situations and, yes, they are valuable. It is a nurturing atmosphere that has an element of regression to the parent–child relationship. It can be a relaxing, supportive moment, but the bathroom type encounter must never be the mainstay of emotional care because the clear focus of the event is the activity of bathing and the talking is secondary to this. Moreover, the social asymmetry is very marked, with one person in uniform and the other naked.

(d) Communicate safety through obvious and relaxed acceptance of personal feelings

The underlying theme to this section is that emotional care depends on a sense of safety being experienced by the people you are working with. This implies that they feel safe with you, in that they can trust you. The word 'trust' is used in a specific sense here, namely that your patients rapidly discover that they will not be contradicted, continually interrupted, embarrassed, humiliated, judged inadequate or left feeling devalued. *This atmosphere of trust may only be generated by the character and tone of your reactions to their disclosures.* Either this trust will already exist as a result of previous encounters with you or it must be established very early on. Your replies must convey that you are relaxed with what they want to talk about and that their disclosure of personal feelings, worries, regrets, anger, sadnesses, dark thoughts and tears are all welcome and appropriate in this type of encounter. Further, that you will not be reacting with stifling and compulsive reassurances, censure, indignation, embarrassment or harshness. Nor will you leave them with a 'blocked out feeling' or experience of not being listened to. They will then sense that *you are safe to talk to* and so talk with you.

How is this all achieved? Many of you will be good listeners (as described earlier), and this is a key ingredient. But it is important to have thought through how you will react in the first instance to the initial statements of your patients. People who are not used to talking with others in depth often begin in a wary, defensive state. It feels a little foreign to them and they often worry what you will think of them. Generally, though, they will not shy away from the conversation unless you introduce something that compounds their defensiveness. You do, therefore, need to acquire the habit of giving encouraging and supportive reactions that allow and encourage emotional expression, rather than responses that may well be meant in a kindly way, but in reality are blocking responses. Often a situation that lends itself to an opportunity for initiating emotional care goes awry because of this effect. Let me give a couple of admittedly rather 'heavy handed' examples of kindly blocking responses:

John (our patient in the cardiac unit): 'My wife is such a worrier, sometimes I feel more bothered about her than myself.'

Nurse (kindly but blocking response): 'It's silly for you to be worrying about things like that at this stage. Your job is to rest and get some strength back and you won't do that fretting about other people. She'll be all right, I'm sure. I'll have a word with her.'

Comment. This is a rejecting communication that opens with the nurse referring to John's feelings of concern for his wife as 'silly'. This does not say to him, 'I recognize and value your feelings, so feel relaxed in talking more about them to me, I am safe to talk to.' In fact, it says the opposite: 'There is something wrong about you having these feelings and raising them now, so squash them away and do something else, it is not safe to talk about them here.'

A more helpful alternative would be:

Nurse (with a facilitating response): 'I can understand what you are feeling, John. Would you like to tell me a little more about your concerns? What is it particularly that is in your thoughts and feelings for her that troubles you?'

Comment. This is a facilitating response because it carries the statement that John's disclosure has importance for the nurse. She sees it as worth spending time on and worth elaborating. There is no judgement, no evaluative comment and no blocking effect. It gives him the sense of the nurse being safe to talk to – so he will go on to talk more and emotional care can take place.

A further example:

Consultant (during ward round with a post hysterectomy patient): 'How are you this morning? Nurse tells me that you have been a bit upset.'

Patient: 'Yes, I've been feeling very low, quite depressed. I'm afraid I'm going to be tearful.'

Consultant: 'Absolutely no reason for you to be upset or depressed, my dear, everything has gone very well, it is all healing up nicely. Just a bit of post-op blues I expect. You'll have to try and get things like that out of your head. I'll get nurse to give you some tablets to shift it.'

Surprisingly, I still meet people who, in telling me of their experiences in hospital, reveal that this particular brand of blocking response is alive and well. The denial of the function of feelings as a part of normal process and the reflexive recourse to compulsive reassurance and anti-depressants can be very destructive. It also promotes a situation where emotional care is denigrated. I hope this style and outlook is nearing extinction. How could (or should) a very pressed consultant respond in order to be congruent with the aims of emotional care? He or she will, of course, realize that, although a relief for some women, hysterectomy is a significant psychological blow for others. It involves the end of fertility and a major change for some women in their sense of womanhood and self-image. Naturally, there can be some intense feelings and important emotional processes involved. Therefore, something like the following is needed.

> Patient: 'Yes, I've been feeling very low, quite depressed. I'm afraid I'm going to be tearful.'
>
> Consultant: 'I understand, truly. There has been a lot of strain for you. We would like to help you with that too. It is important to us because we know that hysterectomy can be a complicated and upsetting experience. I hope that you will forgive me that I can't discuss it with you personally, now. I have to be in theatre in a few minutes and so I am going to ask Annette, our nurse counsellor, to meet with you to talk it through. She will be along shortly to make an arrangement if you would like this. I hope that you will feel able to talk with her in depth.'

A minor and quite common version of the consultant's blocking response is the familiar 'Don't upset yourself love, sit down there and I'll get you a cup of tea.' (Have you have come across this recently?) Thus, a key question for all of us is:

> **Do I have characteristic blocking responses that reduce the sense of my safety as a person with whom personal feelings might be shared?**

If the answer is 'perhaps' or even 'yes' then you have some work to do before undertaking emotional care work. As has been established, emotional care is about helping people to *express* their personal feelings and responses that block this are the opposite of emotional care. Moreover, they reveal a stance to emotion in others that is really one of 'flight to a safe distance'. In other words, personal feeling and emotional expression are something of a threat.

• *Give 'permission' for emotions and emotional expression during the session*

Very similar in theme and approach to the last strategy discussed, this item is just a reminder to carry on what has been started. Often people are taking risks when they make very personal disclosures to you. You must always, therefore, be assiduous in preserving the sense of safety in the encounter through the character of the responses that you make. It is not so much a case of your working to 'say the right thing', because that would introduce a 'performance anxiety' for you to have to deal with, which would be intrusive. It is more a matter of maintaining the atmosphere of relaxed acceptance and helping your patients to express their experience and feelings without judgement, anxious reassurance and tension from you. Another example will help to illustrate this. We will join Debbie and John D again. It is the fourth night after his heart attack. They have talked for a little while about his frightening experiences when actually having the heart attack and also about worries for the future. This has led on to him telling her:

John: 'Actually, over the last day I have started to feel quite down, Debbie. I know I should feel grateful for everything that has been done but there are some black thoughts.'

Nurse Debbie: 'Are they thoughts that you feel like sharing with me?'

John: 'Well, last night . . . I haven't told anyone, my wife would be really upset. I expect you'll think it is stupid . . . I've been feeling guilty about it.' (He is giving a warning that he is about to reveal something that makes him feel vulnerable – extra support is needed.)

Debbie: 'Take your time, John. Just say what you feel like saying. You have had a very difficult experience and it is bound to stir up a lot of feeling.'

John: 'I find myself thinking (he chokes on emotion a little) . . . I find myself thinking that now I've got heart disease the best part of my life is over. I don't mean that I want to do myself in but yesterday I thought "Maybe it's best if I have another coronary, quick, clean and fatal and that finishes it." I'll never be able to keep the business going at full pressure like I need to. I was near top of the squash ladder, really strong for my age, really fit and, I hope you don't mind my saying it, pretty good in bed. It all seems like it's all gone now. I keep remembering my Dad in his wheelchair, after his stroke. I don't want to be like that.' (At this point tears trickle down John's face and he cries quietly for a little while. He cannot continue talking.)

Debbie: *(She says nothing, puts her hand on John's hand and simply gives him a tissue and a little time in silence, still sitting with him and looking at him in a relaxed way. She is at ease with his emotion, feels for him, empathizes with his turmoil but does not give way to any reflex to rush in with reassurances or platitudes about positive thinking. She cares about his feelings and his situation but is aware that this is an opportunity for John to search into his personal feelings and share them with a trusted person. If she starts offering views or information to correct the worst of his fantasies or challenges his feelings then the moment will be lost. If she tries to make the situation easier for herself by saying in some way 'don't feel like that' she will have committed an error in emotional care – she will have been caring for herself. But she didn't.)*

John: 'I'm sorry to take your time making a fuss like this. I'm making a fool of myself. What are you thinking of me, that I'm ungrateful?'

Debbie: 'It feels like a terribly sad experience that you are going through and that is no surprise for me, to be honest. But I can see that you are not used to sharing your feelings with other people, John. You seem so condemning of yourself, using words like "stupid" and "fool". Is that how you actually see yourself at the moment?'

John: 'Well, maybe not quite like that. I was a bit embarrassed, new territory for me. Thanks for listening, it helps a lot.'

Debbie: 'I think that it is important and I'm glad that you have been able to talk to me. You were saying that sometimes you feel finished and would be happy for it to end with another heart attack.'

John: 'That's right. I don't feel like that all the time, it sort of comes in waves. You must think that I'm very ungrateful after all the work the staff have put in . . . What do you think? Will you tell me what you think?'

Debbie: 'All right. I'm glad that you have been able to talk to me like this. You have had a severe shock and things are going to change a lot for you for a while. It has been frightening and the future must look frightening. So it is bound to stir up some intense feelings. That is how it is for people who have had heart attacks. I hope that it helps if you share these thoughts and feelings with me, much better than being alone with them. So, my main feeling just now is that I'm really pleased that you were able to tell me. I think that it is a step forward. I have to get some more observations done now so I hope that we can talk about it some more tomorrow. Is that OK?'

John: 'Have you got the time? I would appreciate that. It is a relief to talk about it. I couldn't tell Gail, she would be horrified, poor soul.'

You can see what is happening here. John is, in effect, exploring the effect of his expression of personal feeling. There is a theme to his question to do with 'What do you think of me now that I have told you about my depressed feelings, now that I have shown you my emotions?' It is a critical moment. Debbie does well. She shows no discomfort and makes no value judgements. In fact she shows herself to be at peace with his expression of personal feeling. The result is that he trusts her and benefits from the brief session. He wants to follow it up with another. (Incidentally, this was based on an actual incident related to me by a nurse in a supervision session.)

• Listening and facilitating emotional expression

To continue the tutorial. Once the person that you are working with trusts you, feels safe and is talking to you, the next requirement in emotional care is active listening and occasional facilitation as required. Once *you* can relax into the situation and accept that you do not have to say anything clever and insightful and that you do not have to solve your patients' problems for them on the spot, then the listening should be easy. Your task is to help the person search into their thoughts and feelings and talk through these with you. At times it will feel uncomfortable, perhaps, holding back from 'jumping in' with helpful reassurances, suggestions or corrective information. *The key point, though, is that emotional care is about facilitating the identification and expression of personal feelings in order to assist normal emotional processes and processing.* Such progress normally adds positively to the patient's general well-being. Furthermore, it is a means of adding support and companionship to your care regime. Counselling and psychological therapy will take things further and emotional care may well progress into these when undertaken by practitioners with that type of training. Similarly, something said by the patient may indicate that informational or educational care is needed. This can take place later. *But the emotional care session is about emotional care, so later is the operative word.* Your main role is thus facilitating, listening and sharing. This can be somewhat unnerving to practitioners who have not had counselling training and are from professions where active intervention is the natural order of the day. It may be of help perhaps if, prior to some of your initial sessions, you arm yourself with the following thoughts:

> **In an emotional care session the process is as important as the content.**

And

> **Emotional care is about facilitating the identification and expression of personal feelings in order to assist normal emotional processes and processing. Furthermore, it is a means of adding support and companionship to your care regime.**

The first of these adds up to saying that you are trying to create a situation where the *style of interaction* between your patient and yourself is an important experience because of the way in which it is conducted (as distinct from the actual content and meaning of the words used). The content of relaxed acceptance and respect for personal feeling, together with the experience of respect, support and companionship, promotes a process of in-depth relating and intense sharing; in other words, the opposite of the distant 'detached concern' of the classic doctor–patient relationship.

It is time now, perhaps, for a summary of where we have got to, with a list of skills for listening to and facilitating the expression of personal feeling, followed by an example.

| • **Sitting close (but not too close).**

- Allowing no distraction from extraneous sources.

- Making eye contact with a steady natural regard (not forced – it does not need to be a near permanent stare).

- Showing in your behaviour that you are attending closely – an occasional nod of the head. Brief statements such as 'I understand' and 'Tell me a little more about that.'

- Occasional use of the reflection technique (a very brief summary statement from you of, at most, two or three sentences, given in your own words to check that you have understood accurately and show that you have followed what has been expressed.

- Helping with short questions and requests for amplification of statements to do with personal feeling (facilitating emotional expression).

- Drawing your patient in to talk in greater depth about feelings or redirecting them if they have gone off-track or are avoiding feelings.

- Avoiding evaluative comment or correction of information unless requested.

Let us return to John D and Nurse Debbie for an illustration of some of these:

John: 'When Doctor P said that I would have to find another sport because I would not be able to go on with highly competitive squash, it really got to me. I was in quite a black mood for an hour or two. Might have been a bit rude to one of the nurses actually, but I didn't mean it. Funny, isn't it. I should be grateful to be alive but I'm moaning about squash. Anyway, then the family came and I had to cheer myself up. We had a look at a few invoices and letters and . . .'

Debbie: 'John, let me just stop you there for a moment because you mentioned feeling really bothered about the squash and then skated over it. Take it a bit more slowly and work out why it bothered you so much.' (**Facilitating – bringing John back to focus on feelings.**)

John: 'Well, it was after he had gone. I realized what he had said and my heart turned over – you know.'

Debbie: 'Try and bring back the actual feelings.' (**Facilitating emotional expression.**)

John: 'Well, it might start me off again.'

Debbie: 'Then if it doesn't feel comfortable leave it for now.' (**Maintaining safety.**)

John: 'No, I do feel better when I get things off my chest and you are the only one that I talk to like this. I don't tell Gail, she has enough on her plate without me adding to it again.'

Debbie: (Silent, but looking at John and waiting, she nods understanding. **Facilitating behaviour.**)

John: 'I suppose I was imagining going back into the club. I've been playing there for eight years. I was doing well, very well in my league and in my team.'

Debbie: 'And what hurts most?' (**Facilitating emotional expression.**)

John: 'Well, having them see me like this. Well, they won't see much difference but they will know about me and all I'll be able to do is sit and watch, a has been. That's what got to me, the thought of turning up like a cripple. I was very fit before the heart attack, people used to comment on it.'

Debbie: 'And that makes you feel?' (**Facilitating emotional expression.**)

John: 'Angry, really wild, I could smash something. I can't stand feeling out of it, not able to compete, not having any strength. It's the same sort of feeling about my business too, it has been expanding really nicely. I've always been competitive, a fighter. Now it's like I'm a spectator. And in here you keep getting an underhand message that it's your own fault that you've had a heart attack. Like if you had done things differently it wouldn't have happened, you would still be fine. So yesterday I was thinking that I'm to blame, I've knocked myself out of things. That really made me angry.'

Debbie: 'So you feel really mad that you have lost your strength and been reduced to a spectator and find yourself thinking that it is you own fault?' (**Reflecting back.**)

John: 'Yes, that's right. That's exactly what it feels like. I hate it.'

They continue for a while.

I hope that this example helps to clarify how, by catching things at the right moment, Debbie helped John to examine and express his feelings about the consequences of the heart attack in much greater depth than he was likely to if left to his own devices. She *facilitated* the process.

• Communicating understanding, acceptance and empathy: reflecting back

Debbie showed understanding and acceptance in this exchange. At no point did she make incidental remarks of the 'it's silly to feel like that' or 'try not to upset yourself' type because she had kept in mind that her task was to facilitate emotional expression and help along John's normal emotional processes. Nor did she divert into informational care, problem-solving counselling or other interventions. Instead she listened intently, gave occasional encouragements for John to talk in greater depth and rounded off by **reflecting back** with the briefest of summaries. Reflecting back is an important skill for you to practise, since it conveys understanding and empathy in itself and also offers a natural closure. (Alternatively, if by some chance Debbie had got it wrong, it is an opportunity for John to sort that out.) With these techniques Debbie enabled John to experience the extent of her understanding. He must also have felt her acceptance and support. Further strategies to consolidate this atmosphere of acceptance could come through communications from Debbie to emphasize her *empathy*.

A person with good empathic ability accurately identifies what another person is feeling, perhaps experiencing something similar to them in emotionally provocative situations. Sometimes this is achieved at an intuitive level, without directly being told of those feelings; sometimes it comes from listening to a clear account and then 'resonating' emotionally – that is, responding with the same emotional pattern as the person with the primary experience. Letting the person you are working with know that you empathize helps in maintaining the safety and depth of the encounter, and it is often an encouragement for that person to continue talking to you. In addition, just very occasionally sharing your own feelings and reactions can have a similar effect. It can be very supportive. But this latter option comes with a caution. It is something that one does with care and discipline and only, I repeat, very occasionally. Thus, Debbie might have made the following types of intervention:

Debbie: 'Yes, I do understand, I can sense a real feeling of bottled up anger. It feels like it must be very frustrating because you are such a 'doer' and at the moment you can't do much. If I am right, there is something else to do with being cross at yourself and having no way to get rid of the anger. It's not like you can have a row with someone and clear the air.' (**Empathizing.**)

John: 'Yes, that's right. I never know what to do when I'm angry at myself.'

And

Debbie: 'I can get a good sense of what you feel, John. Just saying a little bit about myself that might fit in here, I broke my leg some years ago skiing. It took ages and ages to heal and I got really cross with it and cross with myself for being careless on the ski slope. I know from first-hand experience that that kind of anger is really disturbing.' (**Sharing personal experiences, solidarity.**)

Not all counsellors and psychologists would agree with personal revelations, I ought to say. But sometimes, in my judgement, they can provide a helpful facilitating boost to a conversation and help to establish closeness and trust. It has to be a matter of judgement at the time. It would be a bizarre stance in giving emotional care if you were to set out to hide your own feelings and remain stonily detached. At the same time, over-identification with and great emotional involvement in your patient's situation does not help and is not appropriate. The best approach is to keep a check on how often you do make personal revelations, and if you are finding yourself using this technique regularly then it needs to be discussed with someone in a supervision session, because you may need to explore your motive.

• Giving support

Definitions of support are vague. Suffice it to say that if *you* have been supported recently you will know it. There will be a lifting of isolation, a sense of relief from the oppressiveness of a disturbing emotion or situation. The change will be because you will have been listened to and will have shared the personal feelings involved with another. That person will have been attentive, given you full attention, helped you express your feelings and discussed things in an easy way with you. That act will have given some respite from the feelings – you will have felt supported psychologically, perhaps even hopeful. There are, of course, various forms of support. If someone is being very helpful in a practical way then that would be social support.

In some ways support is a product rather than an activity *per se*. The package of skills involved in emotional care are a composite that provide the basis of intense support – for those that seek it, that is. Thus, if you have been having sessions similar to those described above with patients who had initially responded positively to the opportunity to talk about their reactions, then it will almost certainly have been supportive for them. How can we tell? Listen to the things that people say after the event, typically 'Thanks so much, it has been a help to talk about it' and 'I want to thank you for listening to me the other day, it felt like getting a weight off my shoulders.' As a patient said to me, 'I would not have expected it, frankly. *I am not one for making a scene but after we talked I did feel an unexpected sense of release and it has stayed with me.*' **That** is support.

• Ending an emotional care session

Although the ideal is for prearranged sessions of a reasonable length (20 minutes), the reality of busy schedules has to be acknowledged and we need to recognize that a significant proportion of emotional care interventions will be fairly brief, impromptu events. In this case, it is best to have your patient take some note of the time limitation at the outset. Something like:

> 'John, if you would like to talk with me about that for 10 minutes or so it might be helpful. I have to be on Oak ward at four, so that gives us a good 10 minutes.'

the position is similar with scheduled visits. It can be helpful to say roughly how much time you have and, possibly, to remind the person that you are working with that you need to round off as the departure time approaches:

> 'John, we will have to finish in five minutes, is there anything else that you would like to mention today in the time that we have got left?'

On most occasions, finishing will present no problems. Just do it naturally as with a normal clinical encounter. If it has been a relaxed atmosphere, simply check how your patient is feeling after talking and then bid him or her goodbye, perhaps arranging for a means of further contact as you do so.

On occasions, though, the atmosphere might have been very emotionally charged, with your patient going through some distressing or disturbing material. In this instance you need to use your last few minutes to bring them back to the here and now and try to effect a sense of completion where possible. It is a useful approach to check how the session has left them and how they feel about the next event in their day. For example:

> 'We must finish in a few minutes, John, so let's start winding down a little. Tell me how you are feeling at the moment and how it has been for you talking to me about such personal things.'

Then

> 'That's good. I'm very glad that you have been able to talk with me. Now, just before I go, I expect that you will have visitors shortly. Are you OK with that?'

'But I feel that I want to *do* something': further care, counselling and referral for psychological therapy

The truth is that most of us in the caring professions do have a near compulsive need to say or do something practical and helpful for our clients. The entirely disciplined 'emotional care only session', as I have described above, might well leave you with a feeling of things left undone. Well, that is fine: once the session is finished you can get on and do what you feel is required. Debbie would have almost certainly felt that a little more informational care work was necessary because John's picture of his future was overly pessimistic. The emotional care would also be continued by her on an 'as required' basis. Moreover, she might have judged, accurately in this case, that John could well benefit from a session or two with a clinical psychologist or counsellor. Since

Debbie had not had training in counselling herself, the latter could well be a nurse or social worker with special training. *It would all depend on local resources.* In this case, Debbie would need to check that John would like further help of this kind and make arrangements for a referral. Again, the procedure for this depends on local arrangements. For example, I regularly receive direct referrals from nurses, physiotherapists and occupational therapists, as well as medical staff. Such referrals are either in verbal form or as a standard clinical letter. If you are thinking of becoming more active in psychological care it is worth meeting the people to whom you might make referrals and negotiating how it should be done and what transfer of information with the referral is best.

How does one know which cases to refer for further psychological assistance? Probably the simplest way of viewing the issue of referral is to observe the following. **If you feel that your patient's emotional needs or difficulties go beyond psychological *care* because they have a troubling depth and persistence that exceeds the limits of your training and your available time, then psychological therapy or counselling is probably called for. In that case, you should consider making a referral and discuss this with your patient.**

You do not have to make the decision alone. It is always useful to consolidate and review your thoughts by discussing them with a colleague; also, importantly, discuss them with your patient. I hope you will have read Chapter 2 and its review of psychological reactions to illness and injury. You may find it helpful to reflect on the patient or partner you are working with and consider if they report a type of reaction similar to one (or more) of those listed. If so, the key question has to be: *is their reaction causing sufficient distress or becoming sufficiently disabling to merit referral to a clinical psychologist for therapy or referral to a counsellor?* Again, I must emphasize, your patient should be asked for their view because a referral for psychological therapy or counselling should be because the person involved wants it. *On no account should people be sent for therapy or counselling without having indicated that they want to attend and are positively motivated.*

The link between counselling and psychological care

I may have created an ambiguity on the issue of counselling that I must address. In the breakdown of psychological care skills given in Chapters 1 and 3, counselling is included as one of the components of psychological care, but in the case of John and Debbie I mention that she could refer him for counselling. The position is that emotional care can often very well blend into counselling care, *if the health care practitioner involved is trained and able to offer this*. In fact, the ideal situation is where the nurse, occupational therapist, physiotherapist etc. who is giving psychological care is able to offer at least basic, supportive counselling to patients, since it saves referral hassles. Whether this applies to you or not depends on whether you have had counselling training. Training is essential, because it is not appropriate to just have a go at counselling. Debbie stopped at emotional care because she had not yet attended counselling training.

Psychological care, as presented in this book, is a set of practices that are quite close to basic, supportive counselling but do not depend on counselling training. This is because psychological care is rather different in aim and style to counselling. For one thing, it is primarily about *preventive interventions* linked to medical treatment or phases of rehabilitation. There is also a strong component of information provision. Neither of these are the usual focus of effort in counselling.

Those of you who feel drawn to psychological work should, if you have not already done so, consider further training in counselling skills. This will help you in aspects of psychological care work. Counselling training courses are plentiful and there is a rich stock of relevant, well written books that serve as excellent primers. For example, Freshwater (2003) writes under the title *Counselling Skills for Nurses, Midwives and Health Visitors*. Similarly, Davy and Ellis (2000) write under the title *Counselling Skills in Palliative Care*. These are relevant as a guide to those of you thinking of professional development in this direction. They also serve as an independent indicator that such skills are seen as important assets in the practice of nursing and other health care professions.

Because of limits on space and also because there is such a good provision of literature on counselling these days, I am not providing an extended section on counselling. I will, though, set out a few notes in order to clarify the links between psychological care, counselling and psychological therapy to give enough information for those of you who feel under-informed on these resources.

A briefing on counselling and psychological therapy

When you provide an emotional care session for a patient you are creating an encounter that comes close to basic, supportive counselling. It also has some elements common to psychological therapy. The emphasis in emotional care is on 'process as a component that has equal weight to content' (see earlier in this chapter), and a style of interaction based on listening, facilitating emotional expression and providing a safe, supportive atmosphere. This also applies to counselling and various psychological therapies. They cannot really proceed without these. But some trained counsellors and most clinical psychologists are usually much more *interventionist* – that is, actively intervening to achieve change, as opposed giving care.

There is some confusion in the use of the term counselling and, as a way of clarifying things, I find it helpful to use two terms:

- *Advisory counselling.* This is a type of intervention where information, advice and guidance comes from the advisor or counsellor. The counsellor is the active participant (similar in form to informational or educational care). Thus, one can receive fertility counselling, sexual counselling, legal counselling or careers counselling.

- *Personal counselling.* This is a type of intervention in which the counsellor helps clients to talk in as much depth as possible about issues that trouble them. The client is usually the most active in terms of the amount of talking. The counsellor is in the role of a facilitator and listener, helping clients to explore the feelings, thoughts, perceptions and motives related to whatever situation concerns them. Ideally, this leads on to improved insight and progress in dealing with personal problems and a generally improved sense of well-being. *Usually,*

> *when we talk of patients needing counselling, we are referring to*
> *personal counselling.*

Davis and Fallowfield (1991) give an account of counselling in health care that is useful as an overview and general guide to principles and applications. Egan (1990) provides a good illustration of the basic elements of an interventionist style of counselling that may be used in a health care setting. It is relevant to extract some of his key points. He proposes a three-stage scheme:

1 *Exploring and clarifying the problem situation.* People turn to counselling when they are unhappy, confused or distressed. Quite often, though, they will not be truly clear about what exactly is disturbing them, but are only able to report the consequences, such as anxiety or depression. Thus, the special working relationship in counselling is focused progressively on encouraging in-depth 'self-exploration', so expanding the person's contact with her personal feelings and perceptions. With the counsellor's helping interventions the nature of the difficulty becomes clarified.

2 *Setting goals based on dynamic understanding.* The client is drawn into piecing together disclosures and discoveries from stage 1 and generating a clearer picture of herself and others in the problem situation. This process involves focusing on the 'dynamics' of the situation – that is, the psychological forces (motives, needs, fears, blocks etc.) that have emerged from the discussion. In other words, a deeper understanding is achieved, including, perhaps, recognition of issues that previously have been blocked from conscious awareness. Unlike some forms of psychological therapy, counselling does not usually involve major inputs from the counsellor. The skill is in leading the client to achieve insight by helping her to discover for herself what is within.

3 *Facilitating action.* Egan's approach is very much action-oriented, so the end point of such sessions is using the knowledge gained to declare targets for change and resolution. These might be very concrete targets, such as making headway with the business of social integration after a long disabling illness. For other clients the issue may be one of achieving

acceptance of the loss of a body part or adapting to an illness that narrows life down. Whatever the nature of the problem, the counselling *relationship* is used to help the individual to change. *Reappraisal, confronting awkward issues, taking initiatives, seeking ways out of an impasse and testing out the reality of feared situations become the focal point for action and change.*

In essence, then, the basic relating skills for counselling are much the same as in emotional care – that is, providing a warm, working relationship that emphasizes listening skills, communicating understanding, empathy and support. However, at times some counsellors will shift into another mode, known as 'challenging skills'. Despite the title, these are still gentle, supportive interventions, but they help a client to redirect thoughts or explore feelings at greater depth. They are used to help to probe and explore aspects of a client's life and expose problems that do not emerge of their own accord in the conversation because there is a lack of insight, denial or evasiveness. Such an approach is common to both the more interventionist styles of counselling and psychological therapy (as practised by clinical and health psychologists).

As a low-key illustration, here is a brief extract from an average sort of counselling/therapy session with Anna and her unit psychologist. At this point in the encounter the psychologist is *operating in an exploratory counselling style* and not following the pathway of any particular style of therapy. Anna's husband has suffered renal failure and she has become very stressed and physically strained in recent months. She is buckling under the strain of coping with his needs, the needs of the children and two part-time jobs. Recently she had a brief 'stress breakdown' and is now talking about this with the psychologist. It has emerged that Anna has created a very physically arduous life pattern at present and is becoming physically exhausted to the point of being ill with fatigue:

Psych: 'So what is the situation today, Anna?'

Anna: 'I'm pretty tired. I was on night shift at the nursing home last night and I'm feeling a bit lightheaded, not been to bed yet.'

Psych: 'Are you telling me that you are working some nights as well as daytimes now? How are you feeling physically?'

Anna: 'I don't let myself feel anything because if I stopped and thought how tired I was I would collapse in a heap. I have to keep going somehow . . . I'm doing my best but (breaks off and hides her face in her hands for a while) . . . I know what you're thinking. But I do have to keep going. The trouble is I'm not sure how much longer I can.'

Psych: 'Anna, take your time with this but try and capture what it is like when you wake in the morning to another day of pushing yourself so hard – what is the feeling and what are the thoughts that you become aware of when you wake?' (**Exploring feeling and perception.**)

Anna: (Long pause) 'I wake up tense, worrying. I have this feeling that I must keep things together as they are, not let them change for the worse. I don't want Peter's kidney failure to harm the kids and I don't want him to feel guilty about not being able to work and the finances falling apart. It's worry about money, I suppose. I don't want the children to start finding that they can't have things or go on trips. Their exams are in a few months and . . . you know, children are such a worry.'

Psych: 'Just money, or are you trying to protect them from knowing in full what the situation is?' (**Probing.**)

Anna: 'Partly, I suppose. I just want things to seem as normal for them as possible. Peter is still in shock really, he doesn't need any more burdens like them getting upset. And the children, well, as I say, exams are soon, I don't think that they should be distracted or have to suffer any more worry than is necessary.'

Psych: 'And so?'

Anna: 'And so . . . so . . . I don't know really. And so I feel that I have got to push myself. I must not let them see that we're in difficulties. Yes, I'm frightened of them seeing how things are. They could lose their father. The trouble is I'm running out of steam.'

Psych: 'What makes you so sure that the children could not cope if you told them more?' (**Confronting.**)

Anna: 'Well, Lucy is quite sensitive. Martin would seem all right on the surface but I think he would fret about things inside. It's hard to tell. In a way I'm reliving the time when Mum had cancer and Dad sort of went to pieces. We had to cope for him. It affected me quite a lot.'

Psych: 'Perhaps it still does. Do you think that your anxiety about the children finding out how things are might be more about you than about them. That you are driving yourself to the point of illness yourself because this is stirring up all the old feelings in you from when your mother was dying?' (**Confronting.**)

Anna: (Long pause) 'Do you think that I have become neurotic? I have been putting off telling them or letting anything seem different. Deliberately. It's a help for me to be so busy in one way, like it blots everything out – but I know I can't keep it up. I don't want them to see me . . . what's the word I want . . . weakening. Keeping busy helps. Pretend things haven't changed.'

Psych: 'And if you become ill too?'

Anna: 'That mustn't happen.'

Psych: 'Then we have to think through other ways for you to handle it, because that is one of the real risks at present. How are you feeling talking about it with me at the moment?' (**Moving to problem-solving.**)

This is a slightly edited and shortened version of the actual encounter but you can see that there are examples of 'challenging interventions' within the exchange. Nevertheless, there is the same atmosphere of caring concern and attentiveness to feelings of the moment that is prevalent in emotional care. The psychologist, though, is more active in exploration, interpretation and problem identification. Later they move on to problem-solving. Counselling and psychological therapy thus build on the base of emotional care.

As additional reading to develop your knowledge of counselling I can recommend Nelson-Jones (1990), who gives a helpful and practical tutorial on counselling skills and objectives.

In what way does psychological therapy differ from counselling?

You will encounter two terms for psychologists who work in the health care system and concern themselves with the care of ill or injured people. 'Clinical psychologist' is probably the commonest name, but some practitioners are now using the terms 'clinical health psychologist' or 'health psychologist' to signify a specialization in physical health issues. They are different titles with, sometimes, slightly different training routes, but the approach and practice involved are much the same. Consider them as interchangeable.

Clinical psychologists will usually have had more intensive and specialist training in particular approaches to therapy than counsellors, and are chartered to work with mental health problems as well as problems in living and adaptation to illness. Thus, patients with phobias, anxiety states, post traumatic stress reactions, progressively deepening depression, eating disorders, obsessive disorders, alcohol and drug dependency problems, sexual problems, brain damage, psychotic reactions and so on fall within the scope of psychological therapy and the clinical psychologist. Having said that, many clinical psychologists now work in the health care setting and focus their approach to therapy on the problems of the average patient, as, clearly, do I. They are to be found in all sorts of settings, dealing with respiratory disorders, neurological damage, chronic pain, cardiac issues, still births, renal failure, hearing problems and so on. Sometimes they will function in much the same mode as a counsellor – it all depends on the issues that concern the patient or partner.

Some clinical psychologists work within a formal system of therapy that has specific procedures and targets – for example, cognitive behavioural therapy, cognitive analytic therapy, family therapy, psychodynamic therapy. These therapies can be much more probing, analytic and sometimes confrontational (in a constructive, caring way). Nevertheless, like emotional care, all these approaches depend on the 'therapeutic relationship', which is the common base for most psychological interventions. For more on psychological therapies and clinical/health psychology in general, Trull and Phares (2001) give a useful review.

Counsellor versus clinical psychologist

The issue of choosing between a counsellor and psychological therapist for referral will probably not arise that regularly because, in relative terms, there are not that many of them around. Thus, the answer to the question is usually a practical one, namely what you have got available locally. It is not that common to have a choice between a counsellor and clinical psychologist, but one or the other can usually be found in the locality. Clinical psychology and clinical health psychology is expanding in the health service in Britain, which is a great help. The trend is towards increasing numbers of psychologists working both in the community and in the hospital services. Similarly, many general practices have counsellors offering regular sessions and a few have sessions from clinical psychologists. Finally, some hospital departments also have dedicated counsellors, e.g. 'the stroke counsellor'. So, with a little exploration you should be able to find some resources to supplement your own psychological care.

Where do psychiatrists fit in?

Unlike clinical psychology, which is a 'stand alone' profession, psychiatry is a branch of medicine. Psychiatrists are doctors who have taken postgraduate training in the treatment of mental disorder. The general pattern is for psychiatric colleagues to take responsibility for significant and disabling mental disorder that requires diagnosis and formal treatment regimes, usually with medications. Psychiatrists differ in how psychologically minded they are, and range between those who rely primarily on drug treatments and those who have moved into an emphasis on psychological therapy or behaviour therapy. In the latter you will find interest and support for psychological care and, possibly, a willingness to accept referrals. It will need to be discussed face-to-face to establish mutual positions.

Discussion time

If you have the opportunity of a tutorial style discussion group then it will be useful to review some of the main issues raised in this chapter. For example:

- What are the main assumptions in emotional care? Do you agree with them as stated?

- Do you see emotional care work as relevant and appropriate to your own health care profession?

- What are the necessary personal characteristics for staff providing emotional care? Where do you stand in relation to these characteristics? Do you need further personal development work to make yourself suitable?

- Can you provide some case examples where emotional care was needed? Do you have case examples of both good and bad emotional care? Do you have personal examples of emotional care work?

- What are your current training needs in relation to emotional care or counselling, and how can these be attended to?

6 Professional issues and the provision of psychological care

In this short final chapter I want to deal with some issues that need to be kept in mind and blended into the professional practice of psychological care. I will discuss:

- advocacy;
- identification, over-involvement and difficult cases;
- supervision, support and self-care for staff giving psychological care;
- developments and opportunities in the health care professions;
- is it worth the effort and can psychological care be evidence-based?

Advocacy

One element in the diagram giving the components of psychological care (Figure 1.2) has yet to be mentioned. It is the notion of representing the needs of your patients and their partners in situations where: (a) those needs might not be taken into account; or (b) there is some conflict between the patients' needs and those of the staff. Advocacy is about acting as a 'go-between' on psychosocial issues when that is something that the patient wants and when it is likely to make a significant material difference to those involved. The go-between function will be in the form of gentle representation and negotiation on behalf of the patient by yourself. Examples include: the patient who is claustrophobic and needs some special help with an MRI scan; the patient who gets into an anxiety state in a waiting room situation and is helped by having the first appointment of the day; the patient who has an important request for the doctor and feels unable to make it personally; the patient who could cope with a procedure if there was to be a general anaesthetic but does not think she will be able to cope if the usual local anaesthetic is used.

> Eileen, a 65-year-old lady, got off to a bad start on her first visit to the diabetes clinic. She felt that she was told of her need for regular insulin injections in an insensitive manner and that the subsequent interviews with the diabetes nurse and dietician had lacked privacy (it was an open plan setting) and were inappropriately friendly (she disliked first name terms). It was a clash of unit culture and expectations. However, Eileen was greatly upset and her reaction undermined the regularity of her insulin injections. The person handling her psychological care spoke to her consultant personally and explained the situation tactfully. The consultant was pleased to help and agreed to a fresh start on a home visit basis. Peace was restored.

I have put this function in the section on professional issues because it is something that has to be done with careful thought and professional neutrality. Sometimes a discussion with a colleague to check your judgement on matters before intervening can be a good idea. It is easy to cause 'ruffled feathers', in which case the impact can be negative and unhelpful.

Identification, over-involvement and difficult cases

While we are busy sensing, monitoring and empathizing with our patients' psychological reactions, we should also keep a little bit of our awareness engaged in the task of sensing and monitoring our own reactions to individual cases. In particular, we should be on the look out for situations in which the reactions and circumstances of our patients, or their partners, interact with our own psychology – for example, the possibility of becoming overly identified with our patients' feelings and circumstances, so that our own behaviour becomes influenced by unrecognized reactions on our part.

Jane, a community nurse with counselling training, noticed that she would sometimes make extra efforts and even worked beyond her hours visiting certain types of patient. In contrast, she did not make this sort of effort for other types of patient. Having lost her own husband through a brain tumour, she realized, on discussing the issue with her supervisor, that she tended to make an extra effort to visit homes where one of the partners was likely to be left on their own because of the possible death of their partner. She was unconsciously identifying with partners who faced a situation similar to that which she had encountered.

All of us will vary in our reaction to the different types of people. It is unlikely that we can get along with every patient or relative that we meet and have to work with. Similarly, some patients and partners will feel that they merit special efforts. This is a predictable effect that is linked to our personal history and psychology. It has to be dealt with in a practical way. *Thus, it is important for you to be aware of the pattern that your interaction with specific patients follows.* If, for example, you find yourself angry and drawing a breath before making reluctant contact with a patient or, in contrast, engaged and motivated to help at a level that is above average for your usual pattern, then this should be thought about and discussed. If you have a supervision arrangement then this is the type of issue that should be discussed regularly at supervision meetings. If not, then, as a minimum, talk it through in general terms with a colleague who is capable of listening. It can often be the case that just talking it over helps you to identify the issues and enables you to resolve them. It is important for both you and your patient not to get trapped in psychological care work when you are uncomfortable with it. There might even be times when you would be advised to ask someone else to take on the psychological care for particular cases.

Supervision, support and self-care for practitioners giving psychological care

In view of these points concerning the pattern of relating between yourself and your patients, if you become committed and regularly involved in psychological care work then some sort of supervision and support should be sought. I am talking not about situations where the work is limited to occasional bits of informational care but about those where there is regular involvement with emotional care or counselling. Involvement of this type can be immensely satisfying as an extension of care but it does impose loads and can 'use' you more than might be apparent.

Supervision means a regular and scheduled opportunity to discuss your work and reflect on it with a colleague who is able to give constructive feedback and help you explore your thoughts and feelings in relation to individual case experiences. As well as this, your own well-being needs to be reviewed regularly, since continual exposure to the distress of others can have tiring and damaging effects. For those of you with very busy practices and duties, supervision may seem like a distant luxury. However, the general trend in thinking these days is that the absence of support, supervision and opportunities for continuing professional development (CPD) is unacceptable for health care practitioners. In my view, sessions designed to review psychological care work are legitimate professional development experiences and so the time involvement can be linked to CPD time allowances, which are mandatory for most British health care practitioners. What sort of time consumption are we talking about? It does not have to be excessive. A half-hour session each month provides a minimum that is a great step forward from no support and supervision arrangement at all. I would not want to be prescriptive about the amount of time, since local resources and situations are governing factors, but any advance on half an hour a month is to be valued.

Obtaining support and supervision is all part of the *self-care* necessary for health care practitioners. In Nichols (1993) I give more space to the theme of self-care than is possible here, but the basic points should, at least, be summarized.

Key point. To accept a role in health care that is known to be stressful without, at the same time, maintaining a personal programme of preventive self-care is a form of self-neglect. To allow such a situation to prevail is an abandonment of professionalism. In other words, practitioners in busy, demanding and stressful health care professions should feel an obligation to practise self-care in a professional, planned way.

Box 6.1   Common stress indicators

- *Behavioural*: continual rushing, burdened by commitments and deadlines, missing meals, excessive eating, sleep loss, 'wound up', angry outbursts, increased smoking and alcohol intake.
- *Emotional*: feeling emotionally fragile, fraught, on a 'short fuse', low, tearful, agitated, anxious, trapped.
- *Physical*: can't relax, tense, headaches, fatigue prone, muscular aches (neck, back), sense of physical strain, prone to illness, skin conditions, changes in menstrual function, asthma, ectopic heart beats, high heart rate and blood pressure.
- *Cognitive*: frequent worrying, poor concentration, distractable, perception of entrapment, too many demands and pressures, perception of powerlessness and hopelessness.
- *Interpersonal*: less able to cope with the needs of others, 'difficult' with others, inclined to row, impatient, over-controlling, inclined to withdrawal, dependent, needing continual support.

Each of us has our own characteristic combination of stress indicators.

The basic skills of self-care include:

- Learning to identify your own personal indicators of strain, stress and distress and developing the habit of *self-monitoring as a preventive skill*. The common stress signs are well known and regularly repeated in many books and magazines. A very brief summary in Box 6.1 serves as a relevant reminder as you consider your own self-care. This gives features of the stressed state, with, obviously, some mutually contradictory elements such that they cannot all apply at the same time. It is best to consider each item as a dimension rather than a 'yes or no' category and then to ask yourself where you are on each dimension and note your general trend of change for that dimension.

- If you believe that you are drifting up the dimensions of stress, early action is much better than late. Seek out support and discussion and try to understand why it is happening. Engage with a personal counsellor if you have the opportunity. *Under-*

> *stand that seeking support or supervisory contact is an act of maturity and strength and not a sign of weakness.*

- Be 'stress defensive' in your general working behaviour. In particular, don't go at a sprint pace if you want your career to be a marathon, because you probably won't last. Adopt a pace and load that are sustainable over the years. This includes emotional loads when your work includes emotional care and counselling.

Pam worked as a nurse in palliative care. She loved the work but, after several months of intense pressure owing to staff sickness, realized that she was becoming emotionally drained and physically exhausted. On returning home from work one evening she drew up outside her house, sat in the car for 10 minutes and then drove away again to sit by a local river for an hour. She felt that she could not go in because the children would rush at her with demands and her husband would want to know about her day and to sort out dinner with her. She just felt that she had to be alone and away from any further demands. If she had gone in she would have become cross and bad tempered quite quickly. These were the first signs of a stress-related breakdown.

When there are no support and supervision resources available locally

If you find yourself in a situation where you cannot find assistance with support and supervision from clinical psychologists or counselling trained colleagues, then consider gathering a small group of your own colleagues to form a support network that is based on a *self-help support group*. Nichols and Jenkinson (1991) give practical guidance on how to set up a support group in the absence of a formal, qualified leader. With guidance of this type it is perfectly possible to set up a group of about six or so colleagues who meet perhaps once a month for an hour or more for general support and basic peer supervision. In addition, members of such groups can be available to one another on a network basis for unscheduled meetings (probably in pairs) should there be a need for further support or peer supervision between group meetings. Nichols and Jenkinson acknowledge that it is generally better to have an experienced leader for support groups, but this is by no means essential. So if resources are thin locally, a preventive support group facility can still be put together and run successfully. What you will need as a participant in such groups includes:

- an understanding that seeking and receiving support is a necessary strength for preventive self-care;

- an ability to identify, value and disclose your relevant personal feelings and thoughts;

- an ability to receive the time, attention and care of colleagues;

- an ability to return attention, genuine listening and care to colleagues.

Sutherland (1997) gives a useful overview of the importance and benefits of support for health care practitioners.

Developments and opportunities for psychological care within the health care professions

The master skill in psychological care is identifying the needs of your patients and responding appropriately. No health care profession has a monopoly on this skill, it has to be said. There are, though, other factors that lead to certain professions being, perhaps, a little better placed than others to provide a significant input in psychological care on level 2 (all should contribute on level 1). It is the case, for example, that some professions have a greater emphasis in their training on psychological issues than others and, therefore, when it comes to noticing and thinking about the psychological needs of patients they are probably better prepared. It is also the case that some health care practitioner roles allow a less pressured, face-to-face contact with patients that provides an opportunity for psychological care work to be blended in with the primary roles. My personal view in relation to just a few of the professions that I hope will become more involved in psychological care can be summarized as follows.

Nursing is a powerful profession in terms of numbers. Thus nurses are in an excellent position to make a major contribution in the development of psychological care in the community and in hospitals. The training in nursing is increasingly holistic and, therefore, has a basic psychological bias. Nurses are often in roles that put them into contact with patients at times that are critical for information provision and emotional care. *Community nurses and health visitors* have roles that include visiting and listening. *Midwives* have close contact with pregnant women and are essential for immediate psychological after-care in difficult cases, e.g. miscarriage. *Practice nurses* often have fast turnover clinics but those that I have spoken with accept that it is possible to find time for some psychological care work, and would like to develop that side of their role. Much the same can be said for *hospital nurses* in departments of oncology, renal, respiratory, cardiac, orthopaedic and neurological medicine – to name just a few specialities. *Psychiatric nurses* could also improve the quality of care offered by adopting aspects of psychological care within their field of mental health.

Occupational therapy is a profession similarly well placed for involvement in psychological care. A substantial part of the training is slanted towards psychological issues and the clinical role takes occupational therapists into the type of interpersonal contact that is wonderfully suited to psychological care work. (On a personal note, I hope that a name change might be possible for this profession one day, to 'Rehabilitation Therapists' or something similar that describes their role rather better – but I gather that this is a difficult issue.) As one occupational therapist said to me recently, the tendency in hospitals at the moment is for them to be used as discharge facilitators. This is not a surprise in the rushed, assembly line culture that has become predominant in British hospitals. She saw this as impeding advances in psychological care by occupational therapists, but at the same time thought that there was a basic readiness within the profession to take on more psychological care work.

Speech and language therapy provides a perfect setting for psychological care – that is, intense, one-to-one encounters that are usually centred on speech and communication and are usually scheduled for a sufficient length of time for psychological care to be blended in. Often there are repeat appointments, which also helps. Although comparatively few in number, speech and language therapists are very well placed to contribute to psychological care.

Dieticians also have a pattern of work with patients that emphasizes one-to-one, conversation-based encounters. These encounters naturally lean towards information provision and can readily be extended a little for more general informational care, when appropriate. Similarly, conversation with the dietician can easily be moved into territory concerning reactions to illness and treatment and so offer opportunities to provide a little emotional care, if that is necessary, or arrange a referral for psychological assistance.

Physiotherapy. Conversation with physiotherapist colleagues confirms that, as in many other health care professions, physiotherapy training and practice is tending towards a rather more psychosocial perspective and approach. This is excellent news, because physiotherapists often have contact with patients early on in treatment or recovery from trauma, when they are shocked, vulnerable and in the early stage of appraising their situation and reacting to it. Physiotherapists are, therefore, in an excellent position while working with patients to monitor their psychological state and assess the need for psychological care, this being provided either by the physio or through arrangement with other colleagues. Added to this, the 'investment element' comes into play, in that success with physiotherapy treatments is inevitably linked to patients' attitudes, perceptions and emotional status.

Hospital doctors and general practitioners can play a vital part in creating a culture that promotes psychological care. It is a sad thing when psychological care is conducted *despite* the doctors rather than with their involvement and encouragement. To those in the medical profession who have read this book I do want to convey the importance of your personal contribution to the development of psychological care. Your time pressures and waiting lists may deny an involvement other than monitoring psychological state, but your referrals and encouragement to colleagues in allied professions to provide psychological care, together with representations to management to secure understanding and resources, will have enormous value.

I hope that the health care professions that have not been mentioned will not be offended, but I am now tight up against my word limit for this book. Probably the same type of comments will apply to your profession as those above and I hope that you will all be encouraged to pursue developments in psychological care. As for the alternative, readers will know my views well enough by now to realize that if any health care practitioner sidesteps the basic functions of psychological care on level 1 then, I, at least, regard it as a form of professional negligence and failure in basic care.

Is it worth the effort and can psychological care be evidence-based?

In some ways this question, which is a favourite at conferences, is an odd question. Psychological care is about identifying and meeting the needs of our patients. The question thus actually translates into, 'Does meeting the needs of our patients work?' We could go around in circles with this one. It is better to ask, 'Does psychological care meet the needs of our patients and their partners and is it helpful for them?' In order to engender confidence in my case I have given reference to various studies that offer supporting evidence to these questions throughout the book. It is appropriate, though, to cite one or two more good pieces of research that will give a positive conclusion to my quest to convince you of the need for psychological care for the ill and injured.

The core function in psychological care is to monitor psycho-logical state. This includes assessing the patient's level of information and their reaction to that information. Information is then provided as necessary. Is this justified? An excellent example of evidence on this point comes from the field of oncology. Few people in this country can know more about cancer patients' needs for information than Leslie Fallowfield. Fallowfield *et al.* (1995) reported research in which the information needs of 101 patients with cancer were assessed in detail. The findings were that '94 per cent expressed a desire for as much information as possible'. In discussing the damage done by withhold-ing information from the victims of cancer, Fallowfield *et al.* (2002) cite a very large survey of 2331 patients with cancer. Of these, '87 per cent wanted all possible information'. To fail to provide informational care is, therefore, clearly negligent of patients' needs.

When provided, does information and informational care help? Is it a good investment of effort? Ley (1989) describes a group of meta-analytic studies (these combine results from large collections of research studies of known high quality). The reports reveal that 61 per cent of people receiving informational care after a heart attack or heart surgery progress better than those receiving no informational care, that good informational care reduced hospital stay times in surgical patients by an average of 1.21 days and that psycho-educational tech-niques reduced levels of distress and gave higher rates of recovery after invasive procedures in 57 per cent of patients.

As for support, emotional care and counselling care, Billings *et al.* (1996) describe the 'lifestyle heart trial'. This was an intensive form of cardiac rehabilitation, with physical exercise, diet change, education and an emphasis on support with informal emotional care through regular group support work. The key variable measured was the extent of narrowing of coronary vessels. It was found that, compared with a control group, the patients so treated registered a small *reduction* in the extent to which the coronary arteries were narrowed. The support and emotional care component were an essential element of the successful regime.

More specifically, a controlled study of the efficacy of emotional care and supportive counselling given by a registered nurse to post heart attack patients is provided by Thompson and Meddis (1990). This 'counselling' was primarily emotional care: 'The counselling focused on the patient's reactions to and feelings towards the heart attack ... encouraged ventilation of both positive and negative feelings ... helping resolve immediate problems.' In comparison with a control group receiving routine care only, the group receiving psychological care were significantly less anxious and less depressed during the six months of the study (the Hospital Anxiety and Depression Scale was used for assessment). A companion study reported in Thompson and Meddis (1990) went through the same routine with 60 wives of heart attack patients. One group received education, support and emotional care. Once again this treatment group was significantly less anxious than the control group over a period of six months.

Mathieson and Stam (1991) write under the intriguing title 'What good is psychotherapy when I am ill?' This is a convincing review of many studies looking at the benefits of psychological therapy for people ill with cancer. Saxby and Svanberg (1998) give a broader ranging review under the title *The Added Value of Psychology to Physical Health Care*. Both of these reviews cite many high quality studies that provide us with an evidence-based rationale for psychological care. Thus it can be said:

Psychological care is needed.
Psychological care works.
These claims are evidence-based.

Some areas of nursing and medicine are focused primarily on the provision of *basic care*, as opposed to improvement and rehabilitation. *Palliative care for people who are dying is the foremost example.* It becomes absurd in a sense to require evidence to prove that dying people need and benefit from a multidisciplinary care regime that has, as part of its basis, good psychological care. Payne and Haines (2002) show that it is not safe to assume that all health care practitioners have this perception, however. Mixed attitudes in palliative care work did, for some years, lead to a suppression of psychological care. Now, though, as Payne and Haines demonstrate, the case is well established and the cause is supported by government papers based on inquiry and investigation detailing the optimum approach for palliative care. The recommendation is for a balanced approach with a strong emphasis on psychological care as a key component to the care of the dying.

A. Overton (personal communication, 2002) made a strong case to me that my views on psychological care should be expanded to include the field of *mental health* treatment. People receiving treatment for mental health problems have, she argued strongly, the same needs for informational and emotional care as patients in a hospital. I think that she is right, but can, at this point, find space only to recognize the issue as important and worthy of development.

Finale

It could be said that I have constructed this book in the spirit of a somewhat complaining prophet. That's as may be. But at least it allows me to finish like a prophet. I hope that you have been converted to the cause and can have confidence in the need for and value of your psychological care for the ill and injured. If you have, then 'go forth and give psychological care' and enjoy seeing the benefits to your patients and feeling the rewards of providing a more complete form of health care.

Keith Nichols   October 2002

Discussion time
Developments on 'your patch': issues to be resolved

- What is our current provision of psychological care? What developments are needed?

- What are our arguments for developing psychological care?

- What sort of organization of psychological care best suits the needs of our unit, ward, service or health centre?

- Who can we call on for guidance, training and support or supervision?

- Are all our staff suited to psychological care work? Who on the staff should undertake psychological care on level 2?

- Can we expect opposition? Where will it come from and how can we deal with it?

- Do we need to improve our own self-care and support? Would a support group be viable and helpful?

Appendix
Observations for psychological care

PATIENT: ....   DATE: ....

RECORD MADE BY: ....   NOTES: ....

PREDOMINANT MOOD STATE? anxious, tense, agitated, fraught, worried, stressed, tearful, low, guilty, depressed, negative, withdrawn, confused, frustrated, angry, aggrieved? Relaxed, cheerful, calm, positive, good morale? Other?

....

Comments: ....

....

HOW WELL INFORMED/OUTLOOK AND EXPECTATIONS?

....

....

....

PSYCHOLOGICAL OR BEHAVIOURAL DIFFICULTIES?

....

....

....

ACTION TO BE TAKEN?

....

....

....

References

Allen, R. (1997) Digestive tract cancer. In A. Baum, S. Newman, J. Weinman, R. West and C. McManus (eds) *Cambridge Handbook of Psychology, Health and Medicine.* Cambridge: Cambridge University Press.

Allen, J. and Brock, S. A. (2000) *Health Care Communication Using Personality Type.* London: Routledge.

Baum, A., Newman, S., Weinman, J., West, R. and McManus, C. (eds) (1997) *Cambridge Handbook of Psychology, Health and Medicine.* Cambridge: Cambridge University Press.

Becker, M. H. (ed.) (1974) The health belief model and personal health behaviour, *Health Education Monographs*, **2**: 324–508.

Beer, A. (1995) *Springing the Care Trap: Carers Speak Out.* Exeter: Department of Psychology, University of Exeter (unpublished research report).

Bennett, P. (2000) *Introduction to Clinical Health Psychology.* Buckingham: Open University Press.

Bennett, P. and Carroll, D. (1997) Coronary heart disease: impact. In A. Baum, S. Newman, J. Weinman, R. West and C. McManus (eds) *Cambridge Handbook of Psychology, Health and Medicine.* Cambridge: Cambridge University Press.

Bennett, P. and Connell, H. (1998) Couples coping with myocardial infarction: the partner's experience, *Coronary Health Care*, **2**: 140–4.

Benyamini, Y. and Leventhal, H. (1997) Coping with stressful medical procedures. In A. Baum, S. Newman, J. Weinman, R. West and C. McManus (eds) *Cambridge Handbook of Psychology, Health and Medicine.* Cambridge: Cambridge University Press.

Bigler, E. D. (1989) Behavioural and cognitive changes in traumatic brain injury: a spouse's perspective, *Brain Injury*, **3**: 73–8.

Billings, J. H., Scherwitz, L. W., Sullivan, R., Sparler, S. and Ornish, D. (1996) In R. Allan and S. Scheidt (eds) *Heart and Mind: The Practice of Cardiac Psychology.* Washington, DC: American Psychological Association.

Broome, A. and Llewelyn, S. (eds) (1995) *Health Psychology.* London: Chapman and Hall.

Davidson, G. and Neale, J. (2001) *Abnormal Psychology.* New York: John Wiley.

Davis, H. and Fallowfield, L. (1991) *Counselling and Communication in Health Care.* Chichester: Wiley.

Davison, K. P. and Petrie, K. J. (1997) Emotional expression and health. In A. Baum, S. Newman, J. Weinman, R. West and C. McManus (eds) *Cambridge Handbook of Psychology, Health and Medicine.* Cambridge: Cambridge University Press.

Davy, J. and Ellis, S. (2000) *Counselling Skills in Palliative Care*. Buckingham: Open University Press.

Dixon, M. and Sweeney, K. (2000) *The Human Effect in Medicine*. Abingdon: Radcliffe Medical Press.

Earll, L. and Johnston, M. (1997) Motor neurone disease. In A. Baum, S. Newman, J. Weinman, R. West and C. McManus (eds) *Cambridge Handbook of Psychology, Health and Medicine*. Cambridge: Cambridge University Press.

Egan, G. (1990) *The Skilled Helper*. Monterey, CA: Brooks/Cole.

Elian, M. and Dean, G. (1985) To tell or not to tell the diagnosis of multiple sclerosis, *Lancet*, **2**: 27–8.

Erikson, E. H. (1959) Growth and crises. Reproduced in T. Millon (ed.) (1967) *Theories of Psychopathology*. Philadelphia: Saunders.

Evans, P. E., Clow, A. and Hucklebridge, F. (1997) Stress and the immune system, *The Psychologist*, July, 303–7.

Fallowfield, L. (1997) Breast cancer. In A. Baum, S. Newman, J. Weinman, R. West and C. McManus (eds) *Cambridge Handbook of Psychology, Health and Medicine*. Cambridge: Cambridge University Press.

Fallowfield, L. and Clarke, A. (1991) *Breast Cancer*. London: Routledge.

Fallowfield, L., Ford, S. and Lewis, S. (1995) No news is not good news: information preferences of patients with cancer, *Psycho-oncology*, **4**: 197–202.

Fallowfield, L., Jenkins, V. and Beveridge, H. (2002) Truth may hurt but deceit hurts more: communication in palliative care, *Palliative Medicine*, **16**: 297–303.

Faulkner, A. (1998) *When the News Is Bad*. Cheltenham: Stanley Thornes.

Fishbein, M. and Ajzen, I. (1975) *Belief, Intention and Behavior*. Reading, MA: Addison-Wesley.

Frasure-Smith, N., Lesperance, F. and Talajic, M. (1993) Depression following myocardial infarction: impact on 6 month survival, *Journal of the American Medical Association*, **270**: 1819–25.

Frasure-Smith, N., Lesperance, F. and Talajic, M. (1995) Depression and 18 month prognosis following myocardial infarction, *Circulation*, **91**: 999–1005.

Freshwater, D. (2003) *Counselling Skills for Nurses, Midwives and Health Visitors*. Buckingham: Open University Press.

Gath, D., Cooper, P. and Day, A. (1982) Hysterectomy and psychiatric disorder: levels of psychiatric morbidity before and after hysterectomy, *British Journal of Psychiatry*, **140**: 335–42.

Goldstein, D. and Hoeper, M. (1987) Management of diabetes during adolescence: mission impossible?, *Clinical Diabetes*, **5**: 2–10.

Goldstein, L. H. and Leigh, P. N. (1999) Motor neurone disease: a review of its emotional and cognitive consequences for patients and its impact on carers, *British Journal of Health Psychology*, **4**: 193–208.

Hemingway, H. and Marmot, M. (1999) Psychosocial factors in the aetiology and prognosis of coronary heart disease: systematic review of prospective cohort studies, *British Medical Journal*, **318**: 160–7.

Hughes, J. E., Royle, G. T., Buchanan, R. and Taylor, I. (1986) Depression and social stress among patients with benign breast disease, *British Journal of Surgery*, **73**: 997–99.

Jacobsen, P. B. and Holland, J. C. (1991) The stress of cancer: psychological responses to diagnosis and treatment. In C. L. Cooper and M. Watson (eds) *Cancer and Stress*. Chichester: Wiley.

Janis, I. and Levanthal, H. (1965) Psychological aspects of physical illness and hospital care. In B. Woolman (ed.) *Handbook of Clinical Psychology*. New York: McGraw Hill.

Johnston, M. (1997) Hospitalisation in adults. In A. Baum, S. Newman, J. Weinman, R. West and C. McManus (eds) *Cambridge Handbook of Psychology, Health and Medicine*. Cambridge: Cambridge University Press.

Kaplan De-Nour, A. (1994) Psychological, social and vocational impact of renal failure: a review. In H. McGee and C. Bradley (eds) *Quality of Life Following Renal Failure*. Chur, Switzerland: Harwood.

Kennedy, P. (1991) Counselling with spinal cord injured people. In H. Davis and L. Fallowfield (eds) *Counselling and Communication in Health Care*. Chichester: Wiley.

Kennedy, S., Kiecolt-Glaser, J. K. and Glaser, R. (1988) Immunological consequences of acute and chronic stressors: mediating role of interpersonal relationships, *British Journal of Medical Psychology*, **61**: 77–85.

Lacey, J. and Burns, T. (1989) *Psychological Management of the Physically Ill*. London: Churchill Livingstone.

Lane, D., Carroll, D., Ring, C., Beevers, D. G. and Yip, Y. H. (2002) The prevalence and persistence of depression and anxiety following myocardial infarction, *British Journal of Health Psychology*, **7**: 11–21.

Lewin, R. (1995) Cardiac disorders. In A. Broome and S. Llewelyn (eds) *Health Psychology*, 2nd edn. London: Chapman and Hall.

Ley, P. (1982) Understanding, memory, satisfaction and compliance, *British Journal of Clinical Psychology*, **21**: 241–54.

Ley, P. (1988) *Communicating with Patients*. Beckenham: Croom Helm.

Ley, P. (1989) Improving patients' understanding, recall, satisfaction and compliance. In A. Broome (ed.) *Health Psychology*. London: Chapman and Hall.

Ley, P. (1997) Written communication. In A. Baum, S. Newman, J. Weinman, R. West and C. McManus (eds) *Cambridge Handbook of Psychology, Health and Medicine*. Cambridge: Cambridge University Press.

Ley, P. and Llewelyn, S. (1995) Improving patients' understanding, recall, satisfaction and compliance. In A. Broome and S. Llewelyn (eds) *Health Psychology*, 2nd edn. London: Chapman and Hall.

Llewelyn, S. and Payne, S. (1995) Caring: the cost to nurses and families. In A. Broome and S. Llewelyn (eds) *Health Psychology*, 2nd edn. London: Chapman and Hall.

Long, C. (1995) Renal care. In A. Broome and S. Llewelyn (eds) *Health Psychology*, 2nd edn. London: Chapman and Hall.

Lynch, J. (1977) *The Broken Heart*. New York: Basic Books.

McAvoy, B. R. (1986) Death after bereavement, *British Medical Journal*, **293**: 835–6.

McVey, J., Madill, A. and Fielding, D. (2001) The relevance of lowered personal control for patients who have stoma surgery to treat cancer, *British Journal of Clinical Psychology*, **40**: 337–60.

Maeland, J. G. and Havik, O. E. (1987) Psychological predictors for return to work after a myocardial infarction, *Journal of Psychosomatic Research*, **31**: 471–81.

Maguire, P. (1997) Breaking bad news. In A. Baum, S. Newman, J. Weinman, R. West and C. McManus (eds) *Cambridge Handbook of Psychology, Health and Medicine*. Cambridge: Cambridge University Press.

Martin, P. (1997) *The Sickening Mind*. London: HarperCollins.

Mathieson, C. M. and Stam, H. J. (1991) What good is psychotherapy when I am ill? Psychosocial problems and interventions with cancer patients. In C. L. Cooper and M. Watson (eds) *Cancer and Stress*. Chichester: Wiley.

May, R. (1960) *Existential Psychology*. New York: Random House.

May, R. (1977) *The Meaning of Anxiety*. New York: Norton.

Moffic, H. S. and Paykel, E. S. (1975) Depression in medical in-patients, *British Journal of Psychiatry*, **126**: 346–53.

Moos, R. H. and Tsu, V. (1977) The crisis of physical illness. In R. H. Moos (ed.) *Coping with Physical Illness*. New York: Plenum.

Nelson-Jones, R. (1990) *Practical Counselling and Helping Skills*. London: Holt, Rinehart and Winston.

Nichols, K. (1984) *Psychological Care in Physical Illness*. Beckenham: Croom Helm.

Nichols, K. (1987) Chronic physical disorder in adults. In J. Orford (ed.) *Coping with Disorder in the Family*. Beckenham: Croom Helm.

Nichols, K. (1989) The care trap. Unpublished talk given at Newcastle University, Australia.

Nichols, K. (1991) Psychological aspects of acute pain, *The Pain Society*, **9**: 51–5.

Nichols, K. (1993) *Psychological Care in Physical Illness*, 2nd edn. London: Chapman and Hall.

Nichols, K. (2003) Initial reactions to renal failure: a clinical briefing. In R. Dingwall (ed.) *Psychosocial Care in Renal Failure*. Lucerne: EDTNA/ERCA.

Nichols, K. and Jenkinson, J. (1991) *Leading a Support Group*. London: Chapman and Hall.

Nichols, K. and Springford, V. (1984) Psychosocial difficulties associated with survival by dialysis, *Behaviour Research and Therapy*, **22**: 563–74.

Owen, R. L., Koutsakis, P. D. and Bennett, P. D. (2001) Post-traumatic stress disorder as a sequel of acute myocardial infarction: an overlooked cause of psychosocial disability, *Coronary Health Care*, **5**: 9–15.

Payne, S. and Haines, R. (2002) Doing our bit to ease the pain, *The Psychologist*, **15**: 564–7.

Pennebaker, J. W., Kiecolt-Glaser, J. and Glaser, R. (1988) Disclosure of traumas and immune function: health implications for psychotherapy, *Journal of Consulting and Clinical Psychology*, **56**: 239–45.

Reynolds, M. (1978) No news is bad news – patients' views about communication in hospital, *British Medical Journal*, **1**: 1673–6.

Richards, C. (1981) Communication – the patient's point of view, *Nursing*, **27**: 1189–90.

Rumsey, N. (1997) Dysmorphology and facial disfigurement. In A. Baum, S. Newman, J. Weinman, R. West and C. McManus (eds) *Cambridge Handbook of Psychology, Health and Medicine*. Cambridge: Cambridge University Press.

Rutter, D. (1989) Models of belief–behaviour relationships in health, *Health Psychology Update*, **4**: 3–10.

Salmon, P. (2000) *Psychology of Medicine and Surgery*. Chichester: Wiley.

Saxby, B. and Svanberg, P. O. (1998) *The Added Value of Psychology to Physical Health Care*. Leicester: Division of Clinical Psychology, Occasional Paper No. 2.

Skevington, S. M. (1995) *Psychology of Pain*. Chichester: Wiley.

Skirrow, P., Jones, C., Griffiths, R. D. and Kaney, S. (2001) Intensive care: easing the trauma, *The Psychologist*, **14**: 640–2.

Sutherland, V. (1997) Psychological support for health professionals. In A. Baum, S. Newman, J. Weinman, R. West and C. McManus (eds) *Cambridge Handbook of Psychology, Health and Medicine*. Cambridge: Cambridge University Press.

Tabrisi, K., Littman, A., Redford, B., Williams, J. R. and Scheidt, S. (1996) Psychopharmacology and cardiac disease. In R. Allan and S. Scheidt (eds) *Heart and Mind: The Practice of Cardiac Psychology*. Washington, DC: American Psychological Association.

Thomas, V. and Clarke, J. M. (1997) Nurse–patient communication: nursing assessment and intervention for effective pain control. In A. Baum, S. Newman, J. Weinman, R. West and C. McManus (eds) *Cambridge Handbook of Psychology, Health and Medicine*. Cambridge: Cambridge University Press.

Thompson, D. R. and Meddis, R. (1990a) A prospective evaluation of in-hospital counselling for first time myocardial infarction men, *Journal of Psychosomatic Research*, **34**: 237–48.

Thompson, D. R. and Meddis, R. (1990b) Wives' responses to counselling early after myocardial infarction, *Journal of Psychosomatic Research*, **34**: 249–58.

Trull, T. J. and Phares, E. J. (2001) *Clinical Psychology*. Belmont, CA: Wadsworth.

Wells, D., Clifford, D., Rutter, M. and Selby, J. (2000) *Caring for Sexuality in Health and Illness*. London: Churchill Livingstone.

Weinman, J. (1997) Doctor–patient communication. In A. Baum, S. Newman, J. Weinman, R. West and C. McManus (eds) *Cambridge Handbook of Psychology, Health and Medicine*. Cambridge: Cambridge University Press.

Wilson-Barnett, J. (1989) Distressing hospital procedures. In J. Lacey and T. Burns (eds) *Psychological Management of the Physically Ill*. London: Churchill Livingstone.

Woodhams, P. (1984) Nurses and psychologists: the first hand experience, *Nursing Times*, 11 January: 34–5.

Yalom, I. D. (1980) *Existential Psychotherapy*. New York: Basic Books.

Index

non-integrated psychological care, 105–7
non-retrievability of information, 124,
    129–30
notes, 145
nurses, 12, 103, 120, 233
Nursing, 23, 118

observations for psychological care, 92–3, 94,
    95, 240–1
occupational therapists, 12, 121, 234
older people, 83–4
open questions, 99
organic effects, 19
organization of psychological care, 90,
    105–11
    fully organized and integrated, 105,
        108–10
    part-integrated, 105, 107
    referral or expert-dependent, 105, 111–13
    solo, non-integrated, 105–7
orthopaedic ward, 119–20
over-involvement, 227–8
overload, 124, 127–8
Overton, A., 238
Owen, R.L., 48

pain
    informational and educational care,
        116–7
    psychological reactions to, 53, 61–2
palliative care, 238
panic attacks, 22, 23
part-integrated psychological care, 105, 107
partner crisis, stress and guilt, 43, 70–6
passivity, 124, 131–2
patient-centred communication, 97–102
patient contact, health practitioners with,
    7–8
Paykel, E.S., 86
Payne, S., 238
Pennebaker, J.W., 185
Penny, C., 121
peritoneal dialysis, 61, 79, 110–11, 134,
    162–4, 171
peritonitis, 163
permission for emotions/emotional
    expression, 200–2
personal control, lowered, 55–8
personal counselling, 219–20
personal emotional development, 191–2,
    193
personal feelings, 192–3, 204–6

personal psychology
    and emotional care, 196–200
    and informational care, 159–63
personal revelations, 214
Petrie, K.J., 185
physical contact, 157
physical symptoms, responses to, 43–4,
    55–8
physiotherapists, 12, 235
post traumatic stress reaction (PTSD), 18,
    46–7, 48–9
practice nurses, 12, 102, 234
preventive psychological care
    informational care, 165–8
    vs psychological therapy, 14–16
primacy effect, 174
primary health care, 12
problem clarification, 220
procedures, 53
    preparing people for, 153
productive anxiety, 195–6
professional development, continuing,
    230–1
professional issues, 231–41
    advocacy, 227–8
    developments and opportunities in health
        care professions, 233–5
    identification, over-involvement and
        difficult cases, 227–8
    supervision, support and self-care,
        229–32
    value of psychological care, 233–6
professionalization of information provision,
    142
psychiatric nurses, 234
psychiatry, 225
psychological care, 3–30
    awareness, 6–12
    components, 5, 6
    efficacy of, 237–9
    evidence-based, 237–9
    health care practitioners' involvement, 7–8
    importance, 58
    interventions, 10, 12–13
    as an investment, 28–31
    key concept, 5–18
    lack of in general hospitals and health
        centres, 20–5
    link with counselling, 217–18
    observations for, 94–5, 96, 97, 240–1
    organization of, *see* organization of
        psychological care

COUNSELLING SKILLS FOR NURSES, MIDWIVES AND HEALTH VISITORS

Dawn Freshwater

Counselling is a diverse activity and there are an increasing number of people who find themselves using counselling skills, not least those in the caring professions. There is a great deal of scope in using counselling skills to promote health in the everyday encounters that nurses have with their patients. The emphasis on care in the community and empowerment of patients through consumer involvement means that nurses are engaged in providing support and help to people to change behaviours.

Community nurses often find themselves in situations that require in-depth listening and responding skills: for example, in helping people come to terms with chronic illness, disability and bereavement. Midwives are usually the first port of call for those parents who have experienced miscarriages, bereavements, or are coping with decisions involving the potential for genetic abnormalities. Similarly, health visitors are in a valuable position to provide counselling regarding the immunization and health of the young infant. These practitioners have to cope not only with new and diverse illnesses, for example HIV and AIDS, but also with such policy initiatives as the National Service Framework for Mental Health and their implications.

This book examines contemporary developments in nursing and health care in relation to the fundamental philosophy of counselling, the practicalities of counselling and relevant theoretical underpinnings. Whilst the text is predominantly aimed at nurses, midwives and health visitors, it will also be of interest to those professionals allied to medicine, for example physiotherapists, occupational therapists and dieticians.

Contents
Introduction – The process of counselling – Beginning a relationship – Sustaining the relationship – Facilitating change – Professional considerations – Caring for the carer – Appendix: Useful information – References – Index.

128pp   0 335 20781 2 (Paperback)   0 335 20782 0 (Hardback)

PARTNERSHIPS IN FAMILY CARE

Mike Nolan, Ulla Lundh, Gordon Grant and John Keady (Eds.)

- What are the key features of partnerships between family and professional carers?
- How do partnerships change over time?
- What is needed to help create the best working partnerships?

Forging partnerships between service users, family carers and service providers is a key theme in both the policy and academic literatures. However, what such partnerships mean and how they can be created and sustained while responding to change over time, is far from clear.

This book considers how family and professional carers can work together more effectively in order to provide the highest quality of care to people who need support in order to remain in their own homes. It adopts a temporal perspective looking at key transitions in caregiving and suggests the most appropriate types of help at particular points in time. It draws on both empirical and theoretical sources emerging from several countries and relating to a number of differing caregiving contexts in order to illustrate the essential elements of 'relationship-centred' care.

Partnerships in Family Care will be important reading for all health care students and professionals with an interest in community and home care for the ill, disabled, and elderly.

Contents
Preface – Introduction: Why another book on family care? – Part One: 'Recognizing the need' and 'taking it on' – The dynamics of dementia – Early interventions in dementia: carer-led evaluations – Seeking partnerships between family and professional carers – Part Two: Working through it – Quality care for people with dementia – Partnerships with families over the life course – 'I wasn't aware of that' – Caring for people with dementia – Family care decision-making in later life – Part Three: 'Reaching the end' and 'a new beginning' – The evolving informal support networks of older adults with learning disability – Relatives' experiences of nursing home entry – Placing a spouse in a care home for older people – Creating community – Forging partnerships in care homes – Conclusion: New Directions for partnerships relationship-centred care – References – Index.

Contributors
Christine Bigby, Louise Brereton, Denise Chaston, Chris Clark, Sue Davies, Irene Ericson, Gordon Grant, Ingrid Hellstrom, Prue Ingram, John Keady, Gwynnyth Llewellyn, Ulla Lundh, Rhonda Nay, Mike Nolan, Asa Paulsson, Alan Pearson, Jonas Sandberg, Bev Taylor, Roger Watson, Bridget Whittell.

320pp   0 335 21261 1 (Paperback)   0 335 21262 X (Hardback)